—————— Praise for ——————

THE CLINICIAN'S GUIDE TO
Treating Adult Children of Narcissists

"As more therapists are working with clients who are excavating the fallout of having narcissistic parents, this book provides actionable guidance."

—Ramani Durvasula, PhD, licensed clinical psychologist, author of *Should I Stay or Should I Go?* and *"Don't You Know Who I Am?"*, and founder and CEO of LUNA Education, Training and Consulting

"This is the most comprehensive and useful clinical training book on this population I have ever read. Remarkably readable, *The Clinician's Guide to Treating Adult Children of Narcissists* presents a vast amount of material in such an organized, relatable way that you know you can use it right away to do a better job. Using perfect teaching metaphors, the authors offer a rare combination of practical aids and deep insight into unconscious factors. Their sensitivity to cultural issues also provides a long overdue boost in awareness for any therapist. The client handouts, charts, and questionnaires alone are worth the purchase, but read it all to get every drop of these master clinicians' wisdom."

—Lindsay Gibson, PsyD, best-selling author of *Adult Children of Emotionally Immature Parents: How to Heal from Distant, Rejecting, or Self-Involved Parents*

"This book is a must-have for clinicians, whether a client's parent has narcissistic tendencies or narcissistic personality disorder. Marlow-MaCoy and Kempe approach the issue of narcissistic abuse globally, looking at the damage caused not only by the narcissistic parent but also by those who enabled them."

—Stephanie Moulton Sarkis, PhD, NCC, LMHC, author of *Gaslighting: Recognize Manipulative and Emotionally Abusive People—and Break Free*

"Wow! I wish I'd had this wonderful resource much sooner in my career! I frequently work with the college student population, and many of them are navigating the first steps away from a narcissistic parent at the same time as the transition to adulthood. Marlow-MaCoy and Kempe have written a very thorough guide for the clinician, clearly defining concepts and sharing important history and research. The case studies are in-depth and quite illustrative. I especially appreciate the takeaway questions for further exploration at the end of each chapter, and the *very* helpful appendix, which is chock-full of resources. I'd say that this book would have a home on my practice's bookshelf, but I know that it will likely be off the shelf and on my desk, with many pages bookmarked and text underlined for emphasis."

—Kelly D. Shea, LMFT, trauma specialist

"*The Clinician's Guide to Treating Adult Children of Narcissists* is an easy and informative read. Not only do the authors provide an in-depth understanding of narcissism in all its forms and how it can impact children in their adulthood, but they also provide resources to assist in further therapeutic understanding. This, in turn, will guide and benefit treatment greatly. This book will be an invaluable tool in furthering my practice."

—Shannon Innes-Bloom, B.Psych. (Hons.), M.Psych. (Clin.)

"This book is expertly crafted to be easily accessible and supportive of clinicians working with individuals who have been impacted by narcissism. Treating an adult child of a narcissist can be complex and confusing for a clinician who has limited knowledge, understanding, experience, and training on this particular (and often overlooked) population. The clear, concise definitions and examples of narcissistic tendencies provide a detailed picture of how clients may have experienced narcissism from their parents while offering an opportunity for clinicians to deepen their insight and awareness of this very prevalent issue to best support clients in the healing process. The combination of examples, definitions, reflection questions, interventions, worksheets, and more lays a firm foundation for a clinician to become competent in providing well-informed, nonjudgmental care to individuals in need of support and understanding as they heal. As a clinician, I feel better equipped and informed entering into work with an adult child of a narcissistic parent, as well as more confident to support clients who have other experiences with narcissism in their lives, due to the expertise and resources shared within this book."

—Stephanie Kilper, LPC, BC-DMT

"What a welcome, thoughtful, and thorough analysis of how adult children of narcissistic parents can be affected by being raised in a relationship that is often confusing and harmful. Marlow-MaCoy and Kempe give an in-depth look at what a client with a narcissistic parent may be experiencing and needing during psychotherapy, as well as steps the psychotherapist may take in assisting the client to heal from the relationship. This is the best book I have read on the topic to date. I would recommend it to clinicians and clients alike."

—Kristin Young, LMFT

"As a clinician who specializes in treating abuse survivors, I am so pleased to have this book in my library. Many of the previously available books on the subject of narcissistic abuse are intended for clients and/or are heavy on the theory without much in the way of practical application—but not this one! In addition to providing a thorough conceptual framework for understanding the dynamics of family narcissistic abuse, Marlow-MaCoy and Kempe give clear clinical interventions and workbook-style exercises that are actually useful for everyday work with clients. They also do an excellent job of encouraging clinicians to consider cultural factors that may affect treatment, and identify ways to tailor treatment accordingly. I highly recommend this book to all clinicians—and for those of us who focus on attachment and trauma, it's a must-read."

—Monique Dauphin, LMHC

"This is a highly informative and comprehensive guide for any clinician who works with adult children of narcissists. Highlighting the important details of therapy with these clients, Amy Marlow-MaCoy and Amy Kempe cover all the bases—the therapist's approach, the characteristics and behaviors of the individual with narcissistic qualities, the intense struggles of the spouse/other parent, and the siblings' experiences and wounds. A deeper and more vast context of this family dynamic is clearly presented and the impacts on the family and the individuals explored, including their views of self and future relationship difficulties."

—Kaitlin Wenger, LCSW

"*The Clinician's Guide to Treating Adult Children of Narcissists* is a timely, eye-opening, and comprehensive guide for working with those who have experienced and/or still are experiencing narcissistic abuse. Marlow-MaCoy and Kempe brilliantly display their experience and passion for working with these clients, and they present a myriad of techniques to adequately equip clinicians in treating this traumatized population. As a clinician, I greatly appreciate the client stories, metaphors, charts, and reflection questions, which drive the key points home. This book beautifully demonstrates ways to empower clients and boldly holds the clinician accountable, challenging us to look within and address self of the therapist issues. The reflection questions provide an incredible launching point for self-exploration and understanding for how we show up in the therapy space and therapeutic relationship. The authors also offer detailed, empowering language to use with clients and show the importance of using both a holistic and systemic approach, addressing societal influence, family roles, and culture, among many other things. This book belongs in every mental health academic program and on every clinician's bookshelf, regardless of their specialty or career stage. It is an invaluable tool that will make our work with clients—and especially with this population—that much more impactful. I have already begun to use this book to hold myself accountable, and I look forward to sharing this with my clients."

—Jennifer Rhodes, LCMFT, MS

"*The Clinician's Guide to Treating Adult Children of Narcissists* contains a wealth of knowledge on a complex and often misunderstood issue. Full of helpful tools and case examples, this guide will be a valuable resource for clinicians in the assessment and treatment of narcissistic abuse. The care and dedication the authors have given to helping this population heal clearly shines through the pages of this comprehensive, well-written book."

—Brittny Jordan, MS, LPC

"This book offers insight and support for various types of clinicians. Whether you support individuals, families, or couples, this book provides important information to be better able to spot narcissistic dynamics and to treat folks who are experiencing symptoms related to their interactions with those with narcissistic traits. A number of concrete tools, interventions, and worksheets that can be used with clients in an easy-to-understand format are included. The authors also provide important opportunities for self-reflection for clinicians, and attention is paid to treatment implications for marginalized communities. I definitely recommend this thorough and well-rounded read as an addition to your clinical library!"

—Christine Baldwin, LCSW

"*The Clinician's Guide to Treating Adult Children of Narcissists* is my new go-to volume on the subject. The authors provide an extremely rich and comprehensive look at this subject, covering soup to nuts. Clinicians will learn not only what narcissistic abuse is, but how to spot it within individuals and systems, how a person heals from this complex trauma, and how to care for themselves as clinicians while working with these presenting concerns. This book is a must-read."

—TJ Walsh, MA, LPC, NCC, CCTP, CMHIMP

"This is a must-read for all clinicians. In my experience, it is not uncommon for clients who initially seek treatment due to anxiety, depression, or relationship issues to uncover childhood relational traumas that they were completely unaware of. Marlow-MaCoy and Kempe provide a clear and concise guide to understanding the impact of narcissistic and immature parenting on the emotional and interpersonal development of children and the patterns of relating that continue into adulthood. Full of vignettes and practical tools, *The Clinician's Guide to Treating Adult Children of Narcissists* is a framework from which clinicians can confidently support and guide clients in healing their relational wounds. Most of all, the authors are delicate in their discussions with a sensitivity to family systems, intergenerational trauma, cultural trauma, and oppression, holding space for authentic healing that can impact both future and past generations."

—Jodi Silverman, LCSW, RMT

"*The Clinician's Guide to Treating Adult Children of Narcissists* is a hands-on, comprehensive guide that is a must-read for clinicians who are working with adults living with the impact of narcissistic abuse. Through the synthesis of client stories, research, reflection questions, and accessible tools for clinicians to use in and out of sessions, this book invites clinicians into an expansive understanding of the nuance and depth in supporting this population. This is an invaluable resource for new and seasoned clinicians alike!"

—Sarah Herstich, LCSW

THE CLINICIAN'S GUIDE TO

Treating
Adult Children of
Narcissists

Pulling Back the Curtain on Manipulation, Gaslighting, and Emotional Abuse in Narcissistic Families

Amy Marlow-MaCoy, MED, LPC
with Amy Kempe, MS, LPC, NCC, CSAT

Published by
PESI Publishing, Inc.
3839 White Ave
Eau Claire, WI 54703

Cover: Emily Dyer
Editing: Jenessa Jackson, PhD
Layout: Emily Dyer & Gretchen Panzer

ISBN: 9781683736059 (print)
ISBN: 9781683736066 (ePUB)
ISBN: 9781683736073 (ePDF)

PESI Publishing
pesipublishing.com

About the Authors

Amy Marlow-MaCoy, MEd, LPC, runs a private practice specializing in supporting adult children of narcissists in healing from complex developmental trauma. She has spent more than 10 years working with adults to heal from chronic and complex emotional abuse and neglect. Amy utilizes her advanced training in multiple models of trauma treatment to support clients in healing. She has completed level 1 and 2 training in internal family systems, phase 1 and 2 training in brainspotting, and basic training in EMDR. Along with her clinical practice, Amy provides supervision to pre-license candidates and professional consultation for clinicians wishing to deepen and grow their strengths in working with survivors of narcissistic abuse.

As a therapist, speaker, and author of *The Gaslighting Recovery Workbook: Healing From Emotional Abuse* (Callisto Media, 2020), Amy is regularly invited to speak on gaslighting and narcissistic abuse. Amy is a continuing education provider with PESI and has appeared as a guest expert on numerous podcasts focused on narcissistic abuse. She was an expert panelist at a screening of *A Place Among the Dead*, a film using allegory to depict the effects of narcissistic abuse, starring Juliet Landau. Amy was recently the keynote speaker at an Intimate Partner Violence Awareness program for military leadership, civilian contractors, and service personnel at the McGuire-Dix-Lakehurst Joint Military Base. Amy received her master's degree in counseling psychology from Temple University.

Amy resides in the Philadelphia suburbs with her family. In her free time, she enjoys reading sci-fi novels, snuggling with her cats, and tending her growing collection of plants.

Amy Kempe, MS, LPC, NCC, CSAT, founded, owned, and ran a successful private practice specializing in narcissistic abuse recovery and complex posttraumatic stress disorder. She saw the need for more expansive care and became a co-owner and founder of a new healthcare practice focused on trauma-informed, complete medical health, mental health, nutrition, and fitness.

Amy is also a certified sex addiction therapist who works with individuals and couples whose relationships are impacted by out-of-control sexual behaviors. She earned her master's degree from Villanova University and is trained in internal family systems, brainspotting, and eye movement desensitization and reprocessing.

Through her years of practice, personal exposure, and education, Amy has gained a wealth of experience supporting adult children of narcissists in healing and recovering from abusive relationships. From the start of her work, she was able to see the differences between complex posttraumatic stress disorder and the nuance that is needed to effectively work with individuals who have been abused by those with higher narcissistic traits. Amy is innovative in her approach to therapy and passionate about helping others understand the multifaceted ways in which narcissistic abuse affects ongoing development and creating ways to cultivate understanding and healing.

Amy lives outside of Philadelphia with her family and often spends quiet time in her garden. She enjoys finding inspiration, bringing play and fun to life, and finding novel concepts and creative expressions.

Table of Contents

Acknowledgments

Amy Marlow-MaCoy

There are many wonderful, special, and important people who have helped me grow as a person and a clinician. I would like to recognize and express my heartfelt appreciation to all of you.

To Ryan Bartholomew and Kate Sample at PESI, for providing a space to lean into my love of this client population and for allowing me to share what I have learned through my many years in practice. Thank you to Jenessa Jackson, our patient editor who helped cut through the chatter to the heart of our messages.

To those who knew I would be here long before I did: To Elizabeth Venart, who encouraged me to listen to my intuition and inner wisdom. To the many wonderful colleagues who supported and encouraged me through the years. To the professors from whom I learned the art of meeting heart-to-heart with another person. And to the many phenomenal clinicians and educators who helped me deepen the skills I use daily with my clients.

To my clients, who are my best teachers and models: Your resilience, courage, and resolve are a true inspiration. Every word was written with you in mind.

To Amy Kempe: We did it! From the moment we met, we knew this day would come. I am so proud of us and so grateful for your spirit, energy, and confidence throughout this process. Thank you for doing this with me.

Finally, to my family: To my parents, who always knew I would be an author, thank you for supporting my creative expression. To my children, Caelyn and Eleanor—you are a joy and an honor to care for with your strong and bright spirits. And to my husband, Tom—you are my loving partner, my stable ground, my encourager and supporter, my quiet certainty, and the one I truly trust. Thank you for being you.

. . . .

Amy Kempe

My life's work and the writing of this book would not be possible without the support and wisdom of many whom I would like to acknowledge and thank.

To Kevin: You are the best thing that ever happened to me. I would not have been able to do this without your unwavering support and strength. Your love is a gift of a lifetime, and I am often awestruck that I get to spend my life with you. I love you.

To Will and Adam: You are my greatest joys who inspire me to dig deeper and to go for it. Words are not enough to express how deeply I appreciate and love you, in this life and the next.

To Jessie: I would not have been able to write this book without your support, confidence, and friendship. There is no one else in the world I would want to brave this frontier with. You are a warrior.

To Amy Marlow-MaCoy: We did do it! Thank you for seeing me in this work, for our combined vision, and for all of the discussions, editing, and unsaved drafts. We grew during this process, and I am grateful our paths were intertwined.

To Ryan Bartholomew and Kate Sample at PESI: Thank you for providing me the opportunity to use my voice and share what I have learned. A huge thank you to Jenessa Jackson, who took on the not-so-small task of editing two passionate, verbose women. You are a gift, and this would not be possible without you.

Finally, to all the teachers, clients, healers, and friends in my life: I am forever grateful, honored, inspired, and humbled by the lessons you have taught me. I am because you are. Thank you.

Introduction

Imagine entering a therapy office for the first time in your life. After years—decades, even—of wondering what was wrong with you, you have gathered the courage to sit down with a perfect stranger and share your life story in the hope of finding some relief. Imagine inviting this stranger into your reality and sharing your story with them—the story you hid from yourself for years until you were forced to face your truth. The story that's been hurting you from the inside for all this time. The life story in which you were the victim of someone else's black hole of needs.

The one in which you were raised by a narcissist.

Now, imagine pouring out your heart to this perfect stranger sitting in the therapist's chair, hoping they will hear you, validate you, and help you understand what has happened to you—only to hear them tell you that you're wrong.

> *"I can absolutely validate that you feel hurt by some of your mother's parenting choices, but I don't know if it's fair to label her a narcissist. Real narcissists are extremely rare, actually."*

> *"You know, a lot of people use words like narcissist and gaslighting, but those are nowhere near as common as social media makes out."*

> *"Your father probably didn't mean it that way. Don't take it to heart. A lot of men just aren't socialized to be emotionally attuned."*

> *"I can hear that you feel very hurt by the way your parents raised you. Parents are humans, too, and we all make mistakes. I wonder how it benefits you to hold on to your resentment instead of moving on from the past?"*

> *"I really can't support cutting off family members; there is always a chance to improve the relationship if we keep trying. Let's have a family session and see where you can compromise so you can all be reconciled. After all, relationships are a two-way street."*

To make yourself so vulnerable as to share the reality of growing up with an emotionally abusive, manipulative, and immature parent is a gut-wrenchingly scary step. To take that step and then be invalidated by the person you have gone to for healing is not only pouring salt in the wound, it's a slap to the face. Sadly, this is the reality for many survivors of narcissistic abuse who seek therapy to heal from their toxic families of origin. Time and time again, we have heard the same story: A client reaches out for help to heal from narcissistic abuse, only to be inadvertently gaslighted and invalidated by a well-meaning therapist who doesn't have a deep enough understanding of narcissistic relationships.

Many clinicians are underprepared to work with adult children of narcissists because they are only familiar with narcissism as it is depicted in pop culture and social media. Most of those depictions are overly simplified, casting the narcissist as a scheming villain out to ruin their victims' lives or absolving them of all wrongdoing in the face of the narcissist's own trauma history. Some depictions are more of a caricature than an accurate portrayal of the complex humanity that even the most self-absorbed narcissist contains. In addition, there is a relative lack of resources clearly outlining and describing the dynamics of narcissistic abuse (Ackerman et al., 2017; Miller et al., 2017), and graduate education programs typically underemphasize the scale and impact of narcissism in relationships. As a result, clinicians often brush aside descriptions of a narcissistic loved one, which does a grave disservice to clients whose family members do not match the mental image of a "narcissist" but whose emotional abuse and manipulation leave equally deep wounds.

While most everyone can relate to having someone dismiss, downplay, or question their reality, this experience is especially painful for adult children of narcissists because they carry a lifetime of being told that their feelings are wrong, their memories are unreliable, and their perceptions are flawed. They have been raised to believe that they are in the wrong in any disagreement. Being invalidated yet again by a therapist—someone with all the presumed authority of knowledge and expertise—can be a devastating blow to a client's sense of self.

As clinicians, we have the power to further undermine our clients' self-trust or to be a strong source of support, affirmation, and acceptance. If we attempt to treat adult children of narcissists without fully understanding the full scope of the issues they face—including complex developmental trauma, deep attachment wounds, ingrained shame and guilt, and lack of self-identity (to name just a few)—we put our clients at risk (Grossman et al., 2017). We play into the continuation of the abuse cycle without realizing it. But if we can understand our clients' lived experiences and validate their reality, we have an opportunity to be the first source of emotional safety that they have ever encountered. That is what we are here to do with this clinician's guide: to help you gain a deeper understanding of narcissistic abuse so you can support clients in healing from it.

In this book, you will find the tools and resources you need to understand and explore a client's experience of love bombing, devaluation, triangulation, gaslighting, hoovering, and more so you can fully support them in healing from this relational abuse. We provide a thorough, in-depth description of what narcissistic abuse looks like, how it harms clients, and what differentiates narcissistic abuse from other forms of family conflict. We have also woven in a variety of client stories to illustrate what treating narcissistic abuse can look like in practice. In addition, we have included an appendix containing several handouts and worksheets to aid you in applying these concepts to your work with clients.

We wrote this book to assist clinicians who work closely with adult children of narcissists, including, but not limited to:

- Licensed professional counselors

- Social workers

- Marriage and family therapists

- Eating disorder treatment teams

- Clinical educators and supervisors

- Psychiatrists

- Psychologists

- Substance abuse treatment teams

The work of healing from narcissistic abuse is deep and complex. As conversations about narcissism in personal and global contexts increase, the need for well-trained and experienced specialists is greater than ever. Caring, competent, and well-prepared clinicians can be instrumental in changing a client's life when they truly understand the depth of the issues and dynamics at play. Having worked closely with this population for many years, we are honored to have gathered the wisdom of our clients, as well as our own experiences, and to share what we have learned with you. It is our hope that in reading this book, you will feel the same sense of respect, compassion, and pride in these clients that we do. We also hope that it will allow you to become one of those therapists with whom these clients can feel safe to speak their truth. Because there is nothing in the world quite like the feeling that someone, somewhere, finally *gets* it.

PART 1

· · · · · · · · · · · · · · ·

Understanding
Narcissistic Abuse

· ·

CLIENT STORY: Lydia

Lydia began seeing Marcel for therapy when she was 27 years old. Marcel's first impression of Lydia was of a thoughtful, intelligent young woman full of nervous energy and curiosity. When she entered Marcel's office, she responded positively to his warm welcome, the tension in her shoulders easing ever so slightly as he invited her to find a seat on the couch. As they settled into the get-to-know-yous of a first therapy session, Lydia identified the concerns that had led her to call Marcel: a difficult breakup, low self-esteem, lifelong anxiety, and dissatisfaction with her body.

"I think I need to deal with my anxiety," Lydia began. "I just got out of a long-term relationship, and I can't stop replaying everything that happened. I know Scott—my ex—did things wrong, too, but I feel like if I weren't so anxious all the time, I would be easier to be with." Lydia could easily list all of her own flaws and expressed concern that her inability to make her most recent relationship work meant she would end up alone—a deep fear that she had rarely voiced until now. "I tried so hard to make it work with Scott, *so* hard. And for it to fall apart anyway, and be alone again at 27, makes me feel like I'll never be good enough for anyone."

Marcel's ears perked up at that phrase "never be good enough." From the way her body language shifted and the quiet defeat in Lydia's voice, it was clear that this belief was deeply ingrained. It was also clear that it had taken root long before she met Scott. Curious, he made a mental note to track this in future sessions.

· · · · · · · · · · · · · · · · · ·

The Early Sessions

Lydia's first several sessions were primarily focused on coping with her breakup. As she processed the grief and loss of the relationship falling apart, Marcel noticed Lydia had a habit of questioning her own memories, feelings, and experiences. When he pointed this out, her eyes teared up.

"Well, it's true, I don't trust myself. I thought Scott was a good guy, different from my other exes. He was so sweet and attentive in the beginning. I was totally swept off my feet. I fell for it hook, line, and sinker. Obviously that didn't work out, so my judgment can't be trusted." Lydia then outlined other data points to support her own unreliability, such as becoming overly upset when Scott came home hours later than promised or feeling hurt when he made teasing remarks about her weight.

1

"Can we check that out for a minute?" Marcel asked, slowing Lydia in her litany of self-criticism. "What is wrong with feeling upset about him being late without telling you or making jokes you find hurtful?" The surprise and confusion on Lydia's face confirmed Marcel's hunch that she had been a victim of frequent gaslighting. This conversation marked the beginning of a different phase of Lydia's processing, as Marcel explained what gaslighting, manipulation, and emotional abuse might look like in a relationship.

"Maybe that's why I felt almost relieved when the relationship finally died," Lydia pondered. "I thought that was just more proof that something is wrong with me, that even though I was sad about breaking up, I also felt freer." Marcel nodded, pleased to see her consider the possibility that her intuition was correct, rather than shutting herself down immediately. Her eyes took on a faraway look as she sat with the possibility.

"That would make a lot of sense," Marcel said, validating her ambivalence. "I'm curious—you looked for a moment like you were thinking about something else other than Scott. Have you ever experienced any of the patterns we talked about in any other relationships?" It was a little risky, calling attention to the signs of slight dissociation he'd noticed, but Marcel was confident in their rapport and in Lydia's willingness to explore new insights. Lydia paused, briefly looking far away again before nodding slowly.

"I guess it kind of reminds me of how I feel with my mom," she said after a long pause. "Our mother-daughter relationship has always been... complicated. She's not abusive—she's actually very loving and my biggest cheerleader—but for some reason I keep thinking about her when we talk about Scott." *There it is*, Marcel thought. And so the next phase of Lydia's process began as they took a closer look at her relationship with her mother, Evelyn.

. . . .

Going Deeper

Although Lydia described Evelyn as a loving mother, she also made reference to her "mean side," in which Evelyn would become viciously critical of Lydia, particularly if she thought Lydia was "getting a big head" or feeling too proud of herself. Lydia's friends and teachers were rarely exposed to this side of Evelyn because in public, she appeared to be the most devoted and vocal supporter Lydia could ask for. She told everyone, including Lydia's friends and teachers, that Lydia could easily become the president of the United States one day. In private, though, Evelyn had another side.

In addition, Evelyn emphasized the importance of outward appearances and frequently commented on Lydia's changing body as she went through puberty. One time, Evelyn even gave Lydia a book on weight loss as a birthday gift. A competitive swimmer in high school, Lydia had always maintained a strong, fit physique but frequently worried about her size. Lydia's lifelong body image concerns now made even more sense, although she had never really considered her mother as a source of those concerns.

"I think she just didn't want me to gain too much weight because it might affect my swimming," Lydia said. "It hurt my feelings, but I was also really sensitive as a kid. It probably wasn't as bad as I remember." Here, again, Marcel could see evidence of the gaslighting she had experienced over the years, causing Lydia to blame herself for feeling hurt, rather than holding her mother responsible for saying those hurtful things in the first place. This time, Marcel felt Lydia was ready to confront the issue more directly.

"Sometimes it doesn't matter what the other person intended," he said calmly. "If your mom's advice was hurtful, your feelings are valid regardless of what she intended." Lydia's discomfort was immediately palpable as she froze in her seat and stared at Marcel.

"I can't be mad at her," Lydia said, somewhat defensively. "She did so much for me as a single mom. She did her best and I love her." Lydia's resistance gave Marcel another piece of important information: that acknowledging her mother's words as hurtful immediately triggered guilt, shame, and a need to defend Evelyn. Trusting their rapport, he gently pressed a little more.

"Okay, I hear that it's really hard to talk about how your mom might have hurt you," he gently reflected. "I'm wondering what feels wrong about that. Do you think it's possible to love someone *and* acknowledge the ways they have hurt you?" Lydia's knuckles turned white as she squeezed her hands tightly together and bit her lips.

"I don't know," she finally said, very quietly. "It makes sense in my head, but it doesn't feel right to talk about her like this. I feel like I'm not giving her enough credit for how hard she tried. And it feels wrong to complain about her to you. Mom used to get really upset if I told anyone what she said about my body or about the diet book. She said talking about stuff like that outside was 'airing our dirty laundry' and 'low class.'"

A few more pieces of the puzzle clicked into place as Lydia spoke. The secrecy, the feeling of disloyalty when she spoke about her mother's hurtful behaviors, the conditioning to paint her mother in the best possible light—Marcel's suspicions were confirmed. Lydia was almost certainly the adult child of a narcissistic parent.

. . . .

The Heart of the Pain

Lydia struggled with feelings of guilt and shame as she slowly allowed herself to acknowledge how her mother had hurt her. She ricocheted back and forth between feeling rage at the critical things Evelyn told her and feeling remorse for "talking badly" about her mother.

To help her process these conflicting feelings, Marcel and Lydia spent a great deal of time practicing "yes, and" sentences: Yes, Evelyn was a single parent who tried her best, *and* she also said and did things that were deeply hurtful. Yes, Evelyn attended every swim practice and meet to support Lydia, *and* she was relentlessly critical of Lydia's performances every time. Yes, Evelyn purchased trendy clothes and accessories for Lydia to wear to school, *and* she sometimes purchased them a size too small to motivate Lydia to go on another diet.

Eventually, Lydia's impulse to defend her mother gave way to the heartbreaking questions every adult child of a narcissist must confront sooner or later:

"Why couldn't she just love me?"

"Why couldn't I just be her daughter instead of having to be this star athlete and straight A student?"

"What do I have to do to make her happy?"

"Will I ever be good enough?"

With these questions, Lydia gradually moved into the heartbreaking but honest acceptance that her mother had emotionally manipulated and abused her throughout her life. With acceptance, Lydia began to separate herself from the idealized version of Evelyn as the heroic single parent that she'd held for so long. Instead, she began to see Evelyn more realistically: as someone whose relational patterns and behaviors had caused Lydia deep pain. And with this acceptance came the next step of healing: grieving the loss of the protective fantasy of Evelyn she had created and grieving the lack of an emotionally nurturing, healthy parent.

. . . .

Growing Through Grief

Lydia's grief was intense, prolonged, and deeply painful. As she worked through her sadness, bitterness, anger, and betrayal, she gradually began to shed the conditioned instinct to protect Evelyn's image from scrutiny. She began to see more clearly who her mother was and how their relationship had influenced the ways she saw herself. Seeing Evelyn's narcissistic traits more clearly gave Lydia insight into why her other relationships, such as the one with Scott, had caused her such pain. As she learned to recognize the patterns of narcissistic abuse, she could now begin to make different choices in her relationships instead of falling into the same traps she had before. Instead of immediately reacting to her mom's demands, she now could pause and make a thoughtful choice for herself. As her ability to self-regulate in the face of pressure and manipulation grew, her self-confidence and assertiveness also grew. Over time, Lydia learned to trust herself more deeply.

Of course, no grieving or healing process is linear. Lydia slipped into old patterns at times. For example, after receiving a negative review at work, she went into a downward spiral of self-doubt, self-criticism, and anxiety. She fixated on the negative comments in the performance review, viewing them as a reflection of her personal worth, and spent days identifying every imperfection she needed to address. But with each slip, she learned more about where she was vulnerable to manipulation. She learned where her unhealed attachment wounds lingered. And she learned that she was stronger and more resilient than she had ever believed.

. . . .

Lydia could not have known when she entered Marcel's office for that first session that the journey she was embarking on would lead where it did. Marcel couldn't have known from her initial request that the heart of their work would ultimately revolve around healing from a narcissistic parent. If they had only focused on coping with her breakup with Scott, Lydia would have just scratched the surface of the healing she needed. Fortunately, in recognizing the subtle signs of narcissistic abuse that peeked through Lydia's story, Marcel was able to help her go much deeper. In the following chapter, we will look more closely at some of those signs so that you, too, can recognize them in your clients.

Let's begin.

CHAPTER 1

What Is Narcissistic Abuse?

Defining Narcissism and Narcissistic Abuse

Narcissistic abuse doesn't exist in the latest edition of the *Diagnostic and Statistical Manual of Mental Disorders* (DSM; APA, 2013), and any two people could give different descriptions of this phenomenon. Narcissism can also wear many faces and present in a number of ways (Cain et al., 2008; Hart et al., 2017; Levy, 2012), which makes it difficult to pinpoint a single, easy-to-identify definition of this nuanced issue. We need *some* guidelines, however, to clarify what we are actually discussing when we talk about narcissistic abuse. With that in mind, we have defined it as follows:

> **Narcissistic abuse:** A persistent pattern of manipulative, abusive, and controlling behaviors that occur within a relationship, with the primary goal being the promotion of the narcissist's well-being at the expense, and to the detriment, of others.

It can be tempting to write off the concept of narcissistic abuse as a pop culture phenomenon that does not have any real clinical value. The lack of a singular, empirically supported definition of narcissistic abuse may seem to support this perception. We disagree. In the field of psychotherapy, we clinicians sometimes become hyperfocused on empirical data as the determinant of a concept's validity. There is a reason for that, as our field has had to work hard to get acknowledgment and recognition from the harder sciences. The problem lies in relying too heavily on data-driven processes that try to quantify human experiences. Not all experiences are quantifiable, but all human experiences are real and valid. Therefore, we encourage you to remain open to more nuanced conversations about narcissism that occur in all kinds of settings, rather than limiting yourself to the DSM criteria for narcissistic personality disorder.

Having said that, since narcissism and narcissistic abuse are not always easy to quantify, where do we draw the line between a narcissist and a non-narcissist? Simply put: We don't. It is far more helpful and realistic to consider narcissism as a *spectrum* of behaviors and traits than a series of discrete boxes to check off. All humans have some narcissistic traits—self-interest, external locus of control, ambition, or pride. These traits are not inherently negative, but they have the potential to cause great harm when they are expressed in ways that hurt, exploit, or devalue others.

For example, in many cultures, high self-esteem and positive self-image are considered valuable qualities. But when combined with a sense of entitlement and lack of empathy, they can become harmful and abusive. Self confidence is not inherently harmful but *can become so* when it is used to dominate or overpower others. Positive self-image is not a problem on its own but *can become so* when used to devalue others, or when it is so brittle that any critique or lack of admiration is tantamount to an attack.

For clinicians who like having clear-cut parameters for diagnosis and definition, the spectrum of narcissism can be a challenging concept to embrace. We encourage you to cultivate a flexible mindset that conceptualizes narcissistic personality traits on a gradient. Recognizing that these traits may not always meet the criteria for a diagnosis of narcissistic personality disorder should not be a reason to dismiss a client's description of their loved one as narcissistic. Embracing the flexibility of assessing traits as opposed to diagnosing another person allows you to meet clients where they are and validate their lived experience without getting derailed by incomplete diagnostic criteria.

The Many Faces of Narcissism: Subtypes and Presentations

One of the most promising branches of contemporary clinical research on narcissism is the growing awareness that there are many potential faces of narcissism (Fossati et al., 2005; Levy, 2012; Stanton & Zimmerman, 2018a; Wink, 1991). Although many of our current diagnostic guidelines for narcissistic personality disorder are skewed toward clients with the *grandiose* subtype—who are easy to identify because their oversized sense of entitlement, shameless demands for admiration, and larger-than-life personalities draw our eyes to them—this is only one form of the narcissistic personality (Ackerman et al., 2017; Levy, 2012; Yakeley, 2018). There are two additional faces of narcissism that are equally important to consider: the *vulnerable* and *malignant* subtypes.

In addition, while some researchers distinguish narcissistic personality on the basis of subtype (grandiose, vulnerable, or malignant), others do so by presentation (overt or covert). Still others use the terms interchangeably. Therefore, in the following section, we will explore each of these subtypes in more detail, including which presentations are commonly linked to each subtype. Being aware of these many faces of narcissism can make the difference between stopping or perpetuating a cycle of abuse.

Grandiose Subtype

The most commonly recognized form of narcissism is the grandiose subtype (Hart et al., 2017; Koepernik et al., 2020; Levy, 2012), given that it is associated with bombastic, over-the-top, and openly self-aggrandizing behavior. For this reason, it should come as no surprise that grandiose narcissism often corresponds with an overt presentation. Grandiose narcissists engage in flashy displays of wealth and power, expect special treatment from others, and present themselves with an exceptionally confident demeanor. They are also quick to anger and are willing to be perceived as domineering or argumentative as long as they get what they want. They can be extraordinarily charming and persuasive—and their extroverted personalities may afford them success in the public sector, such as in the competitive business world or politics—but their public persona can differ sharply from their private one. For adult children of grandiose narcissists, it can be galling to see others react in adoration to their parent's public persona with no awareness of what happens behind closed doors.

CLIENT STORY: Natalie

When Natalie, 44, was in her early twenties, she was presented with a wonderful opportunity: She had been accepted as an intern at a well-known fashion design agency in New York City. Natalie had dreamed of being a fashion designer since she was a little girl but kept her goals to herself after her parents laughed at her for voicing them. She hoped that her acceptance to this competitive internship would finally make her parents see her dream career as respectable, prestigious, and worthy of recognition. Heart pounding, Natalie showed her father, Ray, the letter.

"Dad, look at this! I got accepted for an internship position at a real New York design firm," she said, biting her lip nervously. "I know you and Mom weren't sure about me pursuing fashion, but the agency really liked my work, and they think I could have a career in design." She didn't dare ask the questions she really wanted to: *Are you proud of me? Do you think I can do this?*

Ray stared at the letter, frowning. Eventually he tossed it back at her, and it landed on the floor.

"Natalie, we talked about this before. Your mother and I told you fashion was a frivolous pursuit and a waste of your time. I thought you were smarter than this. What makes you think you know better than me when it comes to what you can do?" Ray seemed to get angrier and angrier as he stood up from his chair and strode toward the door. He stopped in the doorway, giving her one last hard look. "We told you that you needed to think beyond your own selfish desires and consider how it would look for me to have a daughter go into such a pointless line of work. How am I supposed to talk about your career with my colleagues when their children are being recruited to top law firms and medical schools, and my foolish daughter is selling blouses somewhere?" Ray threw up his hands in frustration. "Well, I suppose if you want to be hardheaded, I won't stand in your way. Maybe you'll learn to listen to me when you make a fool of yourself in front of those fashion snobs."

Ray left the room without waiting for a response. Natalie fought back tears as she picked up her letter from the floor and quietly left the room. She knew that Ray, ever concerned with the family's social status and appearances, would not approve of her choosing a career path he considered silly and not respectable. Still, some small part of her had hoped he would understand, just once, that she wanted to pursue something she loved even if it didn't grant her the wealth and prestige he expected her to achieve. *Well, he didn't say I* couldn't *do it,* Natalie thought. *I think I'll give it a try.*

The following week, Natalie walked to the subway station with her father, timid yet eager to start her first day at her internship. While they each waited for their respective trains to arrive, she made small talk with another passenger, who wished her well in her internship. When the passenger left, Ray turned to Natalie with a furious scowl.

"Just who do you think you are, telling some complete stranger you're going to be a fashion designer?" he hissed. Natalie recoiled at the venom in his voice. "You think you're something special? You're not! You're nothing! You're no one! You think you're better than me, with your worthless bachelor's degree when I have a PhD in physics? I'm doing something worthwhile! And what are you doing? Playing dress-up, like a stupid child. You're an embarrassment."

Natalie was devastated. She looked away, trying desperately not to cry. When Ray's train arrived, Natalie watched in disbelief as her father's face abruptly changed from the storm cloud of anger he had showed her to the bright, charismatic, charming face he showed the world. While Ray greeted the train conductor with a grin and a joke, Natalie sat alone trying to compose herself. She tried to calm down and rebuild her confidence, but she couldn't get his harsh voice out of her head. Finally, she admitted defeat and went home. Twenty years later, she could still hear the exact tone of her father's voice, cutting her to pieces at the mere suggestion that she might feel proud of her achievements.

Natalie's father was a grandiose, overt narcissist. He believed that his advanced degree, prestigious engineering job, and status entitled him to dictate Natalie's career path. He enjoyed being in the spotlight and receiving admiration from friends, family, and the community, and he feared losing face among his peers, whose children were pursuing what he considered more illustrious careers. Natalie's internship opportunity, which could have led to her dream career in fashion design, was a threat because it might have brought negative attention or a loss of status if Ray's colleagues judged him for her choices. Conversely, if Natalie found success in her chosen field, she could have risen to fame and fortune, eclipsing Ray's own social position. This could not be tolerated, so he crushed her fragile self-confidence until she gave up on the opportunity. Decades later, she still saw herself as incapable, foolish, and unrealistic to think she could ever accomplish anything worth pursuing.

Vulnerable Subtype

Like their grandiose counterparts, vulnerable narcissists are characterized by pervasive patterns of self-centeredness, lack of empathy, and envy of others (Hart et al., 2017; Masterson, 1995). Unlike grandiose narcissists, though, they are more likely to cloak these traits in the appearance of neediness and frailty to recruit others to fight on their behalf, which makes them more covert in nature. For example, a parent may interfere with their adult child's relationships by continually demanding their child's attention and expecting to be prioritized over their child's partner.

Vulnerable narcissists are also emotionally expressive, showing sadness when they feel hurt, unappreciated, or disrespected as a means of inducing sympathy and compassion from loved ones. They are characterized by a frequent sense of victimization, low or fragile self-esteem, and a tendency toward depressive symptoms. For this reason, the vulnerable subtype is often harder to identify, as it is less characterized by extraversion and outward displays than the grandiose subtype.

Vulnerable narcissists may also express self-aggrandizement by presenting themselves as the unfairly overlooked or injured party in any situation. For example, a vulnerable narcissist may perceive themselves as an unappreciated genius who just never got their break. They might similarly refuse to take an entry level job because they consider it beneath them, despite their lack of skills that would justify a higher position. They may also believe they have been personally victimized by the people or systems that hold them back from realizing their full potential.

To help illustrate how vulnerable narcissism can manifest, let's continue with Natalie's story. Although the narcissism in Natalie's father was easy to identify, Ray was only one of the two narcissists in her family of origin. The other was her mother, Gina—a vulnerable narcissist whose manipulation was not as visible as Ray's. Gina was less aggressive than Ray in that she didn't attack Natalie's personality as directly, but she always managed to turn the focus of the conversation back to her own unmet needs, disappointments, ailments, or unhappiness.

CLIENT STORY: Natalie *(Continued)*

Twenty years after her disastrous attempt to pursue the fashion career her father didn't approve of, Natalie often found herself thinking back to that day and wishing she'd gone through with her plans instead of going home. Over coffee with her mother, Gina, she once again voiced her regret over letting Ray destroy her confidence and walking away from a great opportunity.

"I just wonder what kind of life I could have had if I'd gone to the internship," she sighed. "If Dad had been even a little supportive, maybe I would have a career I could be proud of instead of quitting every career advancement opportunity that comes my way because he's convinced me I can't do anything." Natalie felt tears gathering in her eyes as she felt the familiar heat of shame. She had never really recovered from her father's crushing words. Every time she thought about pursuing an interest or taking a risk, she heard his contemptuous voice in her mind again. *You're nothing. You're no one.*

Gina smiled sympathetically, patting Natalie's hand. A former dancer and singer, she had been a stay-at-home parent for most of Natalie's childhood. She had never pursued her own aspirations outside the home because only Ray's work mattered.

"You know how your father is; he probably thought you had thicker skin and wouldn't be so upset. He just wants to make sure we all do our part to support the family, and we can't jeopardize his career by making poor choices." Gina sighed and gestured at herself. "Look at me. I could have gone on auditions and been on Broadway, but I chose to support your father instead. I sacrificed my future to make sure your father could give you the best life possible. Don't you think we deserve some appreciation for that?" Natalie felt a spike of anger on her mother's behalf. Gina's dreams had also been sacrificed on the altar of Ray's ambition.

"That just means he was horrible to both of us, Mom," she protested. "You shouldn't have had to give up everything just because he had to be number one. He abused you, too. All those fights when he called you washed up, said you were getting fat, said you were delusional to think you'd have made it on Broadway—don't you remember that? He was awful to you when I was a kid. You don't have to make excuses for him." Gina pursed her lips and narrowed her eyes. Despite their tumultuous and often unhappy marriage, she could be prickly about Natalie or anyone else criticizing Ray.

"Nat, I accepted that my life as a woman ended when I became a wife and mother. I couldn't care about myself when I had you and your dad to take care of. We all make our choices in life." Natalie tried to respond, but Gina cut her off and continued, irritability shining through her words. "Maybe it's time for you to own up to your responsibility here, Natalie. Your father wanted you to do something worthwhile, something *important*. You knew he wouldn't approve of fashion, but you ignored him and put yourself in his crosshairs. You think I don't wish I could have just done what I wanted when I was your age? Well, I guess my feelings don't matter to you, either, since you're so focused on what *you* didn't get to do."

As so often happened when talking with her parents, Natalie found herself feeling confused and off-balance. She shook her head slightly, trying to figure out how she ended up on the defense when she'd started the conversation looking for empathy.

"Mom, I wasn't trying to say your feelings don't matter. I was trying to say I get it because Dad has hurt us both. He's been mean to both of us and shut down any chance of us pursuing our dreams. We shouldn't have to justify the things we're passionate about for him to think they're worthwhile." Unfortunately, once the spiral began, it was impossible to stop. Gina was on a roll.

"You need to check yourself, Natalie. You sound very entitled," Gina said coldly. "Your father and I have sacrificed and given up things we wanted to ensure that you would have every opportunity. A little gratitude and grace are in order. Your father is an important person doing important work. Do you really expect him to fawn over you for going against his wishes and embarrassing him in front of his colleagues because you were 'passionate' about selling dresses? Let it go! It's not our fault you haven't done anything else with your life because he said something mean when you were 21."

Natalie bit back an angry retort and forced herself to calm down. The conversation was at a dead end. She knew from previous experience that once the conversation reached this point, Gina would take any critique of Ray as a dig at her own parenting.

"Forget I said anything, Mom," Natalie sighed. "I wasn't criticizing you. I was just trying to commiserate about Dad."

"I don't know why you feel such a need to vilify him. If he's such a bad guy, then I must be just as bad for supporting him. I'm sorry we've failed you so badly as parents that you've thrown away your whole adult life. Maybe when we die, you'll find whatever it is you think we've kept from you," Gina huffed. Natalie's shoulders slumped in defeat. *Why did I think it would be different this time?* She wondered. *I never seem to learn.*

Gina tolerated Ray's emotional cruelty and manipulation because she gained status by association, and she enjoyed the material comforts that his prestigious career afforded the family. At the same time, Gina could gain sympathy from friends and loved ones by presenting herself as a victim who couldn't be expected to stand up to him or to support their daughter.

Gina also learned early on that she could gain Natalie's sympathy by complaining about Ray's verbal attacks, creating an alliance between mother and daughter in which they were both Ray's victims. But when Natalie tried to join with Gina, or when she introduced a complaint about Ray, Gina would turn on Natalie. As a result, Natalie had no real allies at home. Even after Natalie cut off contact with Ray in her thirties, Gina continued to pressure Natalie to reconcile because it made them "look bad" to have a daughter who did not speak to her father.

Malignant Subtype

The third subtype of narcissism is malignant narcissism, which can involve an overt or covert presentation. What separates this subtype from the others is the severity and intentionality of the behaviors (Hall, 2019; Stanton & Zimmerman, 2018b). Contrary to popular belief, narcissists are not always acting with malicious intent. Very often, their manipulative behavior is largely driven by a subconscious desire to make the world feel more tolerable by shutting out anything that threatens their sense of importance. Because narcissists are very skilled at identifying vulnerabilities in their victims, it can feel like they are intentionally adding salt to the wound by behaving in ways they know to be hurtful. But the truth is, many narcissists react on instinct.

The exception is the malignant narcissist, who willfully and intentionally sets out to punish others for perceived wrongs committed against them. While many narcissists are primarily concerned with their own welfare, a malignant narcissist will go out of their way to punish anyone they feel has wronged them. For example, a malignant narcissist who feels that a colleague has disrespected them by disagreeing with the narcissist's decisions on a project might take revenge on this colleague, using malicious gossip, gaslighting, sabotage, and coercion to target and discredit them, all with the goal of silencing and punishing anyone who dissents from the narcissist.

In this respect, malignant narcissism can begin to meld into antisocial personality disorder and even sociopathy. Similar to those with antisocial and sociopathic traits, malignant narcissists often take pleasure in the act of dominating, controlling, and humiliating others. However, there are some subtle differences between these conditions. For example, antisocial individuals are more likely to treat people like toys for their own amusement rather than as tools to elevate their status, as narcissists do (Lay, 2019). Malignant narcissism and antisocial personality disorder also differ in that narcissists are more sensitive to criticism, are more focused on their sense of self-importance, and have superficial concerns such as appearance and material wealth (Shafti, 2019). Finally, while someone with antisocial personality disorder might not care if their manipulation tactics reflect poorly on themselves, a malignant narcissist always wants to present themselves in a favorable light while making their target look bad. Let's look at another case example to illustrate this.

CLIENT STORY: Felise

Felise had been married to Gage for 15 tumultuous years when she finally filed for divorce. After years of belittling, public mockery, and infidelity, she had reached her limit. When she informed Gage that she was contacting a lawyer to file for divorce, he flew into a rage. Gage called her pathetic, weak, and mentally ill. He promised to make their divorce an agonizing experience as punishment for her choosing to leave. Felise had known that Gage could be vindictive when he felt wronged, but she had hoped they could find a peaceful solution in order to spare their three children a prolonged custody battle. She soon learned that this was wishful thinking.

Gage filed for full custody of the children, claiming that Felise was mentally and financially unstable. He used her history of postpartum depression as evidence of her emotional unfitness and her lack of work experience due to being a stay-at-home mother as proof that she could not provide. In an effort to provoke Felise, Gage would send her cruel text messages accusing her of infidelity, of being a gold digger, and of lying for sympathy. When she reacted, he used her response as fuel to gaslight her. "You see?" he would taunt. "You can't even keep your cool in a text conversation. How do you think you're going to manage life in the real world?"

Felise fought for and eventually gained primary custody, but the court hearings dragged out for over three years before they reached a settlement. Even then, Gage continued to disrespect Felise's boundaries by using their children to spy on her. He would call the children during Felise's custody weeks to ask what she was doing with them and whether she had any visitors. He also began to drop by unannounced, bringing expensive gifts for the children and stating he "just couldn't wait" for them to see what he had gotten for them. The kids began asking to go to Gage's house before it was his turn for visitation because they wanted to play on their new game consoles and cell phones. When Felise asked Gage to stop luring the kids with expensive presents, he accused her of jealousy.

Gage also began spreading his own version of their separation through their small community, telling other parents that Felise had left him because she no longer wanted the responsibility of being a wife. He painted her as an irresponsible, selfish woman who only stayed at home with the kids to avoid getting a job but still expected him to put her up in luxury. Felise tried to combat the lies, but the damage was done. Other parents gradually pulled away from her, and her social support dwindled. Unwilling to stoop to Gage's level, Felise tried not to respond but simmered with anger at the bald-faced lies.

Gage was infuriated by Felise's decision to end the marriage, and he made it his mission to punish her and make her regret her choice for as long as he could. Even after finding a new partner and getting remarried, Gage continued to harass and undermine Felise at every opportunity. He was determined to "win" the divorce and did not care who else might be harmed in the process. Felise's story is sadly not uncommon in divorce and co-parenting when a malignant narcissist is involved.

Traits of Narcissistic Subtypes

Grandiose Narcissism	• High in self-esteem • Overconfident • Exploitative behaviors • Domineering • Antagonistic	• Motivated by pursuit of social status, admiration, and power • High in extraversion • Less likely to seek therapy for emotional distress
Vulnerable Narcissism	• Low or fragile in self-esteem • Hypersensitive to criticism • Distrustful of others • Emotionally reactive • Avoidant	• Frustrated by unfulfilled fantasies of success • High in introversion • More likely to seek therapy for emotional distress
Malignant Narcissism	• Opportunistic • Use intellect as a weapon to belittle others • Value others only as a means to an end (their own benefit) • View people as tools or pawns	• More likely to be overtly sadistic and cruel • Emotionally disconnected • Superficially charming • Willing to manipulate others without remorse
Shared Traits Across Subtypes	• Entitlement • Self-importance • Fantasies of superiority • Anger or aggression following perceived slights • Envy of others' success	• Callousness • Lack of insight • Lack of concern for others • Highly image-conscious • Superficial

Ethical and Cultural Considerations in Diagnosing and Labeling Narcissism

Clinicians are taught to avoid diagnosing anyone based on hearsay, yet working with adult children of narcissists would appear to fly in the face of that wisdom. There are certainly risks to accepting someone's description of another person as a narcissist. You are receiving information filtered through the client's experiences, and the client has an understandable bias in how they present the other person. That said, there is genuine value and validity to the observations of outside observers. One of the fundamental traits of a narcissist is a blind inner eye. They lack self-awareness, making the adult child of a narcissist's keen perception especially valuable in understanding the dynamics at work in the family.

Regardless, when working with adult children of narcissists, it is important to be clear about how you use language, including terminology such as *narcissist* and *narcissism*. You want to support clients in using the terms that feel accurate to their experience. Some clients may feel uncomfortable describing their loved one as a narcissist because they don't want to label or diagnose them. These clients may resonate with alternative descriptors, such as *emotionally immature* or *self-absorbed*, which may feel less pejorative. We encourage you to use the terminology that feels best for the client. You do not need to diagnose someone with narcissistic personality disorder to acknowledge how their narcissistic traits have impacted the client.

While we encourage you to practice flexibility in your terminology, we also want to emphasize your ethical obligations and boundaries when it comes diagnosing someone you have not personally assessed. This becomes especially relevant when your client is involved in court proceedings. You cannot ethically diagnose a client's loved one or partner with narcissistic personality disorder or testify to them being narcissistic based on the client's description alone. It is important to be clear and upfront with your client so you are both on the same page in your wording and expectations.

In addition to considering the ethical implications of labeling a third party as a narcissist, it is important to recognize that the definition and diagnosis of narcissism is socially and culturally laden (Foster et al., 2003). For example, in the United States, clinicians are more likely to assess and diagnose narcissistic personality disorder due to its inclusion in the DSM. However, many other countries use the *International Classification of Diseases* (ICD-11; WHO, 2019), which does not include narcissistic personality disorder as a discrete diagnosis (Yakeley, 2018). Therefore, we strongly encourage you to consider the cultural values of your community and those of your clients as you assess for narcissism within the family.

It is also important to take gender, socioeconomic status, and race into account when considering whether someone's behavior is narcissistic or simply a response to a culture that devalues them. Gender role expectations, for example, can have a strong influence on how we perceive the same trait in different individuals (Green et al., 2021; Grijalva et al., 2015; Jack, 2021). Western society tends to value confidence, leadership, ambition, entitlement, and extraversion in White cisgender men, but often punishes or devalues those same traits in virtually anyone else. This is particularly true for Black, Indigenous, disabled, LGBTQ+, and other marginalized communities. This is not to say that White cisgender men do not also suffer from rigid and inconsistent cultural norms, but they also receive more benefits from those norms than others.

Similarly, clinicians need to be sensitive to how different cultures may weigh traits and behaviors on the narcissistic continuum. Clients who come from cultures where deference to parental authority is highly valued may have difficulty distinguishing between appropriate respect for authority and subservience. They may feel unbearably shameful or disloyal if they speak negatively about their parents; they may even risk expulsion from the family if they speak up for themselves. For these clients, the cultural values of family cohesion and community may be simultaneously a source of pride and resentment. Part of the client's healing work may involve grieving the ways their parents' narcissism has warped how they experience their cultural values. They may want to find their own way to relate to their culture as they learn to separate their parents' abusive behavior from the values with which they resonate.

Clinicians also need to be aware of how differences in cultural background may heighten the client's fears of exposing family problems to someone outside the home. Clients may worry that inexperienced clinicians will judge them or assume that their narcissistic parent's behavior is simply a community norm that the client must accept. Be open and humble if your background differs from your client's. The truism that the client is the expert on themselves is particularly important in these cases. Clients need to know that you respect both their individual experience and the community from which they come before they can feel safe enough to show vulnerability.

In addition, it is critically important to respect the client's willingness to explore how their community or culture may have either been supportive or turned a blind eye to the abuse of power they experienced. Some clients may grieve the lack of protection or normalization of toxic family dynamics within their community. They may feel numb, angry, or betrayed by their community. Be patient, compassionate, and nonjudgmental as your clients work through these complicated feelings. They must work to understand the difference between their culture and their abusive family's enactment of that culture, after which they can repair their relationship with the former. Gaining a relationship with those in their culture—one that is separate from their family of origin—is often deeply healing and profound for clients.

Religion and Narcissism

Although religious and spiritual practices are not inherently harmful, they can become vehicles for abuse on both a micro and macro scale. Some religious communities—particularly those with more conservative, fundamentalist, or literal interpretations of religious texts—can be prone to *collective narcissism* (Bent-Goodley & Fowler, 2006; Cichocka & Cislak, 2020; de Zavala et al., 2009). This is a form of narcissism in which an individual gains status and a sense of superiority by virtue of their inclusion in a particular community. In religious groups, it is not uncommon to find strong narcissistic traits among those in leadership positions, as some doctrines describe leaders being "called to a position of authority." Unfortunately, this authority has been used for millennia to manipulate and control others, including women, people of color, and LGBTQ+ individuals, who have historically been discriminated against.

Some religious doctrines also lend themselves to reinforcing narcissistic behavior on a micro level (Lasine, 2002). Children of narcissistic religious leaders are conditioned from an early age to show obedience, respect, and deference to parents and other authority figures. They are expected to maintain an image of godliness that will reflect positively on their parents. Some religions even teach that parents and church elders are essentially the voice of God and that to disobey or question them is to challenge God. Clients raised in these environments may struggle with deeply internalized beliefs about their own "badness" and unworthiness. They may believe that attending to their own wants and needs is selfish, which is often held up as one of the worst character traits a person can possess. These clients will need to spend more time unraveling and challenging the message that self-care is selfish.

We do not wish to suggest that all religious or spiritual practices are harmful. Many people find comfort and fulfillment in spiritual beliefs, and a religious community can be a source of support. However, for those who have been abused and manipulated through religion, it is very important to acknowledge and work through their religious trauma in concert with their family trauma.

Therapeutic X-Ray Vision

The purpose of exploring, questioning, and expanding your understanding of narcissism in family systems is not just to give an accurate description of the problem, but to help you understand that narcissism can hide in plain sight. You may inadvertently rationalize coercion, manipulation, and gaslighting in any number of ways if you aren't paying close attention to the telltale signs. If you fail to recognize the manipulation as an ongoing pattern of abuse, you will fail to give your clients the support they need to cope with narcissistic loved ones. As a clinician, you need x-ray vision to see beneath the surface. You have to be able to see the problem clearly to know how to best support your clients.

Chapter Takeaways

 **Key Points**

- Narcissistic abuse is a pattern of abusive, manipulative, and controlling behaviors that elevate the narcissist at the expense and through the exploitation of others.

- Narcissism is not a monolith. The three primary subtypes are grandiose, vulnerable, and malignant narcissism, which may be presented overtly or covertly.

- Narcissism is not solely restricted to the DSM diagnostic criteria for narcissistic personality disorder. It represents a spectrum of personality traits and behaviors varying in severity.

- How we perceive and label narcissism can vary as a function of gender, race, cultural norms, religious beliefs, and community expectations.

 **Therapist Aid**

- *Glossary of Toxic Relationship Terms* (appendix, p. 126)

 **Reflection Questions**

- We all have internal biases and beliefs that are influenced by our cultural norms and values. How do your biases and beliefs affect your ability to recognize narcissistic traits in your clients' families of origin?

- Clinicians sometimes miss the more subtle signs of covert narcissism. What will you consider differently now that you are more aware of these presentations?

- Some narcissistic traits are easier to identify than others. Which traits are easiest, and which are most difficult, for you to recognize and address with your clients?

CHAPTER 2

The Narcissistic Family Structure, Functions, and Roles

The Spider's Web

In many ways, the structure of a narcissistic family resembles a spider's web, in which everything spirals down to a central point. In narcissistic families, this central point is the narcissist's need for praise, admiration, power, control, and self-promotion. Family members are expected to support, or at least not impede, the narcissist's drive to meet those needs. The wants and needs of other family members are secondary, or even peripheral, to that central point (Donaldson-Pressman & Pressman, 1994).

Just as a spiderweb is made up of fine lines of a deceptively strong substance that is difficult to escape from, individuals in narcissistic families are pressed into specific roles or functions within the family. Each assigned role sets the individual on a designated path along the web, and it is difficult to break away from the assigned path because the narcissist's gravitational pull holds family members firmly in line (Gibson, 2015). For the unlucky family member who becomes entrapped in this web, any attempt to escape may result in increased attention and scrutiny from the watchful gaze of the web-maker, who will then employ one or more manipulation tactics to push the individual back into their usual role. There is simply no graceful exit once someone is caught in the web. They must fight to free themselves, tearing the delicate web and leaving a gaping hole fluttering in the wind.

To make a sticky situation more complicated, family roles are not always consistent or well-defined. A person's assigned position in the family may change based on a variety of factors, such as a change in financial or social status; life events, such as births, deaths, weddings, or divorces; or someone in the family resisting their assigned role or even breaking away entirely. *The Karpman Drama Triangle* handout in the appendix illustrates how family members may shift between specific roles and dynamics over the course of a single argument. The common theme in all family roles is that they are ultimately support roles. The narcissistic parent is central, and all challenges or independent decisions are made at the family member's own peril.

Narcissistic Family Norms: Loyalty, Obligation, and Status

Loyalty

One of the most foundational expectations of a narcissistic family is that of loyalty to the family—specifically, to the narcissist—at all costs. Since the family centers on the needs of the narcissist, children and partners are expected to show their loyalty to the narcissist in every way. This can include following the narcissist's wishes by keeping more rebellious family members in line. It can also involve rationalizing the narcissist's abusive behavior while holding other family members to a more rigid standard. In fact, family members are expected to defend the narcissist against any critique of their actions, whether those critiques originate from within or outside of the family. They learn to adopt the mentality that it is unloving to hold the narcissist responsible for the hurtful, manipulative, or exploitative behavior they demonstrate. The narcissist, meanwhile, is not held to the same standards (Donaldson-Pressman & Pressman, 1994; Gibson, 2015). Instead, they enforce loyalty through manipulative behaviors such as gaslighting, the silent treatment, guilt trips, and withdrawal of affection.

Narcissistic families also tend to reinforce the sticky web of connection by adopting an expectation that love is shown through compliance, and this expectation is extended to the child's friends and romantic partners. Narcissistic parents teach their children to assume that it is natural and reasonable to expect that everyone adhere to the narcissist's wishes. They may label a friend or partner who questions or resists the narcissist as a troublemaker or someone who wants to break up a loving family. All outsiders are potential threats unless they show themselves willing to toe the family line, at which point they may be welcomed in. As with biological relatives, however, their acceptance is always conditioned on their willingness to fall in line.

Newcomers who don't accept the narcissist's dominance may be painted as difficult, stubborn, impossible to please, or rejecting. This puts the adolescent or adult child who wants to introduce an outside relationship to the family in an extremely difficult position, as they are torn between meeting the expectations of the narcissistic parent and protecting the other party. The clashing mother-in-law versus daughter-in-law stereotype, while gendered and sexist, has some roots in the narcissistic family reality.

Obligation

These expectations of absolute loyalty come with a heaping side of obligation. In fact, it is central to a common acronym that describes the ties binding adult children to narcissistic families: FOG (fear, obligation, and guilt). Children in narcissistic families are groomed from a young age to believe they owe their parents for their very existence. They are taught that they can and should repay their parents for having raised them. This repayment can come in the form of good behavior, straight A's, financial success, a prestigious career, undying gratitude, or being an "easy child." If children attempt to set any form of boundaries, this is treated as a rejection of that obligation and evidence of their selfishness. This serves as a powerful deterrent to individuality and personal differentiation.

In addition, when a child has been taught to believe that they owe their parents for raising them, they may not feel comfortable taking credit for their own hard work and achievements. They may state that they never could have accomplished what they did without their narcissistic parent's help. While it is perfectly healthy to acknowledge a loving parent's support, in a narcissistic family it is often the way an adult child relinquishes well-earned praise or recognition for their efforts. They simply defer their success to the parent, whether or not they were actually involved in the child's accomplishment.

Ultimately, narcissistic parents treat childrearing like a payday loan, which children must repay through unconditional loyalty and familial obligation. However, we want to be clear that there is a difference between having a sense of familial responsibility to care for an aging parent and the unfettered obligations that are expected of children in narcissistic families. These obligations are not akin to providing care for an elderly relative who is unable to safely live on their own. Rather, they reflect an ingrained expectation that the narcissistic parent has extended themselves in raising the child.

Status and Power

Narcissists crave status and power, and these traits can play out in the family system as well. Since money is tangible proof of value and social status to a narcissist, they may withdraw financial support from a rebellious child, offer monetary gifts in lieu of an apology for appalling behavior, or use money and gifts as leverage to get their way. For example, an adult child planning a wedding might find themselves increasingly edged out of decisions about their attire, decor, and venue after accepting a narcissist's money for the wedding. Similarly, a young parent may believe their narcissistic parent's offer of free childcare is a generous gift but miss the strings attached to this offer, in which the narcissist may undermine the parents' decisions, criticize their choices, and ignore their wishes.

Narcissistic parents also consider an adult child's financial and material success a measure of the child's quantifiable value (and, in turn, a reflection of the parent's own quality and status). When an adult child of a narcissist achieves a certain level of financial or social success, it may even override other factors that have previously devalued the child in the narcissistic parent's eyes, such as a rebellious attitude or poor academic history. For example, a child who was treated as a scapegoat for failing high school may be elevated in perceived social status if their current entrepreneurial success brings enough fame, wealth, and admiration to the family (Shin & Youn, 2020).

Because narcissistic families often conflate material success with human worth, clients raised in these family systems may have a complicated relationship with money. Some may loathe financial success on principle because their narcissistic parent used wealth to flaunt their power and control others. Other clients may feel incapable of achieving the kind of financial success they long for because they've internalized the message that they are incompetent and undeserving. These clients may even struggle with envy and seethe with resentment when others find the financial success they have yet to achieve themselves (Piff, 2014).

When working with clients from narcissistic families, it is helpful to explore what money and status represent to them, as many clients were raised to overlook the manipulation involved in giving money with strings attached. When asked to look more closely at their beliefs about money and material gifts, clients may be surprised at the depth of their own emotional responses, such as anxiety, defensiveness, shame, and worry. These responses can create a doorway to explore how money and gifts in the narcissistic family become symbols of obligation, rather than gifts freely given.

Money and gifts may also be conflated with love, as some narcissistic parents are more easily able to shower a child with material items than show affection and unconditional positive regard. While some clients may have an internal awareness of how money has been used to manipulate them, they have likely been conditioned to downplay, dismiss, or ignore their instincts. Openly discussing their experiences and values around money in the therapy room can give clients an opportunity to validate and reconnect with their intuition. The *Money Mindset Exploration Exercise* in the appendix provides a structure for helping clients identify and work through their beliefs and values concerning money and material wealth.

"Normal" Family Dysfunction vs. Narcissistic Family Systems

All families have some degree of dysfunction, as families are made up of individuals who are, by nature, flawed and imperfect. A narcissistic family system, however, is formed from a particular set of dysfunctional dynamics that persist throughout the lifetime of its members. In particular, children raised in a narcissistic home are routinely and systematically taught to devalue their own wants, needs, and personhood in order to prop up the narcissist and prioritize their desires. The family functions by revolving around the needs of the narcissist. Those functions are carried out by fulfilling various roles in support of the narcissistic parent.

These manipulative and emotionally immature patterns of behavior begin very early in childhood and continue into adulthood, causing deep and ongoing pain and warping multiple generations of family relationships. Adult children of narcissists are raised to see this lopsided and distorted arrangement as normal. These experiences put them at risk for continued abuse in other relationships, as well as continued abuse within their family of origin. Let's revisit Lydia's story for a moment to see this in action.

CLIENT STORY: Lydia *(Continued)*

As the only child of a single mother, Lydia was in a perfect position to prioritize her mother's needs, and Evelyn did not miss the opportunity to secure Lydia as her emotional caretaker. Evelyn taught Lydia, both explicitly and implicitly, that her job was to take care of Evelyn. During her childhood, it was easy to keep Lydia close and enjoy her full attention. As Lydia entered her teen years, however, the developmentally normal desire to spend more time with friends sent vibrations through the family web, signaling to Evelyn that she needed to reinforce her position.

As an adult, Lydia struggled with chronic but vague feelings of guilt and obligation whenever she considered her own wants and needs. When she explored the roots of these feelings, she began to recall her mother's resistance to Lydia spending more time with friends in high school. In one session, she described a minor argument that ensued following a request to go to a friend's house after school. Evelyn said no, and Lydia pushed back, frustrated and angry at her mother's refusal.

"Fine," Evelyn responded, the hurt and anger filling her voice. "I guess I know where I stand with you now: last! You think you're all grown up now that you're in high school, so you must be too important and grown to be around your family. Go hang out with your friends if it's such an awful thing to spend time with your own mother! One day I'll be old, and then I'll die, and you'll probably be too busy with your friends to even notice."

Lydia immediately felt terribly guilty for hurting Evelyn's feelings. She apologized profusely, reassuring her mother over and over again that Evelyn meant the world to her. She ended up canceling her plans and staying at home, trying to make up for her "callousness" by expending even more time and attention on her mother. While Evelyn was initially cold, she soon warmed up and began to coo over Lydia's loving nature, which reinforced to Lydia that sacrificing her time was a way to earn affection.

Lydia's function in her small family was to support Evelyn's needs by fulfilling the role of Evelyn's emotional caretaker. Spending time on her own social needs would detract from this role, so Evelyn played on Lydia's ingrained values of loyalty and obligation to redirect her attention. It wasn't until Lydia finally moved out of her mother's house for college that she finally had an opportunity to develop a social life, and even then, she often worried that she was leaving her mother behind.

Supporting an adult child of a narcissist is a bit like deprogramming a victim of a cult. Because the family is so tightly wrapped around the emotionally immature parent, the client needs to learn how to view the world through a wider, more inclusive lens—one that includes recognizing and tending to their own wants and needs, which is something they've been taught makes them selfish and unworthy of love.

Narcissistic Family Functioning: Filling the Support Roles

There are a number of supporting roles in a narcissistic family, and sometimes a client may play multiple roles in the same show. In fact, many clients become extremely fluent at fulfilling many different roles, depending on what the narcissist needs at any given time. The client's chameleon-like ability to adapt and revise their presentation can be both a strength and a hindrance, as it sometimes leads to an identity crisis when the client finally has a chance to find out who they are *aside* from the roles they have filled. In the following section, we will look at three primary behaviors that family members, especially children, may take in response to a narcissistic parent (enabling, resisting, and going invisible), then identify specific support roles that they may fill.

Enabling

Enabling is the oil that keeps the narcissistic machine running. The motto of the enabler is "That's just how they are." This family member supports the narcissist in manipulating others by excusing, dismissing, or rationalizing their harmful and abusive behavior. Although the enabler may complain about the narcissist in private, they are unlikely to confront or address problematic behavior. They have learned through observation or firsthand experience that resistance is futile, and they would rather just tolerate the frustration than risk a bigger confrontation.

Anyone in the family can be an enabler, whether it's a child, spouse, sibling, or co-parent (Donaldson-Pressman & Pressman, 1994; Gibson, 2015; McBride, 2008). An enabler may overcompensate for the narcissist's behaviors, act as a peacemaker, or play the role of the "bad guy," in which they are tasked with enforcing discipline while the narcissist gets to be the "fun parent." They might also act as a double agent, offering a sympathetic ear to the narcissist as well as their victim, and then using those disclosures to enhance their standing in the other's eyes.

A family member who enables the narcissist quickly becomes a favorite because their behavior allows the narcissist to design the family system to suit their needs. Because of this favored status, an enabling child is often the "golden child" in the family—which, as the name suggests, is the favorite child who represents everything the narcissist wants to see in themselves. They are the outward expression of the narcissist's sense of grandeur and are often shielded from punishment and elevated above other family members to reward their loyalty and compliance.

An enabler may enter therapy with high defenses and have a hard time looking at how they participated in a harmful cycle of abuse. They may feel deep guilt but find it hard to admit. The enabler may also have acted from a genuine belief that they were helping other family members by keeping the peace and smoothing over conflict. They may have difficulty coming to terms with the negative impact their choices had on other family members. Finally, they may face anger, guilt, and shame for having been an unintentional accomplice who participated in the narcissist's systematic gaslighting and disempowerment of other family members.

Resisting

In contrast to enabling, there are also those who respond to a narcissistic parent by resisting their influence and manipulation. Resistant family members are less willing to comply with the narcissist's expectations and may push back on unreasonable demands. They may be the first or only ones in the family to recognize narcissistic behavior for what it is. The resistor's motto is "You won't get away with this." Because resistors do not allow abusive behavior to go unchallenged, they are frequently the target of the narcissistic parent, who may label them as a "bad child" or use them as a scapegoat. Scapegoats function as the vessel for everything the narcissist loathes in themselves and others. The scapegoat has little, if any, voice within the family and is punished for merely existing. If they express anger or protest their treatment, they are painted as jealous or difficult.

A narcissistic parent who complains of a rebellious child who gives them a hard time "for no reason" may well be describing a resistor child. They may complain about this child's noncompliance and use the child's "rebellious" behavior as a ploy to gain sympathy from others. These dynamics are one of the reasons resistor children will often fly the nest at the earliest possible opportunity, attending college across the country or getting a job very young to escape the home. In some cases, the choice to leave home is made for them when a narcissistic parent becomes fed up and revokes financial support unless the child complies. These threats, whether enacted or not, often propel resistor children to develop a strong drive for independence and autonomy that can make it difficult for them to ask for (or accept) help.

Resistors may enter therapy with more access to their anger than their enabler counterparts. They often feel strongly about breaking generational cycles of abuse and not letting manipulative behavior slide. Their drive to bring the ugly truth into the open can cause problems with family members who are committed to avoiding upheaval, which can be a source of great frustration for the resistor. In addition, their attempts to bring the narcissist's behavior to light may result in being their being ignored, invalidated, or shunned out of fear that the narcissist will retaliate. They may become outcasts even if they remain in contact with the family.

Going Invisible

Some family members become so skilled at meeting the needs of others that they create the appearance of never being in need themselves. These "invisible" family members hold the motto "There's nothing to see here." Invisibility can be embedded in many family roles, such as a parentified child who is forced to parent themselves and their siblings, as well as care for their emotionally immature parents, causing them to miss much of their own childhood (Garber, 2011). Another is that of the overlooked child, who is neither good nor bad enough to merit much notice from the narcissist. They make their way through life in the shadow of the golden child while trying to avoid the pitfalls of the scapegoat. As adults, these clients may be quick to jump into intimate relationships because they crave the attention of anyone who will acknowledge them as a person.

Even a golden child can also be forced to go invisible under certain circumstances. Although the golden child receives some benefits from being the favored child, their position at the top is not necessarily assured, as they are subject to the same conditional love as every other family member. If they fail, bring negative attention to the family, or stop adhering to expectations, they can come crashing down from their perch. In order to maintain their position, the golden child may learn to hide any struggles or personality traits that would displease their narcissistic parent. As a result, they may become very anxious, with high expectations of themselves and a deep fear of abandonment, rejection, or loss if they fail to live up to others' standards.

Finally, invisibility often characterizes the family member known as the "identified patient," who becomes the symbol for all the family's dysfunction. The identified patient expresses the family's unacknowledged problems through their illness or behavior, which can include disordered eating, substance use, depression, anxiety, or behavior problems. The identified patient becomes the lightning rod for family problems and is an easy scapegoat for any narcissistic behaviors that break through the mask of being a "nice, normal" family. However, the person behind the behavior is rarely seen; their personhood is forgotten or erased.

Whether a child is more inclined to enable, resist, or go invisible, they are expected to play a supporting role in the narcissistic parent's world. In the following table, we outline some of the common roles that children are conditioned to fill in a narcissistic family. As you review this list, consider how your adult clients may still be enacting these childhood roles when they come to your office.

Roles of the Children

The Peacekeeper	The child who tries to mediate or prevent conflict by persuading others not to disagree with or resist the narcissist. *"Look, Sis, you know he's just going to keep doing it. Can't you just let it go?"*
The Emotional Caretaker	The child who is designated as their parent's confidant, emotional support child, and sympathizer. *"Mom just gets so anxious. I don't want to stress her out by saying no."*
The Good or Golden Child	The child who casts a positive light on the narcissist through their achievements. *"My parents are so proud of my GPA that they bought me a new car for my high school graduation."*
The Scapegoat	The child who is blamed for negative perceptions of the narcissistic parent or punished for behaviors the golden child can get away with. *"I had a 4.0 GPA, but my parents didn't care because I didn't go to the college they wanted."*
The Identified Patient	The child who displays the family's wounds through illness or dysfunctional behaviors—and whose illness allows the narcissist to present themselves as a saintly, nurturing, and devoted parent. *"My mom was always nicest when I was sick, especially if someone was around to see her tending to me."*
The Overlooked or Invisible Child	The child who is often forgotten or overlooked for being neither exceptional nor problematic. *"I fly under the radar. I don't really get praised, but I don't get in trouble either."*
The Parentified Child	The child who has to take on adult responsibilities (e.g., childcare, disciplining siblings, household management, employment, being a parent's marital confidant) at a young age. *"I would research family vacation plans ahead of time so I knew what snacks and supplies to bring because my parents wouldn't, and they'd get mad if we needed something they hadn't thought to bring."*

The Lead Support Role: The Non-Narcissistic Parent

Children are not the only victims in a narcissistic family, although they are the most vulnerable. Victims can also include the non-narcissist parent to whom the narcissist is married or with whom they are co-parenting. In these cases, the non-narcissistic parent can fall into various supporting roles as well. Depending on the roles this parent filled, clients may enter therapy with several potential areas of concern. Let's explore some of these concerns as they relate to various roles the non-narcissistic parent can play.

Enabling Parents

Growing up with an enabling parent can be a source of deep frustration, resentment, and sadness for adult children of narcissists. The client may have spent their entire life waiting for this parent to rescue them from the narcissist, only to be disappointed time and time again (McBride, 2008). Even though the enabling parent may also have been a victim themselves, the client is understandably angry at their parent's failure to protect them as a vulnerable child. In some cases, the enabling parent may have even become an absentee parent, literally or metaphorically, leaving the client to fend for themselves with the narcissist rather than addressing the abusive or coercive parenting behavior.

It is critically important for you to hold gentle space for the anger, sadness, resentment, and grief that clients often feel toward their enabling parents, as these emotions are often accompanied by immense guilt. Let the client know that it is okay to be angry with their parent for enabling the narcissist's behavior, and normalize any feelings that arise.

Resistor Parents

Resistor parents complain vocally about their narcissistic counterpart in the hope of bringing their sins to light. They don't want to be an accomplice to the narcissist's abuse or manipulation and hope that these complaints will drive the narcissist to improve their behaviors. If the resistor parent is not careful, though, they may fall into another trap by triangulating their child and forcing them to choose between parents. This usually results in the child feeling torn between showing loyalty to both parents or resenting both equally. While the resistor parent may have good (if misguided) intentions in partnering with their child in this us-versus-them role, triangulation always backfires.

For many children, resistor parents may also become the source of intense anxiety because they are unwilling to submit to the narcissist. For conflict-averse children, this can be distressing, as they worry that the resistor parent will provoke the narcissist to rage. They may feel angry that the resistor won't back down and blame them for perpetuating the family conflict. There is often unvoiced grief in this anger, as the child is put in an untenable position by both parents, with no one to truly protect or look out for them.

Invisible Parents

In families where there is a particularly strong enmeshment between a narcissistic parent and a golden child, the other parent may become invisible. This can occur when the narcissist overidentifies with the golden child's potential for success and invests all their emotional and mental energy into ensuring the child reaches that potential. The other parent becomes a background figure, disregarded unless they protest, at which point they are simply an obstacle. An invisible parent can be an overcompensator, who goes to extremes to make up for the narcissistic parent's deficits—in part to camouflage their own enabling ways.

The client may view their invisible parent as weak, inconsequential, or cowardly for not having a bigger presence in the family. They may feel betrayed or feel that they were thrust to center stage by the invisible parent's inability to stand up to the narcissist. They may even feel contempt and have little patience for the invisible parent's complaints of being overlooked and ignored. It is not uncommon for the client to feel guilty for being critical of the invisible parent, in which case they may benefit from additional self-compassion development.

Finally, some adult children may feel protective of the invisible parent, especially if they are enmeshed with this parent and believe this parent was also a victim of abuse and manipulation. These clients will benefit from learning to establish healthy, loving boundaries that allow the invisible parent to resume responsibility for their own concerns rather than placing them on the child.

Rules of the Non-Narcissistic Parent

The Overcompensator	The parent who tries to make up for the narcissist's abuse through excessive praise, gifts, apologies, and expressions of love. *"A new phone will distract you from Dad's criticism."*
The Bad Guy	The parent who must become the disciplinarian or enforcer due to the narcissist's poor and inconsistent boundaries. *"Someone has to be the adult here, so you're grounded."*
The Triangulating Parent	The parent who allies with a child against the other parent, which is very common in relationships where one parent is overtly narcissistic and the other is covertly narcissistic. *"Junior agrees with me—you're being unreasonable."*
The Long-Suffering Spouse	The parent who gains sympathy from their children and others by always being a victim of the narcissist, while never asserting themselves or attempting to protect their children. *"You think he's mean to you? You should hear what your dad says to me!"*
The Absentee	The parent who leaves (physically, mentally, or emotionally) the children to fend for themselves against the narcissist. *"There's nothing I can do. Your mom won't listen to me anyway."*

Navigating Family Court and Custody Battles with Narcissistic Co-Parents

Going through a custody battle with a narcissistic co-parent can be draining and exhausting on many levels. Family courts rarely recognize the devastating impact that narcissistic abuse can have a child's development. Judges and lawyers often perceive the non-narcissistic parent's concerns for the safety of their child as a front for the parent's desire to exact revenge on their partner. Courts regularly dismiss a non-narcissist's claims of abuse or mistreatment by the narcissist as false allegations made to sling mud, particularly when the allegations are made by a non-narcissistic mother (Meier, 2020). Unexamined gender biases, a patriarchal institution, and unspoken beliefs about mothers being responsible for their children's relationships with their fathers all contribute to the difficulties of navigating custody disputes with a narcissist.

A particular source of difficulty is the practice and controversy around the concept of *parental alienation*. This refers to a pattern of behavior in which one parent seeks to separate the child from the other parent or damage the relationship between them. While many non-narcissistic parents could rightfully describe their co-parent's undermining, degrading, and manipulative behaviors as alienating, the unfortunate reality is that narcissistic parents and certain special interest groups have co-opted and dangerously twisted the phrase. The concept and usage of the term has thus become highly contentious, as it has become a powerful weapon to silence, control, or override non-offending parents' concerns for their own and their children's safety.

It is very common for a non-narcissist who reports abuse by their partner or co-parent to be counter-accused of parental alienation in response. This counter-accusation can be devastatingly effective. In Meier's (2020) review of family court cases involving allegations of child or partner abuse, non-narcissistic mothers were particularly vulnerable to harm and backlash within the court system—including losing custody of their children—for identifying and speaking out against their co-parent's abusive behavior. Rather than being validated, these non-offending parents are often painted as malicious or vindictive.

Being repeatedly discredited and portrayed as antagonistic simply for trying to protect themselves and their children can cause non-offending parents to feel depressed and defeated, and to lose hope for justice (Lee-Maturana et al., 2019). For some, the emotional, mental, and financial toll of a protracted court battle may become so high that they feel their only option is to sign over custody of their children to escape the harassment, degradation, and pressure. That this is an anguished decision may not matter to the child left behind, who experiences an additional grief process as they confront the loss of this parental relationship.

When a non-narcissistic parent loses or is forced to give up custody of their child to the narcissist, the relationship becomes a high-value target for the narcissistic parent who does seek to alienate their former partner (Baker, 2006; Garber, 2011). A child in this situation is particularly vulnerable to manipulation by the narcissistic parent, as they may feel sad, confused, angry, and afraid in the absence of the non-narcissistic parent. With the narcissist whispering in their ear that their other parent abandoned them, the child may become bitter and resentful toward the non-narcissistic parent. Alienating the child from the non-narcissistic parent is the final triumph for a vengeful narcissist seeking to punish their ex-partner for ending the relationship.

When your client is a parent legally required to continue interacting with their abuser, remember that their options are limited. They must comply or risk having a custody order revoked, losing child support, or being held in contempt of court. In these cases, they are enabling by necessity instead of choice, and your focus should be on helping them mitigate the risks to themselves and their children to the greatest extent possible. This may include providing family or individual therapy to the children, ensuring support for the non-narcissistic parent, referring the narcissist to coaching or behavioral therapy (if they are willing, which is not common), and encouraging as much age-appropriate autonomy for the kids as possible.

It is critical that clients understand the risks and potential consequences of how they present a case in court, given the significance of the risks they face to themselves and their children. Clinicians should also feel comfortable seeking consultation around these tricky circumstances, as it can feel overwhelming to help clients navigate difficult legal issues.

Collateral Damage: Sibling Relationships

One of the greatest tragedies in many narcissistic families is the severe and lasting damage done to sibling relationships (Agglias, 2018; Finzi-Dottan & Cohen, 2010; McBride, 2008). In an emotionally healthy family, siblings have an opportunity to build deep, stable, and long-lasting relationships. They can form appropriate alliances as members of the same family group, rely on each other for support and connection, and face any conflict with their parents together. No family is perfect, of course, and no sibling group avoids conflict or difficulties forever. But in a narcissistic family, siblings become casualties of parental favoritism and inequitable treatment, where they are encouraged to compete for the narcissist's approval. In rare cases, this competition brings siblings closer as they band together to resist the parent's manipulation.

More often, though, it creates deep fissures in the sibling connection that fuel jealousy, resentment, and contempt (Finzi-Dottan & Cohen, 2010; Stocker et al., 1997).

For example, golden children are often put in a position where they are pitted against their siblings, who are often described as malcontent complainers by the narcissistic parent. The golden child may come to believe that their siblings are overreacting or just impossible to please. Even if the golden child is aware of and sympathetic to their siblings' unfair treatment, they may be afraid to rock the boat and risk joining their siblings at the bottom of the ladder. They may feel they lack the power or right to confront their parents about any inequities. Some golden children are acutely aware of how tenuous their place at the top is and struggle with anxiety, perfectionism, and impostor syndrome.

Down at the other end of the ladder, the scapegoat is often keenly aware of the vast difference in attitude, affection, and treatment between themselves and their more favored siblings. They may harbor deep resentment and even hatred toward their siblings for taking more than their fair share of the available love and affection. Scapegoats often attempt to call attention to these skewed family dynamics but rarely get the outcome they hope for. Instead of getting an apology, acknowledgment, or attempt to change, they are met with contempt, gaslighting, and ridicule.

Scapegoats may even have difficulty relating to their siblings outside the narcissistic home (Thomas, 2016). For example, a golden child who falls from favor, or who struggles for the first time in their adult life, might reach out to their scapegoat sibling for sympathy or support. A scapegoat might understand their sibling's pain but also feel bitter at being expected to care about their sibling's difficulties, especially given everything they've been through themselves.

Finally, a sibling who was historically invisible within their family of origin may get caught in the crossfire when their concerns aren't viewed as valid by their golden child or scapegoat siblings. "What do you have to complain about?" both might ask the invisible sibling. "*You* didn't have to be perfect all the time. *You* didn't get punished twice as hard for the same things as anyone else." Despite the seemingly benign nature of the neglect in comparison to the scapegoat or the lack of pressure relative to the golden child, the invisible child suffers as well. It is painful to feel like a nonentity even in the dysfunction of a narcissistic family.

Gender and Role Assignments

Gender can affect role assignments, depending, in part, on whether the narcissistic parent is of the same or different gender as the child (McBride, 2008). For example, Javon, a 45-year-old father of two, was the son of a narcissistic father and non-narcissistic mother. When his twins, Quamir and Aaliya, were born, he felt an immediate preference and fondness for Quamir. Quamir grew up as Javon's golden child, praised and celebrated for every accomplishment, while Aaliya was tolerated but largely ignored. The exception to this dynamic occurred when Javon got into a verbal altercation with his own father. Suddenly incensed with his father's arrogance, Javon took his wrath out on the closest and safest avatar of male success: Quamir. Javon lacked the insight to recognize that he was projecting his anger toward his father onto his son, punishing someone who had nothing to do with the conflict.

Similarly, some daughters of narcissistic mothers may be treated like life-sized dolls through which their narcissistic mother can relive her glory days or vicariously experience her development into womanhood. Some narcissistic mothers may treat their daughters as best friends and confidants, conditioning them to accept a lifelong role as the mother's emotional caretaker. Others perceive their daughters as competition for attention, even from their own male family members. This can create a particularly sharp enmity if a father has idealized or treated his daughter like a golden child, creating and deepening the narcissistic mother's insecurity. Rather than jeopardize her relationship with her partner, the mother will more likely take her anger out on the daughter by making her a scapegoat. In this way, a child can fill two roles at once, by being the scapegoat for one parent and the golden child for another.

There are unique dangers for a child who does not identify with the gender binary or with their gender assigned at birth. When a narcissistic parent learns that a child they perceived in one way (e.g., as their cisgender daughter) is in fact different from their assumptions (e.g., is actually their nonbinary child or transmasculine son), it can make the narcissistic parent feel anxious, confused, and unsure of themselves. These feelings may trigger defensive anger that the narcissist externalizes toward their nonconforming child. Rather than taking an opportunity to be curious and open to learning, narcissists will often refuse to acknowledge a nonbinary or transgender child's pronouns and identity.

As we have seen, many factors influence the roles that children and parents play in a narcissistic family, and it is not uncommon for the same person to fulfill multiple roles at once or change roles over time. Whatever shape they take within a particular family, these cycles of parental idealization and discard can set an adult child up for years of toxic intimate relationships (Thomas, 2016). Parents and caregivers provide the first relationship blueprints that a child receives. Adult children of narcissists may continue to base their relationships off those distorted blueprints for many years, seeking approval and love from partners who replicate their parents' conditional approval and lack of true acceptance. And this is not limited to romantic partnerships; the effects of growing up in a narcissistic family also resonate throughout the client's relationships with friends, coworkers, their own children, and others.

Narcissistic Families Within the Larger Scope of Society

Social Expectations About Family

In our current society, we are inundated with messages about the overarching importance and enduring nature of family relationships. From targeted advertisements on social media to the greeting card aisle of the grocery store, we are told that family is forever, that no one loves us more than our parents, and that we should overlook and forgive all manner of sins in the name of familial love. For adult children of narcissists, there is a bitter irony in these messages, which may bear little resemblance to their lived experience.

Sadly, clients may still feel obligated to stay connected to their abusive and neglectful families out of fear, obligation, or guilt. And those who do decide to cut off ties (or even contemplate doing so) are often discouraged or pressured by disapproving family members who act as "flying monkeys," reaching out on behalf or in support of the narcissistic parent. "You only get one set of parents," they may warn. "How will you feel if they die and you weren't talking to them because of some childhood grudges?"

These dire warnings can cut deeply, as most clients who limit contact or cut ties altogether do so out of desperation, not hate. Most clients would prefer to have a loving, healthy relationship if it were a real possibility (Agglias, 2018). Cutting ties is a last resort to protect themselves from abuse that will not stop. Sometimes the intensity of the guilt trips and flying monkeys forces the adult child's hand, leading to the loss of the entire family as they must remove contact with *all* family members to escape the narcissist's influence.

It is of absolute importance that therapists working with these clients approach messaging and beliefs about family with sensitivity and compassion. You must be diligently aware of your own biases before the session begins. You should also take care not to minimize or downplay the reality of the fear, obligation, and guilt that keep clients stuck. Even if a client's worst fears do not come to pass, the threat is real and credible.

Religious Beliefs About Family

In addition to larger societal views that influence our beliefs about family, many religions contribute to the pressure that clients feel to maintain family connection no matter what (Bent-Goodly & Fowler, 2006; Thomas, 2016). For example, religious leaders, whether intentionally or not, often counsel victims to reconcile with, forgive, and pray for their abusers rather than affirming their right to respectful and loving relationships. While this is a laudable trait in principle, being merciful without any expectation of changed behavior is an open invitation to continued abuse, and many religions promote this invitation.

In fact, many religions teach forgiveness and mercy as primary moral values with little (if any) consideration for when forgiveness is unnecessary or inappropriate. This allows narcissists to weaponize messages like "love keeps no record of wrongs" (1 Corinthians 13:5) and to place the burden of forgiveness on the victims. Similarly, teachings such as "honor thy parents" become tools to maintain authority over a child even in adulthood. There is also some evidence to suggest that certain religious branches attract and support narcissistic behavior, further complicating the already sticky intersection of spiritual beliefs and self-care in relationships.

This messaging is compounded for clients in marginalized groups, such as racial and ethnic minorities, people with disabilities, and members of the LGBTQ+ community. For example, LGBTQ+ clients may experience the double blow of growing up in a narcissistic *and* religiously oppressive environment where they were taught in every way possible that they are unacceptable and unworthy. Religious trauma is a real and serious concern that can be deeply intertwined with family trauma. As always, clinicians must be aware of their own biases and worldview in order to explore the intersection between family beliefs, societal expectations, and religious practices—and where they have the potential for the deepest harm.

The Clinician's Views on Family

Finally, and perhaps most importantly in the context of this book, it is essential to consider your own views on family (Hopper et al., 2019). So often, outside pressure for family reconciliation comes from figures who should be a source of support: therapists. An uninformed therapist, no matter how well-intentioned, can strike a devastating blow to a client by encouraging or advising reconciliation where it is not advisable. Many clients have come to our offices with horror stories about previous therapy attempts in which they were talked into family therapy with a narcissistic parent, only to find the therapist being steamrolled or manipulated by the narcissist. Other clients worked with therapists who discouraged them from cutting off contact with family members, leading to years of further abuse. We have even heard of therapists who suggested that a client write a letter reinitiating contact after years of estrangement, opening the door to another wave of manipulation and coercion.

Even when they are done with the best of intentions, these interventions and treatment goals can cause terrible harm to clients who are victims of narcissistic abuse. They perpetuate family stereotypes that therapists are taught to believe in graduate school: that family unity is key and that Western-style individualism is overvalued and unhealthy. As you work to decolonize and recontextualize therapy in a diverse and multicultural world, you will find yourself continually revisiting and revising your beliefs about family norms (Donaldson-Pressman & Pressman, 1994; Thomas, 2016). But you must be cautious not to overlook the important contextual clues that help you form a detailed and accurate picture of each client's unique family situation.

In addition, you must remember that clients seeking healing from narcissistic abuse tend to have low levels of self-confidence and trust in themselves. They are often conditioned to be agreeable, as being a people-pleaser was the safest role they could fulfill in their relationships. Even the fiercest resistor clients yearn to be seen, heard, and understood in the therapy room. Your validation, or lack thereof, carries a great deal of weight with clients who lack trust in their own experiences. You owe it to your clients to treat their trust with deep respect and to be very mindful of your own biases and inclinations.

If your client is contemplating setting boundaries with their family, or is already in the process of doing so, you can support them by helping them explore the possible outcomes without judgment. Work with the client to identify how they want to handle the situation, as well as all the possible what-if scenarios that may arise, rather than trying to dissuade them from setting boundaries because of how they *might* feel afterward.

Becoming a Person

A child who grows up in a narcissistic home is like a flower trying to reach the sunlight through dense, thorny weeds. Anytime the client tries to grow and expand, they are hurt by the thorns of their parent's rejection. Adults who grew up in these families often report feeling broken, damaged, or stunted from their childhoods. The only way the flower can flourish is if it is either tended to or transplanted to a more nurturing space. Much of the client's healing work, therefore, involves finding or creating space for their own growth and healing.

As children, these clients were not allowed to develop a sense of individuality unless it benefited the narcissistic parent in some way. They were conditioned to put their parent's needs before their own and were placed in an impossible position where they were expected to excel while also letting the parent shine brightest. For some clients, coming to therapy as an adult may be the first time they have an opportunity to learn who they are as a person. As their therapist, you can provide the safe place they need to blossom.

As you work with the client to help them grow into their own person, we recommend asking them about the positive figures in their life. Having at least one loving, supportive relationship with a non-narcissistic loved one can mitigate some of the damage from the narcissistic parent. This close relationship can involve a grandparent, an extended family member, a community support, another parent, or a stepparent. Although your client may not have been able to rely on their parent, was there anyone else in their life to whom they could turn for support? This may be a starting point to eventually create a new blueprint for how relationships can look.

Chapter Takeaways

 **Key Points**

- The narcissistic family forms around a central point: the narcissist and their needs.

- Loyalty, obligation, and power strongly influence family dynamics.

- Family members are expected to play a number of roles, which may be rigid or changeable, depending on what best suits the narcissistic at the time.

- Family responses to narcissistic parents can be loosely categorized as enabling, resisting, or going invisible.

- Sibling relationships are often severely damaged by parental favoritism and bias.

 **Therapist Aid**

- *Karpman Drama Triangle* (appendix, p. 129)

- *Money Mindset Exploration Exercise* (appendix, p. 131)

 **Reflection Questions**

- Family loyalty and responsibility are not inherently negative values, but they can be used to control others in a narcissistic relationship. How have you encountered expectations of loyalty, obligation, and compliance in the therapy room?

- Clients raised by narcissistic parents often overidentify with the roles they fulfilled in their family of origin. How might you help clients begin to explore their own sense of identity, separate from these roles?

- Sometimes, clients are forced to remain part of the family system despite their desire to escape, as in the case of a co-parent. How can you support these clients in finding the healthiest options available given the limitations of their situation?

CHAPTER 3

Power, Control, and Expectations Within the Narcissistic Family

Ruling the Roost: Narcissistic Parents

In the previous chapter, we shared the mottos of some of the classic supporting roles within the narcissistic family. But what about the star of the show? If narcissistic parents had a personal motto, it would be "There can only be one." Narcissistic parents prioritize their own well-being above everything—and everyone—else. In order to meet their need for admiration, validation, and status, they draw emotional and mental energy from those around them, especially those closest to them. This process is known as gathering *narcissistic supply* (Vaknin, 2018), and it is one of the reasons narcissists are sometimes referred to as "energy vampires."

Within the family of origin, the narcissist's partner or children may be sources of supply, but children in particular seem to be an especially valued resource. Most children admire their parents, wanting to be like them when they grow up. "I'm going to work like Mommy," a preschool-aged child might say, filling a toy purse with small items and heading for the door. "I'm cleaning the pool like Daddy," another might say, poking an empty paper towel tube around the bathtub as they imitate their father vacuuming leaves from the pool.

Non-narcissistic parents usually find these behaviors sweet and endearing, and they strive to set an example they want their children to emulate. For a narcissistic parent, though, the natural and openhearted admiration of a young child is like an elixir that feeds their sense of self-importance, and they will do anything to maintain that source of supply for as long as possible. Of course, children don't stay young and innocent forever. As they mature and develop greater autonomy, the parent must take steps to ensure they retain their source of narcissistic supply. This usually involves pulling from a number of coercive or manipulative tactics to control the child's behavior, discourage their attempts to individuate, and reward compliance and submission.

CLIENT STORY: Lydia *(Continued)*

As a young girl, Lydia looked up to Evelyn and followed her lead with little resistance. But as Lydia grew older, she began to find her mother's stage-parent antics embarrassing rather than endearing. She tried to address it with Evelyn, but she got very different results than she had expected. Here is Lydia's description of one attempt to talk to her mother about a frustrating pattern: Evelyn's public critiques of Lydia's swimming performances in high school.

"I asked her once, just once, not to publicly critique my performance at swim practice, to let the coach handle that," Lydia recalled. "It was embarrassing because no one else's mom was doing that, and I knew it annoyed my coach. My mom got so mad, though. She started yelling at me for being ungrateful, then started crying and saying I was ashamed of her. She stomped off and sat at the far end of the stands until it was time to go. When we got in the car, she said she would just stop going to my competitions altogether since she was such an embarrassment to me, which was not what I'd asked for! I ended up consoling her and feeling like a horrible person."

Evelyn wanted to be perceived as an involved athletic parent because the admiration of other parents served as an important source of narcissistic supply. She also wanted to control Lydia's swimming efforts to ensure they cast a positive light on her. Lydia's request that her mother stop publicly critiquing her performance put Evelyn's self-image into question, causing her to feel embarrassed and rejected. These feelings then ignited Evelyn's anger, which she redirected at Lydia. The net result was that Lydia felt deeply ashamed of having asked for a small piece of developmentally normal autonomy and resumed her role as her mother's emotional caretaker.

Messaging from Narcissistic Parents

"You Can Never Be Good Enough"

Have you ever had a boss, supervisor, or professor who simply could not be pleased no matter how hard you tried? In a narcissistic family, this can be the norm. The narcissist's belief that they are entitled to special treatment drives them to maintain impossibly high expectations for their children and partners. This can be exhausting and demoralizing for family members, especially children, who feel like they're constantly striving to be "good enough" in the narcissist's eyes.

With few exceptions, such as for the designated golden child, this quest to be good enough is destined to lead to disappointment because narcissists are notorious for *moving the goalpost*. This is a tactic in which the narcissist initially establishes one target for winning their approval but then changes that target without warning. As a result, family members are forced to constantly adjust what they are working toward, and even if they achieve the original goal, they do not get credit because the goal has changed. They are stuck in a no-win scenario—no matter what they do, they will never win the narcissist's approval or love. Even if they are lucky enough to figure out the magic formula to pleasing a narcissist, the approval and acceptance are fleeting.

CLIENT STORY: Sanjay

As a child, Sanjay would spend countless hours practicing his violin and mastering increasingly complex pieces of music. His father would often tell him, "Sanjay, you have it in you to be a virtuoso violinist if you're just willing to put the work in. You could be amazing." Sanjay took his father's words at face value, as he truly loved the instrument and wanted to prove his father's predictions accurate. Although Sanjay was often disappointed with his father's lackluster response whenever he played the violin, he was sure it was just a sign that he hadn't reached his peak skill level yet.

When Sanjay was a senior in high school, he was invited to perform in a special concert featuring the most accomplished and skilled musicians in his school. Sanjay flawlessly performed a very difficult piece and took his bow with a deep sense of pride. Now his father would surely appreciate his hard work. When Sanjay met his parents after the concert, his mother was beaming with pride. But to Sanjay's shock, his father gave him a teasing smile and said, "Well, that wasn't too bad. I mean, it wasn't exactly Paganini's *Caprices*, but if you're motivated enough, you'll get there eventually."

Sanjay's smile soured as he realized it wasn't enough to be singled out as an exceptional musician. It wasn't enough to perform a difficult piece perfectly. It wasn't enough to do what his father had expected of him because these expectations were not fixed. If he met one goal, a new one would immediately take its place. There was no way to win, no way to ever be good enough.

Over time, when clients repeatedly attempt to meet a goal that is, by definition, unattainable, it can leave them feeling defeated and hopeless (Gibson, 2015; McBride, 2008). They have already been taught to equate personal value with external measures of success, and if they are unable to attain these external successes, they assume that something must be fatally flawed within them. Love and approval are conditional in a narcissistic family, and accepting this hard truth is one of the most painful realities that an adult child of a narcissist will ever face. Processing this reality takes deep, raw work that reaches the most wounded places inside of them. It triggers terrifying questions about the client's inherent worth, lovability, and hope for the future. *If my own parents couldn't love me*, clients often wonder, *how can anyone else?* Here is where you must help your client understand that their parent's inability to love them is not a reflection of the client, but of the parent.

"But Don't Be Too Good, Either"

The other side of this impossible setup is that no one can outshine the narcissist. Just as narcissistic parents are always moving the goalpost so their children will be never good enough, they also encourage children to be high achievers, but only to the degree that the parent doesn't feel threatened (McBride, 2008). This puts a gifted or high-achieving child in a *double bind*, an unwinnable quandary in which they are simultaneously pressured to excel and then punished for doing so. If the child crosses a certain line (which is always invisible, always in a different spot, and never acknowledged), the parent may retaliate. This can involve taking credit for their child's successes, downplaying or dismissing their achievements, or even sabotaging their progress.

In addition, should a child dare to take pride in their accomplishments, it is almost certain to provoke a negative response from the narcissistic parent, who will ironically project their own arrogance onto the child, accusing them of thinking too highly of themselves. The parent may also aggressively focus attention on the child's flaws in order to "keep them humble." At no point, of course, are the parent's flaws up for discussion.

To put it bluntly, parent-child relationships in a narcissistic family are highly utilitarian. Children are either an extension or a reflection of the narcissistic parent. A child whose success, beauty, intelligence, or popularity eclipses that of the parent (even if the parent set them up to make these achievements) is deemed intolerable, and they are put in their place so the narcissist can maintain their position at the top.

There is another layer to the narcissistic parent-child relationship that further complicates these dynamics. Narcissists have an underdeveloped sense of insight and empathy, which means that they are unwilling or unable to admit how they have hurt their families. One of the single most invalidating experiences that an adult child of a narcissist can have is to confront their parent about the emotional abuse they endured, only to hear the parent refuse to take responsibility. The narcissist will shift blame by any means necessary to maintain their internal feelings of superiority. Many narcissistic parents believe they were excellent parents, despite their children's strong disagreement with that assessment.

Keeping the Kids in Line: Tactics of Manipulation, Coercion, and Control

Imagine for a moment that you wake up and find yourself in a room that looks almost like your bedroom, but not quite. You look around, feeling confused and maybe a bit alarmed. This room is nice enough, with its light blue walls and soft carpeting, but your room, you are quite sure, has cream walls with hardwood flooring. Yet, when you find your way to the kitchen and greet your parents, they insist that your room has always been this way. They look at you like you've grown a second head when you insist that it was cream, even recalling specific decor you purchased to suit the color and feel of the room. You feel bewildered and uncertain.

But it gets worse. Now they are becoming angry with you for not agreeing that you were mistaken. "What's wrong with your room?" your father demands, growing red in the face. "Not good enough for you now?" You try to clarify that you're not unhappy, just confused, but now he's gone on a rant about your lack of appreciation, calling you stupid and deficient, and turning away with an icy demeanor. Your mother is no better: "At least your brother appreciates what he has. Maybe you could learn something from him, since you don't seem to want to set a good example yourself." The whole interaction leaves your head spinning, and you begin to seriously worry that something is wrong with you.

Although this example may seem far-fetched, it illustrates some of the many tactics that narcissists use to exert control over their families. Because narcissists are preoccupied with maintaining the status quo, in which they are poised at the top of the family hierarchy, they will squash or dismiss anything that might undermine this narrative, even when it directly contradicts reality (Dentale et al., 2015). In the next section, we'll take a closer look at some of the tactics narcissists frequently use to manipulate, confuse, and disempower their sources of supply (see the *Narcissistic Abuse Tactics* worksheet in the appendix for a more complete list). Many of these tactics either reward compliance with temporary affection or punish deviation with emotional cruelty.

Gaslighting

Gaslighting is a form of emotional abuse in which one person manipulates another into doubting their own reality (Sarkis, 2018). For example, a narcissist might engage in abusive behavior and then deny that the experience ever happened. They may accuse the other person of being "crazy" or "making things up." As a result, the person who is the victim of gaslighting begins to question their thoughts, feelings, perceptions, and memories. Individuals who have been chronically gaslit may come to believe they are inherently unreliable, overly sensitive, stupid, or unable to accurately read situations. These negative self-concepts feed an overall sense of being unworthy and fundamentally flawed. Gaslighting can be overt or subtle, and clients may be so used to receiving it that they fail to recognize it when it occurs.

SPOTLIGHT: Highly Sensitive People

Adult children of narcissists are often gaslit by being told they are "too sensitive." In fact, they *are* sensitive, but sensitivity is not a flaw or cause to dismiss a complaint. Most children of narcissists learn to scan the narcissist's emotional state as a proactive defense mechanism. They become sensitive to the energy of the narcissist and adapt themselves to what they sense.

And then there are some clients who fall into another category of sensitivity altogether, known as the highly sensitive person (HSP). Researcher Elaine Aron (1998), who coined the term, defines an HSP as someone who has heightened awareness and responsiveness to sensory stimuli. Thought to make up 15 to 20 percent of the population, HSPs are not necessarily emotionally reactive, but they do tend to feel things very deeply and pick up on emotional energy to a much greater degree. Their threshold for noticing tangible and intangible stimulation is much lower than the average person, meaning they can intuitively notice the unspoken worries, moods, and needs in others. For the HSP growing up in a narcissistic family, there is quite a lot to feel.

This increased ability to sense emotional energy can have a number of benefits. The HSP can more accurately anticipate the narcissist's moods, which allows them to sometimes avoid being the target of anger or manipulation. HSPs are also natural chameleons, adapting to the needs of those around them as fits the situation. These traits can endear the HSP to their narcissistic parent.

However, there are also drawbacks to being highly sensitive. Some HSPs find it overwhelming to constantly be aware of others' moods. They may feel compelled to solve others' problems, even when they are too depleted to meet their own needs. HSPs may also overidentify with their narcissistic loved one because they recognize the other person's pain and feel guilty if they don't try to fix it. In addition, their ability to accurately read the subtext of the unspoken can make them more susceptible to manipulation, gaslighting, and people-pleasing.

When working with highly sensitive clients, it is very important to help them differentiate between compassion and emotional caretaking. *Compassion* involves having care and concern for someone else's pain without feeling compelled to resolve it. *Emotional caretaking* involves the expectation that being aware of another's pain obligates one to fix it. Many adult children of narcissists conflate these concepts and struggle with guilt or shame if they do not follow their usual pattern of trying to manage another's emotions. In fact, HSPs sometimes self-identify as empaths and need extra support in developing emotional boundaries.

While some clinicians are skeptical of the concept of heightened sensitivity, we encourage you to consider the expert on their own experience. Anecdotally, we have observed a high rate of crossover between adult children of narcissists and those who strongly identify with being an HSP.

Stonewalling and Rug Sweeping

Narcissistic parents maintain their sense of power by controlling the conversation around conflict. However, conflict can't be resolved without communication and the ability to tolerate discomfort, and these are not within the narcissist's wheelhouse. Therefore, narcissistic parents will often use the silent treatment, which is a form of stonewalling, to thwart a child's attempts at confrontation. Whenever the child brings up a concern, the parent may change the topic, storm off, shut down the conversation, or refuse to acknowledge the child at all.

When arguments or fights do erupt, they are "forgotten about" the next day and swept under the rug. During this time, the narcissist may simmer and seethe, punishing everyone with their sullen anger until someone apologizes or diverts their attention elsewhere. Children who grow up with these models are underequipped to resolve conflict in healthy ways. They may struggle in relationships and believe that intensity and conflict are always the norm.

Withdrawing Affection

When a narcissistic parent disapproves of something their child has done, they may convey their displeasure by withdrawing affection and presenting a cold face. They may even explicitly inform the child that they do not love them when they act a certain way. This disapproval is personal and punitive; by withdrawing affection when their child "misbehaves," they connect love with obedience.

The loss of parental love and affection, or the threat of it, is gut-wrenching for a child. They learn to internalize the shame of behaving in such a way that their parent no longer loves them, rather than learning to distinguish behavior from personal worth. In the long term, these children grow up believing their relationships can only work if they do as the other person wishes, setting up lifelong struggles with perfectionism, people-pleasing, and low self-worth.

Threats (Veiled or Direct)

Narcissistic parents want to maintain a sense of autonomy and power over the family at any cost. If their children deviate from what is expected of them, this is viewed as a threat to their power that must be stopped. In these cases, the narcissist may retaliate by making veiled or direct threats. For example, they may threaten to withhold financial aid, walk back a promise, or imply retaliation to discourage their child from a course of action.

A more indirect way that narcissists may communicate threats (with the benefit of retaining plausible deniability) is to relay a story about someone else who reaped negative consequences when they disrespected or defied a parent. "Did I ever tell you about Joey, from my high school? He had such good prospects, but he thought his parents were being too strict, so he went out and partied until he lost his scholarship. He works as a grocery bagger now. I wonder where he would have ended up if he'd been less stubborn and more willing to listen to reason?"

Invalidation

Narcissistic parents are strongly invested in their self-concept as good or even exceptional parents (McBride, 2008). There is no room in their world for a child's criticism, unhappiness, or disagreement. Therefore, narcissists will invalidate any undesirable emotional experiences by gaslighting, ignoring, mocking, or shaming the child. Even when an adult child can provide dozens of examples of their parent's narcissistic abuse, no amount of evidence is enough to counter the parent's certainty that they have done nothing wrong.

Here is one example: "Marcos, you say I was harsh when you don't even know what harsh treatment is! I was firm with you because I wanted you to have a good life. You fabricate things that never even happened; you're exaggerating a little tough love as verbal abuse. You were never abused. You wouldn't have made it one day in my childhood if you think your upbringing was bad. I'm not going to entertain these lies any longer."

"Change Back" Messages

Increasing independence and autonomy are normal aspects of childhood development, but to a narcissistic parent, they signal the threat of losing control. Narcissists will try to shame their victims out of self-advocacy and pressure them back into their old role of submission or invisibility. For example, when a child tells their parents no for the first time, the narcissist may respond with "I liked you better when you were nicer to me." These messages may go hand-in-hand with withdrawing affection, in which the narcissist only offers warmth and pseudo-acceptance if the child returns to their old role in service to the narcissist.

Guilt Trips

Narcissistic parents routinely capitalize on feelings of guilt and shame to pressure their young or adult children to comply with their wishes. A narcissist may complain that their adult child has abandoned the family because they are prioritizing their new nuclear family instead of putting the narcissist first. These guilt trips may trickle down from other family members as well, including siblings, other relatives, and the non-narcissistic parent.

For example, family members may use guilt trips when a narcissistic parent becomes physically ill or nears the end of their life. "Dad has terminal cancer and you're holding a grudge instead of letting a dying man have a little mental peace. How are you going to feel if he can't pull through knowing his own child wants nothing to do with him?" In this case, the adult child's boundaries are treated as incidents of childish pique rather than a means of protecting themselves from an abusive parent. Once again, the pressure is on the child to assuage their parent's distress by "forgiving and forgetting," regardless of the toll it may take on them.

Flying Monkeys

It is not uncommon for narcissists to recruit others into helping them pressure the child into compliance (Thomas, 2016). A common example of this is when a narcissist complains to a relative that their adult child isn't answering their calls. The relative may then reach out to mediate the situation and urge the child to call their parent, essentially becoming a messenger for the parent by proxy. Flying monkeys can be a source of true torment for clients, who may be reluctant to disclose the nature of their parent-child relationship with the unwitting accomplice.

Smear Campaigns

If all else fails and a client creates stronger boundaries with the narcissist, they may well find themselves the subject of a smear campaign (Hall, 2019). The narcissist may gossip about the client, damage the client's reputation with lies, or publicly attack the client's character. Sometimes, this is done under the guise of kindness, in which the narcissist may ask others to pray for the client for "losing their way." Although the prayer request may appear caring on the surface, the intent is to negatively influence how the client is perceived.

Infantilizing Adult Children

Narcissists do not stop trying to control their children once they reach adulthood. They continue to sabotage their child's bid for independence by infantilizing them and effectively training them to rely on the narcissist for guidance, financial support, or approval. This may look like an adult child who still asks his mother for permission when making large purchases instead of conferring with his spouse. It can also look like a client who believes she can't make good decisions because her father always finds flaws in the choices she makes.

Undermining Adult Children in Relationships

Nothing angers a narcissist more than their adult child choosing to follow their own path, especially when the child sides with a friend or partner against the narcissistic parent. Narcissistic parents can wreak havoc on a marriage, or any other long-term relationship, in a number of ways. For example, they may undermine their child or their child's partner, force their child to choose between them and their partner, or present themselves as a confidant for their child's relationship problems. Any disclosures made to the narcissist are then used to drive a wedge between the adult child and their partner.

Undermining Adult Children as Parents

Narcissists will not hesitate to undermine their adult child's role as a parent if they feel like their child is not respecting their authority and expertise. Because they expect to be honored and respected due to their position as grandparents, they will often force their (unsolicited) opinions on their adult children. Some will steamroll their adult child's parenting decisions by ignoring, ridiculing, or overruling them. Others will present themselves as "trying to help" despite clear evidence otherwise. For example, the narcissist might criticize a new father for not diapering the baby correctly.

This dynamic can be especially destructive for new parents who are insecure in their roles and learning as they go. It is also not uncommon for narcissists to disrespect their adult child's parenting boundaries. For example, they might demand access to the birthing room against a mother's wishes or cause a humiliating scene if they are not given constant access to the baby. For exhausted and overwhelmed new parents, it can be hard to maintain boundaries during such a momentous time.

Inconsistent Acceptance or Approval

As we have discussed, narcissistic parents keep their children chasing goalposts by mixing their emotional abuse with periodic bursts of love, affection, and pride. This pattern of behavior reflects a form of intermittent reinforcement, which, as you may recall from your behavioral psychology textbooks, is the most effective way to turn a behavior into an ingrained habit. When a child is *occasionally* shown warmth, love, and affection, it makes them believe that if they can just figure out what they did right this time, they might be able to repeat it next time. And if they can do that, they have a greater chance of feeling loved and valued more frequently.

The Effect of Manipulation: Shame

Most of the manipulative strategies employed by narcissistic parents are designed to evoke shame. Shame is weaponized to induce compliance, punish disobedience, shut down arguments or challenges, and weaken the client's self-confidence. Therefore, of all the wounds adult children of narcissists carry, the deepest and most extensive are rooted in shame. These clients are conditioned to perceive their worth and value as directly correlated to the service they perform for the narcissist. They learn to associate their personal value with the happiness and love of someone whose affection is as fickle as the wind. This internalized metric carries over into other relationships in the form of chronic anxiety, perfectionism, and people-pleasing. When a client is unable to please their partner, friend, coworker, or superior, it can be devastating because they base their sense of worthiness on their ability to make others happy (Ross et al., 2019).

All adult children of narcissists, regardless of whether they enter therapy aware of this parental narcissism, will wrestle with shame at some point. It is imperative that clinicians working with this population understand how much shame can permeate these clients' lives. However, the clients may have a hard time identifying shame within themselves. The following table contains some questions we have found helpful to begin identifying and helping a client recognize how shame has shown up in their life. Listen for these notes in your clients' descriptions of how they function in relationships, how they react to their own mistakes, and when they feel most at peace with themselves.

Assessing Shame

Question	Low Shame Sample Response	High Shame Sample Response
What is it like for you to express a want or a need?	"I don't mind asking for help when I need it. We all need help sometimes."	"I feel like I'm being selfish by burdening other people with my problems."
How do you talk to yourself? Is your inner voice positive, kind, and gracious or harsh, critical, and stern?	"My inner monologue is kind, compassionate, and fair most of the time. Sometimes I can be a little hard on myself, but I can also congratulate myself when I accomplish something."	"My inner critic is really loud almost all the time. Even when I do something right, I feel like it's never good enough, and my inner critic just tells me how I could have done better."
How did your family react when someone did something they didn't approve of? How did they make their approval or disapproval known?	"My parents were pretty clear about what they expected from us. If we did something they didn't like, they'd tell us, but we knew they still loved us."	"My mom had this *look*, and when you got the look, you just knew she was so disgusted with you. Whatever you did, even if you tried to fix it, she would look at you like you were dirt."

A Safe Space to Speak Their Truth

When adult children of narcissists enter into therapy, they may struggle to find the words to describe their experience, or they may feel a pressing need to share story after story with you in an effort to convince you of their experience (Hall, 2019). Either way, you have an unparalleled opportunity to provide these clients with one of the greatest gifts they will ever receive: a safe space to be their true selves. In your office, clients may have the first chance to describe what happened to them, process how it affected them, and determine what they want to do next without being told they made it all up. You can offer them a place where they *matter*—where they can simply and freely exist.

Chapter Takeaways

 **Key Points**

- Narcissistic families are ruled by the narcissist, and only their version of reality is considered valid.

- Parents gain narcissistic supply through the successes, admiration, or control of their children and partners.

- Narcissistic parents use a number of manipulative tactics to control their family, including gaslighting, withdrawing affection, flying monkeys, and smear campaigns.

- Emotionally manipulative behavior patterns can cause and reinforce shame in victims.

- Perfectionist behaviors can be an attempt to relieve feelings of shame for clients who were taught to equate personal value to their performance.

 **Therapist Aid**

- *Narcissistic Abuse Tactics* (appendix, p. 135)

 **Reflection Questions**

- Many adult children of narcissists struggle with the pervasive feeling that they will never be good enough. Have you had clients struggle with this belief, or have you yourself struggled with it?

- Narcissistic parents continue to mine their children for narcissistic supply throughout the lifespan. How have your clients become sources of supply for their parents?

- Invalidation, gaslighting, and inconsistent and conditional approval can make it hard for clients to feel confident in themselves. How has this shown up for your clients?

PART 2

Spotting the Signs: Patient Presentation and Assessment

CLIENT STORY: Deirdre

Deirdre entered therapy on a mission: She wanted to heal and recover from growing up with a narcissistic father. When she first called to schedule an intake with Martina, Deirdre was ready with a list of her father's abusive behaviors—examples of gaslighting, rejection, and discard—and goals of setting boundaries so he couldn't upset her anymore. Deirdre also came prepared with questions: Had Martina worked with victims of narcissistic abuse before? What kind of training did she have? Had Martina ever experienced narcissistic abuse herself?

Deirdre's intensity made sense to Martina, who had worked with many adult children of narcissists. Some clients were hesitant to ask personal questions, but many had sought reassurance that she did, in fact, understand their family dynamic. Deirdre had seen three therapists in the past, all of whom told her they understood high-conflict families, but when she began working with them, it became clear they didn't grasp the full scope of the problem.

"I don't think poorly of my previous therapists," Deirdre said earnestly. "I think they meant well. But I think unless you really understand narcissism, it's just too easy to make things worse. And those therapists did. They tried to do family therapy, they tried to get me to compromise, they tried to tell me my dad was just from a less emotionally aware generation. They just didn't get it. And I really want to work with someone who does."

Deirdre was an insightful client who was prepared to do hard work. She told Martina story after story about her narcissistic father humiliating her for laughs, lavishing praise on her sister for the same accomplishments he ignored in Deirdre, and putting her down when she showed any self-confidence. She spoke openly and frankly about her decision to pursue her MBA because her father approved, as it felt safer to pick a degree in business than in art history as she had wanted to. She described her previous attempts to set boundaries with him, such as telling him not to make jokes about her weight, all of which he promptly ignored, causing many blistering arguments and fights.

No matter how hard she tried, Deirdre could not gain her father's approval. She sometimes felt bitter and resentful toward her sister, who seemed to live a charmed life as the golden child in their family. However, any attempts to address this favoritism resulted in a scathing lecture from one or both parents about Deirdre's jealousy. Her sister declined to engage in the discussions as well. Instead, she advised Deirdre to try speaking more calmly or being more agreeable, subtly placing the responsibility for the dead-end conversations on Deirdre.

With similar messages coming from all sides of her family, it was easy for Deirdre to second-guess herself and question her memories and perceptions. Deirdre often worried that she was being "too much," overly demanding, or needy whenever she asked her girlfriend for even the smallest of favors. Whenever she did get into a disagreement with her girlfriend, she found it hard to accept critical feedback and would become defensive, causing her to lash out or argue until her girlfriend gave up and recanted her complaint. Although Deirdre recognized this was an unhealthy habit, she was at a loss as to how she could change. She worried about being too intense, too emotional, or too stuck in the past, but she felt helpless to do anything differently.

"I'm sorry if I'm being too repetitive," Deirdre said, apologizing yet again for bringing up a painful memory that she'd previously discussed with Martina. "I just want to make sure I'm seeing things the right way. I really believe my dad is a narcissist, but what if I'm wrong? Maybe *I'm* the narcissist. He's told me that before. He said I'm too stubborn and unwilling to be wrong, and that makes me a narcissist. It makes me feel crazy when he does that because I think maybe I missed something in myself."

For Deirdre, the idea that she could unknowingly be a narcissist was agonizing. She had read extensively about narcissism and emotional immaturity and frequently examined her thoughts, feelings, and behaviors under a microscope for any signs of narcissism. And yet, all her knowledge about narcissistic abuse could not allay her fears that she was reading everything wrong and thus drawing the wrong conclusions.

While Deirdre had already learned a great deal about narcissistic abuse, she still had a lot of healing to do. The early stages of her and Martina's work were primarily focused on giving voice to the experiences that no one had ever validated before. As Deirdre recounted each story, she would watch Martina anxiously as if to read her expression. Over time, she learned to trust that Martina would not dismiss her experiences, and they gradually moved into deeper work. They discussed how her father's gaslighting had affected her self-confidence and how it showed up in her defensiveness whenever she felt questioned or misunderstood. They also explored how her father's favoritism had affected her relationship with her sister.

Martina helped Deirdre process the anger, envy, and grief she felt at being unable to gain her father's approval no matter how hard she tried. Together, they mourned the opportunities Deirdre had lost due to her fear of failure and processed the regret she felt for taking the safer choice in her career to appease her parents. They also worked together to help Deirdre develop self-compassion, particularly toward her younger self who had felt trapped by her father's domineering personality.

Deirdre's work was, at its heart, grief work. And her healing included both accepting the past in all its pain and rediscovering hope for a future that she could choose for herself. As Deirdre healed, she blossomed. She began to see herself as strong, resilient, and capable instead of being mired in the pain of the past. Deirdre couldn't change the fact that she grew up in an emotionally neglectful and controlling environment, but she came to realize that it did not need to define her.

CHAPTER 4

How the Client Shows Up

The Narcissism-Aware Client

With the popularity of social media and easy access to internet articles and videos discussing familial narcissism, it has become more common for clients to enter therapy with some understanding of narcissistic abuse. Like Deirdre, these clients are often well-read and may be very savvy about the terminology used to describe narcissistic abuse. Many are drawn to online communities for adult children of narcissistic parents, where they can connect with others from similar backgrounds (Kostyanaya, 2019).

For this reason, many clients will be very cautious about choosing a therapist who has a solid understanding of narcissism. They may ask during the initial intake or consultation call if you have ever experienced narcissistic abuse or if you have any specific training in this area. Some may want to quiz you on how you would handle certain situations, such as a narcissistic parent requesting family therapy. There is good reason for this, as too many clients have had damaging experiences with therapists who lacked a full understanding of narcissistic dynamics.

Of course, it can be irksome to have your experience and credentials questioned, and many therapists will see these questions as evidence of poor client boundaries. However, we believe that these questions are no different from those you would ask a medical specialist when seeking treatment for a particular ailment. For example, if you were considering having a complicated surgical procedure, before going under sedation you would want to know that your surgeon had the appropriate expertise. The questions your client is asking are no different, and we encourage you to keep that in mind.

Clinical and Pseudo-Clinical Terminology

Narcissism-aware clients often want to show their therapist that they know what they are talking about. They may share innumerable examples of the emotional abuse and neglect they've suffered as proof of this knowledge (Hall, 2019; Kostyanaya, 2019). They may also use a variety of clinical and pseudo-clinical language—for example, by naming someone as a narcissist or identifying gaslighting based on a social media post they read about it. Some clinicians are uncomfortable when clients throw around clinical terminology and, yes, sometimes clients will misunderstand or misuse terms. Laypeople do not receive the training that clinicians do, and sometimes terms become so overused that they begin to lose their meaning. There will be times to address improper use of a term, such as when a client labels someone a narcissist for simply disagreeing with them at any time. With that said, how you respond to a client's descriptions of their lived experiences matters a great deal.

Your primary goal for the early stages of therapy is to develop a relationship where your client can truly and deeply trust in your unconditional positive regard. Only then can you begin to address errors in terminology (as well as any other concerns or problematic behaviors). Allowing yourself to become too hung up on the technicality of clinical terminology will affect your ability to develop strong rapport. And without a solid foundation of trust, you cannot help your clients. Clarify terms and concepts when it is appropriate, but remember that the priority is to affirm the lived experience the client has shared with you.

When a client misuses words to the degree that you must address it, be thoughtful in how you approach the issue. We recommend exploring the client's understanding of the term with openhearted curiosity, which can disarm any potential defensiveness by showing that you want to understand their perspective. One option is to simply invite the client to share what they believe the term means. For example, "I hear you describing your stepmom as a malignant narcissist. Can you tell me what that phrase means to you?" Even if the client has misapplied the label, you can validate their experience and offer empathy for their frustration with their stepmother before providing psychoeducation about how therapists use the same term.

You can make or break therapeutic rapport with just a single instance of correcting or dismissing a client's use of terms. Remember that adult children of narcissists come to you with a lifetime of having their experiences dismissed through chronic gaslighting. They have likely spent many hours reading, researching, and reassuring themselves that they are not miscategorizing their loved ones as narcissists. They may have agonized over whether it was fair to use these terms. To go through all of that, and to then see a therapist who claims to be knowledgeable about narcissistic abuse, only to have their experiences invalidated because they didn't use a term properly, can be devastating. Don't let word choices be the reason your therapeutic relationship fractures before it can begin.

Storytelling and Repetition

Some clients may compulsively repeat stories of their loved one's narcissism as a way to affirm that their experiences are real and valid. They may feel compelled to tell story after story to gain your validation or to reassure themselves that you are grasping the extent of the abuse. Many clients are also incredibly worried that they will one day find out that they were completely wrong in labeling their loved one a narcissist, and recounting these stories is a way to remind themselves that what they experienced was indeed narcissistic abuse. Be patient with repetitive clients, as the driving need behind a sometimes-frustrating behavior is the need for reassurance and validation.

If your rapport is strong enough, you may be able to gradually explore the parts of the client that feel the need to continuously relate these stories. On the surface, they may feel that you believe and validate them, but they may be unaware that on a deeper level, they are still trying to convince *themselves* that they have a right to feel hurt about what happened to them. Spending time with the parts of the client that still feel uncertain or ashamed can be richly rewarding work.

Another option to reduce repetitive storytelling is to have the client practice mindfulness by inviting them to tune into their bodily sensations as they recall their stories. This can be a helpful way for clients to build awareness of the underlying emotions and thought patterns that are driving these stories (Langer, 2014). For example, Ezra repeatedly shared a story about his narcissistic father taunting him as a "spineless wimp" because Ezra was reluctant to physically fight a boy who was bullying him at school. He often concluded this story with "I know I'm not a wimp, but he was just such a jerk about it. Why do I have to throw a punch to prove I'm not a wimp?"

After one such repetition, Ezra's therapist, Vern, interrupted the cycle by reflecting the mismatch between Ezra's words and his body language. Although Ezra would always defiantly assert that he knew his father was wrong, he would habitually duck his head and hunch his shoulders every time he said, "I know I'm not a wimp." Today, Vern called attention to the discrepancy.

"Ezra, I'm noticing something that happens when you share this memory. Whenever you say, 'I know I'm not a wimp,' your head drops down a bit, and your shoulders seem to droop. Have you ever noticed that? Sometimes our bodies respond to our words, and it can be enlightening to see what our bodies are saying to us. What if we tried an experiment? Let's see how it feels for you to repeat that statement while really paying attention to your body. Would you be open to that?"

By helping Ezra build awareness between his words and his body sensations, it became clear that Ezra was recounting this story so many times because he was still trying to convince himself that his father was wrong. Despite his insistence that he knew he wasn't a wimp, his body expressed the shame and uncertainty he still felt. After Vern drew his attention to this, they were able to process Ezra's fear that his father was right about him.

Affirming the Expertise of Lived Experience

As clinicians, we are often taught in graduate school that the client is the expert on themselves. When working with adult children of narcissists, this phrase could not ring truer. There is a real risk that you will retraumatize these clients if you do not believe them when they present their experience. If you make them feel ashamed or foolish by correcting or dismissing their lived experience, it can drive them away from therapy and minimize any chance for healing. This potential for harm is why you must always consider clients the experts on their own experience. While their parent may not check off every box needed for a diagnosis of narcissistic personality disorder, the cumulative effect of narcissistic traits can still be harmful.

If you are truly concerned that a client is mislabeling their parent as a narcissist, check in with your own intuition as a clinician; it is possible your client may have some covert narcissistic traits themselves. We call this *having fleas*, which comes from the old adage "If you lie down with dogs, you get up with fleas." The idea here is that clients who have grown up with narcissism as a relational blueprint may adopt some of those same traits and expectations. That does not necessarily make them narcissists, but it is something that they will need to explore in more depth at some point in treatment.

The Narcissism-Unaware or Unready Client

While some clients enter therapy with their eyes wide open to the narcissistic abuse they and others have experienced, there are also many who are unaware of the dysfunction in their family of origin or who are not ready to face the truth. These clients will often present to therapy with any number of initial concerns, such as anxiety or depression. They may not mention their family of origin at all, or they might shrug off problematic behavior with little apparent distress. If these clients have pursued therapy before, it may have been short term or very solution-focused, rather than the more in-depth work that is generally required to heal from narcissistic abuse.

Many narcissism-unaware clients will describe their family of origin as very close, loving, and supportive. As you learn to read between the lines, you may begin to recognize some subtle indications of emotional immaturity and family dysfunction. For example, a client may describe a trait or attribute they've always considered normal, such as "the legendary Jackson temper." On further exploration, they describe their mother having an extremely hot temper that was easily triggered by anything she considered disrespectful.

While having a temper is not an indication of narcissistic behavior in itself, a temper that is expressed through public putdowns ("You're an embarrassment to this whole family!"), personal attacks ("Why are you such a slob?"), and mockery ("Oh, are you going to cry now? Are you going to cry like a little baby because you had to swallow some truth and you didn't like it?") is a different story. The client may believe this is a relatively common experience, not realizing that most parents can restrain themselves from attacking their children for disrespect or "insubordination." They may also not connect their childhood experiences of being taunted and belittled with their current fear of relationship conflict, but as the clinician, you can help them see the connecting threads.

When you notice these underlying signs of dysfunction, you can educate your client about how family relationships can shape their development even into adulthood, which sets the stage for them to explore their family of origin in more depth (Csillik, 2013). Bear in mind, of course, that cultural and familial norms will influence the degree to which a client's description of their family is an indicator of potential dysfunction. Consider the following examples of client statements that suggest narcissistic dysfunction may be present in the family. Treat each hypothetical statement as a point for further exploration, rather than an absolute indication of narcissistic family traits.

Signs of Narcissistic Dysfunction

Client Statement	Potential Dysfunction	Areas to Explore
"We're always in each other's business."	Enmeshment	Be curious about how it feels for the client to be so involved in family members' lives and vice versa. Does it feel like closeness and care, or nosiness and prying?
"My dad can be overbearing, but it's all out of love!"	Emotional volatility and controlling or manipulative behavior	Does the client genuinely appreciate their father's investment, or does it feel burdensome? What are the client's cultural values around parental involvement and authority?
"My mom gets stressed out really easily, so I try really hard not to upset her."	Vulnerable narcissistic traits and martyrdom	Does the mother's anxiety determine how the family functions? Is the client being considerate or are they parentified?
"My brother is just unnecessarily argumentative. He has to be so confrontational when it would be so much more peaceful if he'd just accept that Dad is the way he is, like the rest of us do."	Scapegoat and golden child roles, sibling favoritism, and blame shifting	How do the client's parents react to the brother when he argues? What is their response to the father's behavior?

Identifying Patterns in Individual Incidents

When narcissism-unaware clients begin talking about problems in their close relationships, they may focus primarily on specific behaviors, phrases, or memories. They may not see these incidents as part of a larger pattern. Your job as the clinician is to listen for stories that all seem to land at the same dead end, with the client feeling left alone and responsible for everything that went wrong in the relationship. Here are a few examples of patterns we often see among clients who grew up in narcissistic families:

- The client develops close friendships or intimate relationships that are initially a frenzy of affection and intimacy, but they quickly lose steam or become distant.

- All is well when the client acquiesces to the other person's wishes, but things become strained when the client can't or won't continue this way.

- Disagreements frequently end with the client feeling confused, questioning their reality, or believing they did something wrong without understanding why.

- The client makes extensive efforts to repair relationship ruptures without reciprocal effort from the other person.

- The client feels like they have to walk on eggshells to avoid upsetting the other person, who will rarely (if ever) extend the same sensitivity to the client.

Although these examples may seem clear to you as the clinician, remember that clients are often too close to the patterns to see them clearly. As the saying goes, they can't see the forest for the trees, and they need help identifying how different experiences can be part of the same theme. You will begin helping them pick out the connecting threads, and over time, they will learn to see the larger perspective for themselves (see the *Family of Origin Levels of Awareness Assessment* and *Getting to Know Your Family of Origin* tools in the appendix).

Camouflaging Presenting Concerns

Because many clients only start to recognize their parent's narcissistic traits after beginning therapy, they may not mention their family as a presenting concern at the start of treatment. However, when you begin to explore the origin of their common complaint, such as anxiety, you may find that the family played a larger role than the client first realized. Of course, not every client with anxiety comes from a narcissistic family, but it can be helpful to understand how some common concerns can camouflage the narcissistic family's dysfunction. Let's look at some of the frequent fliers and explore how these symptoms can relate back to harmful family dynamics.

Anxiety

It is probably no surprise that one of the most common mental health complaints among adults—anxiety—is a problem for adult children of narcissists as well (Dentale et al., 2015). Clients with anxiety may struggle with rumination and always find themselves overanalyzing past incidents. They may become mired in analysis paralysis and have difficulty making decisions because they are always fixating on the worst-case scenario. In addition, they may feel the need to always be in control, potentially resulting in obsessions and compulsions. Although clients may have a hard time identifying the source of their anxiety, as they are in a fairly constant state of worry, when you dig deeper, you'll find that their triggers often involve disappointing people, saying no, or confronting someone.

Depression

Depression is another common reason that adult children of narcissists initiate therapy. They may present with persistent low mood as their baseline, which dips into periodic "double depression" when they are overwhelmed or especially triggered. They may report a sense of impending doom or a feeling of inevitability, particularly with regard to the likelihood of failing at something they might try. These clients may feel largely pessimistic or skeptical about the possibility of positive change. They can feel powerless or helpless, especially when they have no choice but to reside with the narcissist for financial or other reasons. Some clients will struggle with chronic suicidal ideation or self-harm. Most will struggle with self-blame and self-loathing, as they are unable to hold the narcissist responsible for the toxic behaviors in the relationship.

Relationship and Work Problems

Many adult children of narcissists find themselves repeating similar patterns of dysfunction in their intimate relationships. Drawn to the familiar, they may report a history of emotionally unavailable or neglectful partners, feel like they have to walk on eggshells to avoid angering their partner, or frequently sublimate their desires to appease their partner. These clients may be fearful of confrontation or standing up for themselves, and they may defend their partner if they are criticized. Some may wonder if they are a magnet for cruel, manipulative, or selfish people.

Clients may also struggle in the workplace. Adult children of narcissists were taught to yield to authority figures, making them easy targets for manipulative or abusive managers. They may have difficulty asserting themselves with peers, leading them to take on others' workload in the name of office harmony. Some clients may stay in dead-end jobs for years, believing they are not capable of getting a better job. And some will find themselves in a career that makes them miserable because they were pressured by a narcissistic parent to choose a career path the parent approved of, whether or not the client wanted it. In chapter 6, we will more closely explore how narcissistic abuse can lead to these relationship and workplace problems.

Low Self-Esteem

Adult children of narcissists have been conditioned to see themselves as less important, intelligent, or worthwhile than the narcissist. That conditioning is hard to shake off even outside the family home. As a result, these clients may be reluctant to apply for leadership positions or promotions because they doubt their skills and desirability. They may question their own judgment and need frequent reassurance when making decisions. They may quit before they even start a challenging task, sure that they are going to fail in the end (McBride, 2008). When they do succeed, they often find it hard to accept any positive feedback they may receive. While the client may not connect these current difficulties to their family of origin, any client entering therapy with a severe lack of self-esteem warrants a closer look at their family background.

Addictive Behaviors

Narcissistic abuse can make victims susceptible to a variety of addictive behaviors, including substance abuse, compulsive shopping, and out-of-control sexual behaviors. These behaviors develop from an attempt to soothe emotional pain, given the deep wounds these clients carry with them. For adult children of narcissists, pursuing the fantasy of always feeling *this good* may seem like a more reliable source of happiness than any relationship could be (Carries & Delmonico, 1996; Vaknin, 2018). These clients may seek therapy specifically for help with their addictive behavior, or it may become apparent during the course of therapy. Either way, whenever addiction of any kind is part of a client's life, it is important to explore their family of origin and examine how familial relationships, norms, and values may have influenced the client's present behaviors.

Body Image

Many adult children of narcissists are subjected to conflicting and confusing messages about their bodies from a young age. For example, a narcissistic parent may simultaneously praise an athletic child's physical capabilities while harshly criticizing their personal style and closely monitoring their weight. Because narcissistic parents are obsessed with appearance, they make the normally private aspects of body size, weight, and development fodder for public consumption and critique.

Narcissistic parents also sometimes inappropriately sexualize their children. They may present their child as valuable due to their attractiveness or view them as a threat to the parent for the same reason. They may even treat the child as both a desirable asset and a detractor at the same time. As a result, it is common for adult children of narcissists to struggle with body dysmorphia, disordered eating, hypersexuality or sexual repression, and overidentification with perceived positive or negative physical traits (Carries & Delmonico, 1996; Shin & Youn, 2020).

The Risk of Letting Themselves See

Many narcissism-unaware clients remain in denial of their family's dysfunction because they have been so strongly conditioned to uphold that illusion of perfection to anyone on the outside. They may become defensive or angry when asked to acknowledge problems in the family because opening up these closely guarded secrets is viewed as a betrayal of family expectations. As a result, they may rationalize a narcissistic parent's behaviors and make excuses for their chronic gaslighting, invalidation, and manipulation.

A client who is in denial may also shift blame for their parent's behavior onto a sibling, stepparent, or other family member. What many clients don't realize is that although this family member has been portrayed within the family as the *source* of strife and conflict, they are actually the *target* of the narcissist's abuse. Be gentle when pulling at the threads of this tapestry to help the client come to this understanding. When a client realizes that they have been on the wrong side of this conflict, it can be a devastating pill to swallow. They may resist facing this reality even in the face of overwhelming evidence, as their perception of their family was built on the narcissist's version of reality. Changing that perception means reevaluating much of what they believed to be true in their life, and some clients will flee rather than face that change.

For narcissism-unaware clients who are in denial or not quite ready to face reality, discussing their family of origin can be very stressful. This is what makes patience such a vital element in the therapeutic process. Your voice can carry a lot of weight, and it may be the first one to ever question or challenge the narcissist's authority. Be mindful of your client's readiness to hear and process any challenges before you bring them.

Adjusting Client Expectations

Survivors of narcissistic abuse often enter therapy with unrealistic expectations of the process. They may begin therapy with the goal of "fixing" their flaws and see themselves as a project to be completed. They may have a strong internal push for therapy to feel productive, which can make therapy become self-abusing instead of a loving act of self-care. This is especially true for clients who struggle with perfectionism, as they may become overly self-critical if they aren't progressing the way they think they should. They may need repeated reminders that therapy is a process, or they will become discouraged and withdraw from treatment. For these clients, it is important to challenge and reframe any beliefs that equate worth with productivity and perfection.

Some clients may also harbor fantasies that therapy will be a magical experience in which the therapist will cure them of all the pain they've endured. They may place clinicians on a pedestal and take every word as gospel. These clients may be very passive—always asking the clinician to tell them what to do, to approve their choices, or to provide them with repeated reassurance. In turn, they may become frustrated with the pace of therapy or have difficulty going deeper than relatively surface-level behavioral changes.

On the flip side, some clients may be very guarded and provide minimal verbal and nonverbal cues about their internal state. They may take more time to open up in session and have a hard time showing vulnerability. When working with guarded clients, it is important to remember that these behaviors are protective mechanisms that they developed to avoid drawing negative attention to themselves. You must have patience and respect for these behaviors in order to develop a trusting therapeutic relationship with the client.

Whether your client presents as anxious and passive, or guarded and closed off, remember that they are presenting themselves in the way that has been safest for them. If these presentations trigger discomfort or defensiveness for you as a clinician, please take the time to do some internal exploration to better understand your own triggers. Adult children of narcissists can be very sensitive to countertransference due to their heightened awareness of others' moods. Pay attention to your internal responses and create an emotionally safe environment by taking responsibility for your own responses to these clients.

Chapter Takeaways

. . . .

🗝 Key Points

- Some clients enter therapy with insight into their family's dysfunction, but others do not. Match the client's pace and readiness to explore family of origin issues.

- Clients may present with any number of relatively common concerns that stem from their dysfunctional family. Since clients may be unaware of or unready to make this connection, wait until the client is ready to help them connect the dots.

- The effects of family narcissism can camouflage themselves as a variety of client concerns, including substance abuse, disordered eating, depression, and interpersonal difficulties.

- The most important skills that clinicians can use with clients at *any* stage of awareness are patience, empathy, compassion, and supporting client autonomy.

. . . .

🛋 Therapist Aid

- *Family of Origin Levels of Awareness Assessment* (appendix, p. 136)

- *Getting to Know Your Family of Origin* (appendix, p. 138)

. . . .

🛋 Reflection Questions

- Some clients enter therapy having learned a great deal about narcissism. They may quiz you to reassure themselves of your education and competency with these issues. What reactions do you have to clients who want to know if you are narcissism aware?

- Some clients are unaware of their narcissistic family dynamics (or are not ready to face them), and they may be slow to consider their family as part of their current pain. Where might you find yourself wanting to move too fast, push too hard, or do the client's work for them?

- Family dysfunction often underlies many common emotional concerns. How do you address or invite discussion about the client's family of origin in your intake assessments?

CHAPTER 5

Identifying and Assessing Relationship Patterns

Telltale Signs

There are many telltale signs of narcissistic abuse that can provide clues into family of origin dynamics, but if you don't know what you're looking at, it doesn't help you much. In the next section, we will walk you through some of these telltale signs by revisiting Lydia's story. While we always strive to make our examples as clear and thorough as possible, there is also an element of learning to tune into your own intuition. We encourage you to pay attention to your instincts—to your therapeutic gut—and learn to recognize the felt sense that there is more to explore here. Pause after each vignette and reflect on your internal reaction. Do you recognize clients who fit this pattern? Does anything feel familiar from your own experiences? This will allow you to start developing an awareness of when to dig deeper with your clients.

Nonverbal Communication and Guarded Affect

You'll recall that although Lydia initially sought therapy to cope with her breakup with Scott, it became clear that her concerns had much deeper roots than she initially realized. One of the first clues that there might be something deeper to explore was her friendly but nervous demeanor. Lydia's posture was tense, slightly hunched, and very contained. Her body language suggested a need to protect herself, while her face was open and slightly blank. She looked like someone who wanted to be open and expressive but remained at least lightly guarded most of the time.

By itself, Lydia's posture did not necessarily scream "narcissistic family," but it did suggest a certain wariness that is common with adult children of narcissists. Many of these clients learned to appear contained, controlled, and inoffensive as a way to avoid inadvertently offending their narcissistic parent (Gibson, 2015; McBride, 2008). This tendency can show up in session as flat affect, unemotional speech, or the use of intellectualization when discussing very painful topics. Some of these clients may long to be more emotionally expressive but resist showing their feelings out of a deeply ingrained fear of reprisal. Others prefer to avoid emotional expression entirely and want to think their way out of pain.

Whether clients consider emotional expression a goal or something to be avoided, it is common for them to show little in their facial expressions that indicate their emotional state. Therefore, you'll want to look at their body language for internal cues of anxiety, such as clenching hands or jaws, fidgeting, hugging themselves, or holding a pillow as a metaphorical way to provide distance from you in session.

Relationship Déjà Vu

As Lydia worked with her therapist to process her breakup with Scott, she initially focused on examining every possible thing she could have done wrong to cause the relationship to end because she was certain the fault was her own. While Lydia could identify some superficial issues with Scott that had contributed to the breakup, she was much more focused on her own problems and missteps. No matter how Scott had treated her, Lydia automatically assumed she was to blame. Gradually, as she moved through her sadness and began to feel some anger at Scott's cruel behavior, Lydia came to realize that this was not the first relationship to make her feel this way.

This recognition was a journey for Lydia. If, at the start of therapy, she'd been asked whether any of these issues had presented in other relationships, she would have denied it because she was focusing on specific behaviors rather than looking at patterns. For example, one of her previous partners had cheated on her, another had been addicted to cocaine and refused to seek treatment, and another had been sexually coercive with her. While each of these relationships appeared different on the surface, Lydia had to look beyond the specifics to identify the common themes: being taken for granted, being valued for her service rather than her personality, and being expected to meet and fulfill the needs of others first and foremost.

Negative Self-Concept

Lydia was highly self-critical from the start. She so strongly identified with her sense of being needy and overly anxious that she often referred to herself as "clingy" and "neurotic." She also overidentified with her perceived flaws and less-than-appealing traits. While she could extend grace to others when they made mistakes, she struggled to do the same for herself. These are common issues for adult children of narcissists, particularly those who fulfilled the role of a scapegoat or an invisible child in their family of origin. Like Lydia, they are trained to assume fault in any given situation, and they apply this training to all of their relationships without realizing it. These assumptions are driven by deeply rooted core beliefs, such as:

- I am not good enough.

- I will never be good enough.

- I am bad, defective, or broken.

- If I just tried harder, I could get it right.

- Bad things are my fault.

- I am only lovable if I can make someone happy.

These core beliefs tend to be buried quite deeply, and clients may not identify with them at the start of therapy. Your job as the clinician is to listen for conversational threads that point to the client's belief that any mistakes or flaws reflect poorly on their value as a person. You are mentally tracing the present concern back to its genesis.

Repressing "Bad" Feelings

One of the many reasons that it is challenging to identify a client's root concerns is that many adult children of narcissists learn to avoid any emotions they consider bad or negative. For example, Lydia became very adept at repressing her anger because in her relationship with Scott, he would shut her down whenever she expressed feeling hurt with him. Eventually, she learned to ignore these feelings and wrote them off as "being overly sensitive again." When she began reconnecting with her repressed emotions, Lydia struggled to accept her anger, even when she recognized Scott's behaviors as hurtful.

Lydia's tendency to repress her anger could be traced back to her relationship with her mother. Evelyn had a zero-tolerance policy for Lydia's "back talk," which was Evelyn's catchall term for any responses other than acquiescence. When Lydia became frustrated with Evelyn's constant critiques of her swimming performance, Evelyn punished her for speaking up by inducing a guilt trip. In turn, Lydia learned to avoid feeling angry because it led to her feeling like she had wronged her mother.

Like Lydia, many clients feel separated from feelings they deem bad or unloving. They grew up in an environment where speaking their truth risked inviting rage, rejection, and targeted abuse onto themselves, in which case avoidance became an act of self-preservation. Some may have even learned to moderately or severely dissociate when these feelings arise. This is especially true for clients who are people-pleasers or who fulfilled the role of golden child, as they may believe it is disloyal to feel anger, resentment, grief, or envy.

To see if your client has a tendency to repress uncomfortable emotions, listen to how they describe and respond to upsetting events. Here are a few telltale signs to watch for:

- They become visibly uncomfortable when asked to describe their feelings.

- They deny experiencing feelings they perceive as bad or dangerous (e.g., "I don't really get angry, I just feel sad").

- They regularly deflect questions about their feelings by focusing on surface-level content and emphasizing their thoughts about the topic at hand.

- They can name an emotion but quickly move on rather than giving themselves space to feel it.

- They experience physical manifestations of emotions but may be detached from the feeling itself (e.g., having an upset stomach when discussing an anxiety-provoking experience, or becoming extremely sleepy when recounting a traumatic memory).

You can help your clients get in touch with their feelings by slowing down the pace of therapy and helping them develop a greater awareness of how they experience events from a mind-body perspective. For clients who are highly cognitive, or those who try to rush past emotional processing, we suggest emphasizing increased body awareness to help them get in touch with the felt experience of their emotions. The following callout illustrates how you might do this with your clients.

Steps for Enhancing Mind-Body Awareness

1. "Identify an emotion or feeling you would like to explore."

- Some clients may need help naming their emotions, especially if they don't have much nuanced language for their feelings. Help them get specific by fleshing out the broad strokes (e.g., anger) and then home in on the degree and intensity of the feeling (e.g., annoyed or enraged).

2. "Try to recall a time when you felt this emotion very clearly."

- Calling up a memory may be the easiest pathway to exploring emotions for many clients. Have the client paint you a detailed picture of the memory, focusing on how they felt at the time.

3. **"Describe how you experience that feeling now."**

   - Encourage the client to notice how strongly or weakly they experience the feelings attached to the memory they've shared *in this moment*. What is it like for them to notice these feelings now?

   - Some clients may be uncomfortable with noticing feelings that remain (or have grown more) intense since the original memory. For feelings like anger, in particular, they may worry that this means they're holding a grudge. Encourage them to try to notice without judgment.

4. **"Scan your body and observe how your body feels as you experience this emotion."**

   - Invite the client to imagine a circle of light, or whatever visualization they find helpful, that slowly travels from the top of their head to the soles of their feet. As this circle of light travels down their body, they may notice various sensations arise (e.g., temperatures, tension, movements, pain, rigidity, relaxation). Encourage them to simply notice these sensations as nonjudgmentally as possible.

   - If the client is drawn to a specific sensation, stay with it! They can scan their body at their own pace, stopping to mindfully observe their body if they wish.

   - Some clients will feel better having the therapist guide the body scan. If a client prefers verbal guidance, do so in whatever way works best for them.

5. **"Observe your thoughts as you experience this emotion."**

   - Encourage the client to notice their thoughts without fleeing the emotional and bodily awareness they've been developing. For example, you might say, "Observe any thoughts as they cross your awareness, but don't hold on to them. Stay in this observing space."

   - Some clients may become distressed or concerned if there is any discrepancy between the emotion they named and the bodily sensations and thoughts they identify (e.g., if they identify feeling calm but are white knuckling it, grinding their teeth, and thinking, *Am I doing this right?*). Everyone experiences ambivalence or conflicting feelings; normalize this experience and help the client explore the various emotions they noticed.

Helping clients tune into their emotional experience is a necessary step in teaching them to trust their internal emotional compass. Without this internal awareness, they will continue to depend on external sources of validation to know how they "should" be feeling, rather than trusting their own experience (Fisher, 2017; van der Kolk, 2014). The process we've just outlined is one you can use to explore any emotional experience that the client presents with, but many will feel most comfortable if you begin with emotions they find easier to tolerate. As the client becomes more comfortable with the process, they will increase their capacity to tolerate and process harder emotions, experiences, and traumatic memories (Corrigan et al., 2011).

Assessing the Family System: The Circumplex Model

When you begin to explore a client's family of origin, it helps to have a framework to assess the various family dynamics involved. One model that can provide this framework is the circumplex model of family systems, which was developed by Dr. David Olson (2000). This model assesses family health on three primary dimensions: cohesion, flexibility, and communication.[1] Let's take a look at how a narcissistic family might be assessed with the circumplex model (Rogoza et al., 2021).

The Circumplex Model

LEVEL OF COHESION	Disengaged	Separated	Connected	Enmeshed
I-We Balance:	I	I-we	I-we	We
Closeness:	Little	Low–moderate	Moderate–high	Very high
Loyalty:	Little	Some	High	Very high
Independence/ Dependence:	High independence	Interdependent (more independence than dependence)	Interdependent (more dependence than independence)	High dependence

LEVEL OF FLEXIBILITY

Chaotic
- Lack of leadership
- Erratic discipline
- Dramatic role shifts
- Too much change

Flexible
- Shared leadership
- Democratic discipline
- Role-sharing change
- Change when necessary

Structured
- Leadership sometimes shared
- Somewhat democratic discipline
- Roles are stable
- Change when demanded

Rigid
- Authoritarian leadership
- Strict discipline
- Roles seldom change
- Too little change

Balanced · Mid-range · Unbalanced

Adapted with permission from "Circumplex Model of Marital and Family Systems," by D. H. Olson, 2000, *Journal of Family Therapy, 22*(2), p. 148 (https://doi.org/10.1111/1467-6427.00144). Copyright 2000 by the Association for Family Therapy and Systemic Practice.

Dimension 1: Cohesion

Family cohesion describes the emotional bond between family members. At one end of the spectrum is enmeshment and at the other end is disengagement. Both poles may be represented in a narcissistic

---

1. Communication is considered a facilitating dimension that enables movement between the other two dimensions, so it is not included in the graphical depiction of the circumplex model.

family. Enmeshment shows up in the narcissist's expectation that the world revolves around them and that everyone else is an extension of them. No one is allowed to develop independence, make their own decisions, or exist outside the parameters that the narcissist deems acceptable.

An enmeshed narcissistic parent may describe their child as their best friend, or they may be overly invested in their child's success as an opportunity for vicarious glory. This is especially the case for a golden child who is enmeshed with a narcissistic parent. The intensity of this enmeshment may be a proxy for real love and affection, as the golden child may mistake the parent's celebration of their achievements for true affection. However, if the golden child should fall from their perch, they may quickly find themselves forcibly disengaged from the parent, confirming the conditional nature of the relationship. Lydia and Evelyn are a good example of an enmeshed relationship.

At the other end of the cohesion spectrum is disengagement. Disengaged family members have little attachment to the family group and intentionally distance themselves from others. For example, a scapegoat may emotionally disengage from family members who receive the affection they do not. For these clients, it is often easier to separate from their family of origin, though they may still harbor anger and resentment toward family members.

While disengagement may seem like a healthier alternative to enmeshment, it is not without its problems. Disengaged relationships can feel hollow, empty, and on the edge of abandonment. Clients who exhibit this detachment in their relationships may feel alone and unloved, or believe they are unable to have loving relationships. You may pick up some cues indicating disengagement through phrases like "Yeah, I was always kind of the odd one out; everyone else seemed really close" and "They're my family, but I never really felt like I was part of them." Clients with disengaged relationships may be very independent and aloof.

Expectations of loyalty will vary depending on whether a family system is more enmeshed or disengaged. In highly enmeshed systems, there is the unspoken expectation of loyalty regardless of cost or personal opinion. As a result, any betrayals tend to be more covert in nature. For example, a narcissistic parent may try to sabotage a child's external relationships by exaggerating or fabricating negative comments from that child's friend or partner. They may express an us-versus-them mentality that paints outsiders as dangerous, untrustworthy, or inferior to the family circle. If an adult child transfers loyalty to a spouse or to their new nuclear family, this is considered a betrayal (and is the source of many a "nightmare in-law" story).

Conversely, in more disengaged systems, there is little loyalty to others and more of an "everyone for themselves" mentality. Interpersonal betrayals are more open and less surprising because family members have little sense of responsibility for how a loved one might receive their words or actions. Since cutting people off is the norm in a disengaged family, a narcissistic parent may have few adult friends because they frequently burn bridges. Children growing up in these families come to learn that they could be next on the chopping block at any time. For some children, this is strong motivation to stay on the narcissist's good side. For others, it is further evidence of the need to distance themselves from their family so it doesn't sting as much if they are eventually discarded.

Individuation in Enmeshed Families

In enmeshed families, narcissistic parents often discourage individuation because they benefit more from their children's continued enmeshment than from their children developing a strong and clear sense of self. When a client in this situation attempts to differentiate from a parent who views the client as an extension of themselves, this is viewed as a threat that cannot be tolerated. In turn, it is not uncommon for the narcissistic parent to weaponize family loyalty, expectations, and obligations to discourage individuation and punish the client for any attempts at this "rebellion." Becoming one's own person is a dangerous process in a narcissistic family.

Clients who have attempted to develop an individual identity in an enmeshed environment may continue to struggle with individuation even at advanced stages of life. If they have been punished for individuation at earlier stages of development, they may be quite anxious and fearful of doing so now. For clients from communal or multigenerational family cultures, this can be particularly loaded because of compounding family and cultural values. Therefore, be sensitive to family and cultural norms as you support your clients in exploring what level of individuation and family connection feels right for them. You want to be mindful of your own biases about the relative importance of individuation and be careful not to assume a White, Western value structure.

Assessing Family Cohesion

You can learn a lot about a client's family system from common intake questions that you might already ask in your early sessions. We have provided some common assessment questions here, along with some sample responses that could indicate trailheads for further exploration. These are only samples, of course, and not all clients will be this direct in their responses. Your goal is to learn to listen for underlying themes and use those to inform your overall picture of the family dynamics.

Assessing Family Cohesion

Question	Sample Enmeshed Response	Sample Disengaged Response
How close were you with your parents growing up?	"I was extremely close with my mom. She felt more like my best friend than a parent. She would tell me secrets about my dad, and I had to promise never to tell anyone."	"I wasn't super close with my parents. They did their thing, and I did mine. We saw each other at the dinner table and that was pretty much it."
How aware were you of your parents' moods, expectations, and needs as a child?	"I knew what kind of mood my dad was in from the way he closed the car door when he got home. If he slammed it, I would hide in my room until dinner because if he saw me, he'd yell at me."	"I could tell when my mom wanted me to do something for her, but I didn't really feel obligated to act on it."
How involved were your parents in your activities?	"My parents were the definition of helicopter parents. They went to every field trip, class activity, birthday party, athletic event, music performance, and social event. They never wanted me to do anything without them."	"They showed up sometimes but never consistently. If I was getting an award or something, they'd be right there in the front seat so they could show everyone how proud they were, but they weren't really involved in the day to day."
How did your parents feel about you having close friendships or other relationships outside of your family?	"My mom's mantra was 'Family is all you need.' She would only let friends come over to our house; I couldn't go to theirs. I don't think she was very nice to my friends' parents, either, because the friendships always kind of fizzled out."	"My dad had no idea what I was up to most of the time. He'd yell if I came home after curfew, or if I got caught doing something bad, but he was pretty much in his own world most of the time."

Dimension 2: Flexibility

The second dimension of the circumplex model is flexibility, which refers to the amount of change that occurs within the family's rules, roles, and expectations. When there is too little flexibility, it results in rigidity; when there is too much flexibility, it results in chaos. In narcissistic families, the rules, roles, and expectations are rigid in some ways and chaotic in others. For example, the narcissistic parent will always be the ruler of the family, and their word will always be law (rigidity), but how they interpret and apply expectations of other family members may be subject to change on a whim (chaos). Therefore, trying to follow the rules in a narcissistic family is like trying to build a house on shifting sand. There are no consistent parameters; the only consistency is chaos.

Adding to this chaos is the fact that family rules are not always explicitly stated. This allows the narcissist to deny any implicit expectations and to find loopholes for any expectations that no longer serve them. Rules are also inconsistently enforced in that they do not apply to the narcissist. Punishment is reserved for the unexceptional, rebellious, or less-favored family members, while the narcissist feels justified in behaving however they so choose. While narcissistic parents may *appear* flexible from time to time—for example, unexpectedly forgiving an affront or seeming to move on from a conflict—the truth comes out when they later retrieve their grievances and use them against the other person. Clients who were subjected to these seemingly random episodes of punishment during their childhood may struggle with perfectionistic behavior in adulthood.

CLIENT STORY: Chaaya

Chaaya, a high school student, had begun looking at colleges and was now struggling with severe anxiety over which school to attend. Her parents were both Ivy League graduates with multiple degrees, and her older brother was a prolific writer who also attended an Ivy League school. Chaaya knew her parents always had high expectations of her and she was terrified of becoming the "family disappointment." Her parents told her she could choose whatever school she wanted and reiterated that they simply want her to be happy.

After months of indecision, Chaaya took her parents' words to heart and finally decided to take the pressure off herself by spending a semester at the local community college. She felt more confident in her ability to handle the course material there and was less worried about flunking out. When she told her parents of her decision, they were shocked and angry.

"Are you *trying* to shame us?" her father demanded. "We expected you to go to a *real* school and make something of yourself, not waste your time at some community college." Chaaya's parents were disgusted and saw her attempt to prioritize her well-being as a challenge to their authority. While they did not explicitly say so, they expected her to reflect positively on them by enrolling in a competitive, noteworthy program.

Without warning or discussion, they withdrew their offer to pay her college tuition unless she attended a more acceptable school. As an extension of her parents, Chaaya's decision cost *them* status. Therefore, her parents moved the goalpost, and she was left to either accept their disapproval or suffer in order to make them happy. Their apparent flexibility in where she went to college was not what it seemed, as her choice fell afoul of their rigid expectations to bring positive attention to the family.

As Chaaya's story illustrates, many narcissistic families have little tolerance or flexibility when a family member chooses a course of action that doesn't shine a light on the family name. They also have very low thresholds for tolerating imperfections or unappealing traits. While they may profess to be loving and accepting, they will convey their true feelings when a family member falls out of favor. They may give backhanded compliments, make "jokes" with a bite to them, continuously rehash embarrassing stories, and overidentify with that family member's real or perceived imperfections.

Assessing Family Flexibility

Narcissistic families can be confusing because they are often unpredictable and chaotic, but at the same time, the hierarchy is rigidly reinforced. While you may not know from one day to the next if a client's choice will be celebrated or demonized, you can always count on the narcissistic parent to be the one making the call. The following are some sample assessment questions you might use to explore how rigidity and chaos present in a client's family of origin.

Assessing Family Flexibility

Question	Sample Rigid Response	Sample Chaotic Response
What were some of the rules in your family?	"My parents expected us to do all of our chores every day without exception. I was really sick with the flu once, with a 104-degree fever, and my dad got me out of bed to take out the trash because that was my chore."	"The rules were whatever my parents said at the time. But it didn't always stay the same. I just tried to keep up with whatever they said that day."
What were the family rules or expectations regarding physical boundaries (e.g., bodily autonomy, expectations of privacy, locking bedroom doors)?	"I had to keep my bedroom door open at all times because my parents said there should be no reason for secrets. My mom would even go into the changing room with me when I tried on clothes at the store."	"My mom would tell me it was okay to lock my bedroom door, but then she'd change her mind and threaten to take the door off the hinges if I actually did it. Once she did take off my sister's door, and I don't think she'd even locked it—just closed it."
Was there a head of your family? Who was it?	"My dad, 100 percent. My mom could voice her opinion, but my dad was always the one who made the call."	"I guess it was whoever felt like being in charge at the time. Sometimes my mom seemed like this really strong parent who stood up to my dad and asserted herself, and sometimes she just sat back while he took over and ruled the roost."

Dimension 3: Communication

The third dimension in the circumplex model is communication, which is considered a facilitating dimension because it allows families to move through the other two dimensions. For example, a family's cohesion is directly affected by their ability to communicate and understand each other, while flexibility depends on a member's ability to provide clear feedback and assess if a more flexible or rigid response is warranted in the situation.

Communication is measured via several specific domains, including speaking and listening skills, self-disclosure, clarity, continuity, respect, and regard. Each domain is further broken down into specific skills. Listening skills, for example, include the ability to show empathy, listen attentively, and track patterns in one's physical and emotional reactions. These skills are measured on a spectrum, ranging from strong to poor.

Unsurprisingly, communication in narcissistic families is often unclear, one-directional, and inconsistent. These families struggle with expressing empathy, active listening, staying on topic, and demonstrating respect for others. In addition, while the narcissist may have strong self-disclosure skills, others in the family may be unable to consistently or safely express themselves openly (Olson, 2000). The following are some questions you can ask to gauge the communication in your client's family of origin.

Assessing Family Communication

Question	Sample Strong Communication Response	Sample Poor Communication Response
Could your family members ask direct questions of each other and get an honest answer?	"Yes. Sometimes the conversations were hard, but my parents and siblings were generally honest and direct in an age-appropriate way."	"No way! We had to figure everything out by picking up clues along the way. We were the embodiment of 'You can't handle the truth!'"
Can you think of a time when you enjoyed talking to your family?	"I usually enjoy talking to my family. We don't always handle conflict perfectly, but I like talking with my family more than not."	"Um, I'm not sure… maybe when we were on vacation? It was mostly best to try to stay out of the way."
When you talked, did anyone in your family listen? If so, how did they respond?	"My mom was the best listener—I always knew she cared about what I was saying. My dad tried to at least hear me out even when he didn't agree."	"Not really. My parents were the ones who spoke; the kids were just supposed to listen. I just tried to keep up, since they kind of veered all over when they talked."

While the circumplex model provides a solid framework for understanding many of the dynamics at play in narcissistic families, the weaponization of communication to create conflict is a tenet of narcissistic abuse that deserves a more in-depth look. Without strong communication skills, it is all but impossible to handle other common family problems in a healthy way. One key example of this, as we will discuss next, is the inability to address or resolve conflict within the narcissistic family.

Conflict Resolution

In narcissistic families, the word *conflict* is not just a noun but also a verb. As both an action and a way of being, frequent and unresolved conflict is an exhaustingly common way of life in these families. Conflict in narcissistic relationships is not just about disagreements or arguments; it is about the power struggles that occur when non-narcissistic family members resist or fail to comply with the narcissist's expectations. Conflict also serves as an opportunity for the narcissist to discharge their own shame, anger, and dissatisfaction onto others, which shields the narcissist from their own discomfort and shifts the blame to the other person.

As with most things in narcissistic relationships, the rules governing conflict are inconsistent at best (Donaldson-Pressman & Pressman, 1994). If a narcissistic parent determines there is a conflict, then so there is. But if another family member feels provoked or challenged, that is something else entirely. The narcissist will pretend the conflict does not exist by gaslighting the other person or denying it altogether. "If you're still mad about something, that's a *you* problem." To rub salt into the wound, the parent may also openly praise other family members who capitulate or do not acknowledge the conflict. These dismissals can engender immense frustration in the client and lead to outbursts that, more often than not, simply provide more fodder for the narcissist to claim the client is being overly emotional. Trying to make a narcissist acknowledge an unwanted conflict is an unwinnable fight.

SPOTLIGHT: DARVO

Gaslighting is a well-worn tool in the narcissistic toolbox, especially when it comes to shutting down unwanted conflict. One form of gaslighting that narcissists use to avoid being held accountable is DARVO, which stands for *deny, attack,* and *reverse victim and offender.* DARVO is a term originating in the work of Jennifer Freyd (1997). You can recognize this form of gaslighting by listening for these common phrases:

- **Denial:** Refusing to acknowledge or credit the other person's experience.

  - "That never happened."

- **Attack:** Using manipulation and accusations to put the other person on the defensive. Here are some tactics used to achieve this:

  - *Invalidation:* Implying or openly stating that the other person's experience is inaccurate, and then replacing it with one that the narcissist identifies with.

    - "You're not hurt; you're just mad that you didn't get your way."

  - *Projection:* Displacing characteristics or behaviors that the narcissist finds unacceptable onto others.

    - "You're just like your mother, always nagging!"

  - *Dismissal:* Ignoring or brushing aside a concern as exaggerated in order to shut down the conversation.

    - "You're being too sensitive. Let it go."

- **Reversing victim and offender:** Putting the victim on the defensive by claiming they are being manipulative when they resist the actual gaslighter.

  - "I didn't gaslight you, *you're* gaslighting *me!*"

Individuals raised in this kind of environment will benefit from psychoeducation about healthy communication and conflict resolution. This is where models such as the circumplex model may be a helpful resource for identifying the various responses clients may not have realized were available to them. So many adult children of narcissists are conflict-averse due to the ingrained fear that conflict will cause them to lose another person's affection and goodwill. As a therapist, you have an opportunity to provide evidence that counters this fear by openly and compassionately modeling the rupture-and-repair process in the context of the therapeutic relationship. This experience can be both terrifying and world-expanding for clients.

In addition, it is important to help clients understand that conflict is a natural aspect of life that can lead to new, creative solutions to relationship problems. When you reframe conflict as a chance to understand someone more deeply and to solve problems in mutually satisfying ways, it can help clients perceive an opportunity where they have only seen risk. Explore their assumptions about who is right and wrong in a conflict, or whether there is even a right and wrong in every conflict. How different might an argument with a loved one feel if there isn't a "good guy" or a "bad guy" at all, but two people with different and equally valid perspectives? Coming to this realization can represent a paradigm shift for many clients.

Here are a few sample questions to assess for family norms in handling and resolving conflict. For a more detailed questionnaire, see the *Assessing Family Norms in Conflict Resolution* therapist aid in the appendix.

Assessing Family Conflict Resolution

Question	Sample Strong Resolution Response	Sample Weak Resolution Response
How did your family handle disagreements or conflicts between members?	"Any of us could express our opinion, but we had rules about being respectful of each other and not letting it devolve into name-calling or personal attacks."	"My mom would wear you down until you just let her be right. You could never win an argument, so there was no point in trying."
How did family members repair or make up after a conflict?	"We could agree to disagree, but if the argument got heated and we went too far, we'd call a time-out to cool off. And we apologized if we did or said something we shouldn't have."	"Once Dad won the fight, he was happy again. He'd change in a blink, and it was like nothing had ever happened. You'd just sweep it under the rug and move on because otherwise you were holding a grudge."
How do you think conflict reflects on whether a relationship is healthy or toxic?	"Having conflict isn't a bad sign as long as you can talk it out and remember that you care about each other. You don't have to see eye to eye on everything, but healthy relationships work through the hard stuff."	"I try to avoid conflict because it just makes everything worse. I'd rather just do what my partner wants than get into a fight and feel like I'm being selfish or toxic."

Looking at the Big Picture

Working with narcissistic families requires the ability to use both micro and macro lenses. You need to keep one eye on the individual experiences that your clients report and another on the growing web of interconnected relationship patterns. Your work with these clients is not only to help them cope with and heal from their family relationships, but also to expand what they learn into other areas of their lives. No matter what models or approaches you favor as a clinician, the therapeutic relationship and the development of trust are foundational and essential for this healing work.

Chapter Takeaways

 Key Points

- Clients often focus on individual incidents that cause distress. Your job is both to help them process the individual (micro) incidents and also to build recognition of how those incidents create a larger pattern (macro) of interactions.

- All families develop patterns of interaction. Narcissistic family patterns may be a blend of enmeshment, detachment, rigidity, and chaos.

- Clients may have had to struggle to develop an individual identity distinct from their narcissistic parent. They may have little sense of how an individual can fit into a family group, or how families can support individuality within the group.

- Adult children of narcissists rarely experience conflict resolution or the affirmation that their experiences are valid. Therapy can provide an invaluable opportunity to experience both.

Therapist Aid

- *Individual Choice and Consequences* (appendix, p. 140)

- *Assessing Family Norms in Conflict Resolution* (appendix, p. 142)

Reflection Questions

- Many enmeshed families would describe themselves as "close" rather than "enmeshed." How can you help clients differentiate between healthy closeness and an unhealthy lack of boundaries?

- Some clients may be hesitant to describe their family as rigid or enmeshed, since these dynamics can change so quickly based on the narcissist's mood. How can you help clients identify patterns of behavior when their families appear simply chaotic?

- Clients don't always think about things like differentiation and individuation the way therapists do. How can you help your clients explore these concepts in language they can relate to and understand?

CHAPTER 6

The Effects of Narcissistic Abuse Outside of the Family

One of the greatest strengths of a seasoned therapist is the ability to see the connections between two (or more) seemingly unrelated concerns and then help the client understand how one affects the other. While many clients believe their problems will be solved when they change the dynamic of their family relationships, the effects of narcissistic abuse are not confined to the family where the abuse occurred. This is where a clinician's ability to connect the dots becomes truly invaluable.

This process is analogous to viewing a photo mosaic. A photo mosaic is a picture created by arranging dozens or even hundreds of smaller pictures in such a way that the colors and shapes of each individual photo create a larger, cohesive image when viewed from farther away. Each individual picture is an integral part of the work, and no single picture tells the whole story by itself. Together, they create a larger image that can't be seen when looking only at a single photo.

Narcissistic family dynamics are similar in that individual relationships, incidents, and family norms each play a role in who the client is in the present. But it is also important to pull back and see the whole picture—how the narcissistic family affects the client *outside* of the family setting. In this chapter, we will discuss some of the ways narcissistic abuse in one setting can affect clients in other domains, such as their friendships, intimate relationships, workplace, and own nuclear family.

Reenacting Harmful Relationship Dynamics in Other Relationships

Most people will leave their family home at some point. Whether they move out permanently or continue to reside at home but spend more time away due to college, work, or other demands on their time, they will begin to branch out in some form another. However, for clients in narcissistic families, the abuse that began in the family of origin may follow them into other areas of their life. In turn, they may find themselves repeating the cycle of manipulation and abuse that feels both repulsive and familiar (Huh et al., 2014).

For example, consider a young man named Drew, who begins dating Xavier, who mirrors his narcissistic father's obsession with physical appearance. Although Drew found his father's vanity irritating, he admires Xavier's commitment to fitness. He is flattered whenever Xavier invites him to the gym or creates a workout plan for him. Over time, though, Xavier becomes more critical, and his early praise turns into to teasing. He always comments on Drew's "baby fat," poking his sides and calling them "love handles," and jokes that without his encouragement, Drew will have a "dad bod" long before fatherhood. Drew begins to feel the familiar shame and anger he experienced in his teenage years, when his father shamed him for his appetite and for looking "pudgy" instead of chiseled. He promises to work out harder, hoping that if he pleases Xavier and makes him proud, he can put his father's critical voice away once and for all.

Similarly, consider the case of Remy, who begins dating Todd—a man who lavishes her with extravagant praise, gifts, and promises of a beautiful life together. On their second date, Todd tells Remy that he knew she was "the one" from the moment they met. Remy feels like she's in a fairytale as he tells her how they'll honeymoon in Paris and travel the world first class. Unlike Remy's mother, who always felt like she had been cheated out of a wonderful life by marrying a man who didn't think she deserved the best, Remy feels relieved to have found someone who values her and wants to create a life together.

However, when Todd asks Remy to marry him, she is surprised to see him pull out a small, visibly flawed, poor quality diamond ring. Todd had always spoken scornfully of the "cheap trash" in most jewelry retailers' inventory, so she had expected him to propose with a unique, handcrafted piece. Instead, he holds up a tiny ring from one of the very stores he demeaned. Remy doesn't want to seem like an ungrateful gold digger, so she accepts and tries not to think about the discrepancy. When she looks back years later, she realizes this was only the beginning. Todd could spin a tale of glamour and luxury, but the reality rarely matched it. She feels stuck in a frustrating, disappointing reality—just like her mother had been.

Adult children of narcissists who reenact these harmful patterns may identify challenges in their interpersonal relationships but not necessarily recognize how these patterns are connected to the older wounds of parental narcissistic abuse. They may feel like they are drawing narcissistic people into their lives due to some innate character flaw. However, the reality is that they are so accustomed to abusive treatment that they unconsciously accept it in many environments (Hall, 2019; Simonič & Osewska, 2020). It is easy for clients to fall back into this well-established pattern when they have comparatively little experience with anything else. They may not enjoy or want to continue in this dynamic, but fear of the unknown can be an equally strong deterrent.

There are several other reasons why clients can fall into familiar patterns of narcissistic abuse. First, a client might overlook problematic relationship dynamics if their partner or friend's behavior doesn't exactly mimic the narcissistic abuse they experienced from their parent. Clients often do not realize that even though the behavior might look different, the underlying dynamics are the same (e.g., ineffective communication, poor conflict resolution, lack of differentiation). Second, because these clients have been victims of frequent gaslighting, they may override or downplay their intuition. They may recognize the concerning behaviors but convince themselves that they are overreacting or being too sensitive.

Third, most narcissists do not initially present with their most problematic behaviors on display. They possess a charming, socially adept side that allows them to draw people in. Once the narcissist begins to engage in manipulative, controlling, and abusive behaviors, the client may be reluctant to acknowledge or address these behaviors. They fall back into old habits where they ignore or rationalize the narcissist's abuse in order to avoid conflict. This makes it all the more important that you, as the clinician, help them learn to recognize the narcissistic abuse cycle.

The Narcissistic Abuse Cycle: Idealization, Devaluation, Discard, and Hoovering

Narcissistic abuse, particularly in intimate relationships, often follows a distinct pattern involving three primary stages—idealization, devaluation, and discard—which are sometimes followed by a fourth stage called hoovering (Thomas, 2016). We will briefly describe each stage so you can learn to recognize these in your client.

The Narcissistic Abuse Cycle

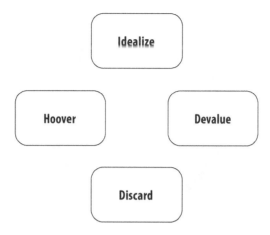

Idealization

During the idealization stage, the narcissist is enamored of their partner and showers them with displays of affection, grandiose gestures, and compliments. This can include constant text messages or phone calls, early professions of love, and pleas to spend every free moment together. Known as *love bombing*, this manipulation tactic makes the victim feel desired in a way they may have never felt before. Love bombing creates an illusion of the ideal relationship, a veneer of intimacy and emotional attunement. For clients with a history of emotional abuse or neglect, love bombing can feel like rain after a drought, making it easy for the narcissist to draw them in. However, because idealization is unsustainable, love bombing eventually leads to the second stage: devaluation.

SPOTLIGHT: Love Bombing

Love bombing is an effective strategy to quickly pull in a romantic partner by creating the feeling of intimacy without any real substance. It also allows the narcissist to gauge how much control they can exert over their victim under the auspices of love and affection. Love bombing overwhelms a client's defenses and interferes with their ability to think critically, making it difficult for them to retain any boundaries they may have had.

Love bombing may not be restricted to individual interactions either. Some narcissists will ingratiate themselves with the victim's friends and family, making it harder for the victim to voice any concerns or address problems in the relationship. Friends and family may be complicit in gaslighting the victim, whether intentionally or not, by using the narcissist's love-bombing behaviors as a counterweight for their abuse. They may suppress the victim's concerns with statements like:

- "We all have flaws; no one's perfect."

- "Wanting to talk to you is a problem? I wish my partner still texted me all the time. I hardly hear from them now that the honeymoon is over."

- "They are just really into you. Enjoy it while it lasts!"

- "Really? You're complaining about them when they just whisked you away for a romantic weekend in Aruba?"

As humans, we rely on the feedback of trusted friends and family to help us judge our choices and the world around us. However, adult children of narcissists are conditioned to excuse boundary violations and downplay their own instincts. Therefore, when their loved ones dismiss valid concerns—perhaps because they're jealous or simply unaware of the relational dynamics at play—the client may remain trapped in an abusive relationship.

Devaluation

During the devaluation stage, the shine begins to fade, and the narcissist gradually withdraws the effusive affection that drew their victim in. They grow colder and more critical over time, then gaslight their victim about these changes. The narcissistic partner will blame their victim for the loss of their fairytale love story, never acknowledging that the narcissist had been the one to create the fantasy in the first place. Convinced that they are to blame, the victim tries everything in their power to please their partner, hoping that they can rekindle their perfect love if they just try harder. However, because the narcissist is always moving the goalpost, there is no way to win. When the victim fails to succeed in this unwinnable game, the narcissist moves on to the discard stage.

Discard

In this stage, the narcissist completely withdraws affection from the client. They may punish the client by giving them the silent treatment, reject their advances, and eventually abandon the client in favor of someone else. However, the narcissist will always blame the victim for the dissolution of the relationship. Once the victim has been discarded, the narcissist no longer recognizes the other person's positive traits or attributes. They now see the victim as undesirable and not good enough, and they may be openly contemptuous toward them.

Hoovering

Once the narcissist has discarded the victim, they may proceed to the next stage, which is to hoover the victim back in by offering them another chance, gaslighting them into believing the narcissist never wanted to end the relationship, or repeating the love bombing that drew them in at the beginning. Hoovering can be very effective when the victim does not want the relationship to end, as they are still invested in correcting whatever went wrong and finding the bliss of the idealization stage again.

If the victim was the one to discard the narcissist by walking away from the relationship, the narcissist may not turn to hoovering but may retaliate for their wounded pride instead. If they do hoover, it may be more focused on the victim's fragile self-esteem. For example, the narcissist may convince the client that no one else will be willing to put up with them. For clients who are still uncertain enough of their value and self-esteem, this may draw them back into the cycle anew.

Although this cycle of narcissistic abuse is most often seen in romantic relationships, it can also occur within families (where the cycle may involve reassigning childhood roles, such as the scapegoat, golden child, and invisible child) and in the workplace (where it may involve giving promotions or demotions, ranking staff by personal preference rather than performance metrics, or having an "inside circle" dynamic). Whatever the specific relationship, the cycle of narcissistic abuse can be disorienting and deeply confusing. It is important to help clients understand these patterns so they can protect themselves from further entanglement.

Attachment Difficulties

Our parents provide our first model for how relationships are supposed to work. As infants and young children, we look to our parents to provide us with safety, to teach us how we can and cannot act, and to affirm that we are loved (and therefore lovable). Emotionally mature parents create a solid foundation for secure, stable attachment based on love, acceptance, and compassion. Children learn that even when they make mistakes or disappoint their parents, they are still loved and lovable. They can explore the world knowing they have a secure home base to come back to.

However, narcissistic parents are inconsistent, unpredictable, and sometimes volatile in their relationships (Donaldson-Pressman & Pressman, 1994; Gibson, 2015; McBride, 2008). A narcissistic parent can't demonstrate unconditional love and acceptance because their warmth and affection are contingent on how well their child performs. They cannot model secure attachment because they don't know what it feels like. As a result, children of narcissistic parents learn that safety, value, and love are inconsistent and conditional. Worse yet, they are taught to believe it is their own fault.

In a narcissistic family, vulnerability is also viewed as a liability. When someone exposes their weaknesses, imperfections, or doubts, they risk being criticized or rejected. Sharing vulnerability with a narcissist is like handing them ammunition to use in the next argument. Narcissists react this way because they lack relational object permanence, which is the ability to remember, when in conflict with a loved one, that the other person is *still a loved one.* For narcissistic individuals, coming into conflict can be like flipping a switch: No longer is this person their child, partner, friend, or relation. Now they are an obstacle to the narcissist's happiness.

Because their family norm is one of insecurity and inconsistency, many adult children of narcissists struggle with *anxious attachment.* They often fear doing anything that might jeopardize their relationships. This anxiety can be frustrating for romantic partners and friends, who can become frustrated with the client's constant need for reassurance and seemingly unquenchable fear of rejection. Particularly in romantic relationships, clients may find the thought of their partner being upset with them overwhelmingly stressful, which triggers further anxiety. In turn, they may become overly clingy, ask their partners to identify the client's "flaws" so they can try to fix them, or perseverate on any disagreements or conflicts.

Some adult children of narcissists exhibit a more *avoidant attachment* style, keeping even close friends and family at arm's length to protect themselves from the dangers of intimacy. In relationships, they may show little emotion, feel uncomfortable with outward displays of affection, and find it difficult to share vulnerable moments with their partner. They may seem distant, emotionally unavailable, and have a hard time with commitment. Many clients with avoidant attachment want to have closer, more deeply connected relationships, but feel incapable of letting anyone in that far. These clients may feel frustrated by their own ambivalence. In the therapy room, these are the clients that it takes years to get to know. They may dole out small details, hinting at traumatic experiences but shying away from discussing them. They've been burned before when they trusted others, and they may be reluctant to risk it again.

Finally, some clients will experience elements of both anxious and avoidant attachment, often swinging between the two styles. They may desperately want to honor their partner's desire for intimacy and try to force themselves to be more vulnerable. The risk here is that they may push past their own emotional boundaries in an attempt to please the other person, which almost inevitably leads to internal backlash. The client may become overwhelmed, leading them to pull away again and distance themselves further. The back-and-forth can be frustrating and painful for both parties.

When working with clients with attachment difficulties, it is important to normalize these polarized cravings for distance and emotional connection. These clients long for unconditional love and acceptance—

things they may never have experienced and have only a vague sense of what they are supposed to be. Whether they present to you as clingy or detached, remember that they are doing their best to create something they've only heard described to them.

Excusing and Tolerating Harmful Behavior

It should come as no surprise that adult children of narcissists have learned to tolerate and excuse behavior that many others would not accept, particularly if they were a scapegoat in their family of origin. For example, a client may excuse a brother-in-law's refusal to acknowledge a text message despite asking him clearly and directly to respond. Another example is a client who makes excuses for a passive-aggressive coworker who treats them disrespectfully, or a client who continuously takes on additional tasks for which they are not being paid in order to please a demanding boss.

These clients are quick to justify and rationalize harmful relationship patterns because they have been conditioned to assume that they must be at fault for any problems that arise. They are so used to receiving abusive treatment that they may not even notice it until it reaches a point of no return, or until someone calls attention to it in a way that they can understand. This early conditioning to accept harmful behavior can make them susceptible to codependency and continued abuse in relationships outside the family. To help your clients gain clarity into harmful behavior such as gaslighting, consider using the *Gaslighting Decision Tree* in the appendix.

SPOTLIGHT: Codependency

The term *codependent* is poorly understood and often misused, both by the general public and within the clinical community. The term originated in the context of substance abuse treatment in referencing a relationship dynamic in which two people become deeply enmeshed and depend on each other's dysfunctional behaviors to feel secure. At its core, codependency is defined as the loss of an individual's sense of self in service to the role they fulfill in a relationship. Individuals in codependent relationships become absorbed in a symbiotic relationship with someone whose dysfunction fits neatly with their own.

A very common combination is that of an emotional caretaker who becomes deeply enmeshed with a needy person. The emotional caretaker may have little personal identity outside of their role as a caretaker and may feel very fulfilled when they are devoting themselves to the other person's needs. The other person, in turn, enjoys the support and sense of importance they receive from the caretaker. Both participants use the relationship to feel needed and to draw their attention away from their lack of self-identity (Hughes-Hammer et al., 1998).

It is important that clinicians help clients accurately identify codependency in their relationships. Desiring a loving, secure attachment with another human is not an indication of codependency, nor is wanting to spend free time with a partner or loved one. As the clinician, you can help your clients learn the difference between finding joy in supporting their partner and believing their worth lies in their ability to do so. As with much of the healing work for adult children of narcissists, clients need your support to find the healthy space between the extremes they are used to.

Listen for some of these common phrases that can indicate a history of excusing and tolerating harmful behavior in relationships. These phases all allow the other person to bypass responsibility and lay blame entirely on the shoulders of your client:

- "I should have known better than to ask about the overdue bill after he got home from work."

- "I know she doesn't mean it in a bad way, but it really hurts when she says I'm being ridiculous for feeling upset."

- "I was probably nagging him. I know that's an annoying thing to do."

- "I provoked her. I shouldn't have brought it up."

- "I can see it from his point of view. I must have been really annoying for him to yell at me like that."

- "I know she has a trauma history, too, so it doesn't seem fair for me to hold her reactions against her."

- "I'm not perfect—sometimes I'm harsh or short-tempered—so I don't feel like I can say anything about him criticizing me."

When working to address harmful relationship dynamics, a particularly sticky point for some clients can be the concept of empathy—the ability to understand what someone else is feeling and vicariously experience these emotions as well. Adult children of narcissists are often very empathetic people by nature and by family training. They are versed in the art of letting someone else's struggles relieve them of any responsibility for their actions.

While there is indeed great value in understanding how another person's struggles can influence their choices, that is not the same as giving someone free rein to engage in abusive behavior. You can help your clients with this concept by holding two beliefs simultaneously: First, that someone can be going through a difficult time that causes them to behave a particular way. And second, that having empathy for someone's struggles does not obligate your client to tolerate abusive behavior.

Boundary Struggles

Many adult children of narcissists lack a clear understanding of healthy boundaries and what they look like in practice (Gibson, 2015; Hall, 2019). Some will set overly rigid boundaries, building impenetrable walls to keep others at a distance and avoid the possibility of rejection. They have difficulty trusting others and fear that if they let anyone into their worlds, they will face scrutiny and rejection. They may be on high alert for minor infractions by others and quick to cut people out of their lives after being hurt by them.

On the other end of the extreme, some clients may have porous boundaries, leading them to overshare personal information and have a hard time saying no to others. They may be recklessly open about deeply personal concerns with individuals who have not proven their reliability or with whom that level of intimacy is not appropriate (e.g., a boss or manager). They may also have a hard time asking for what they need and may appear passive or helpless. These clients have become accustomed to a skewed version of reality in which people-pleasing is the norm, so they allow others to walk all over them.

SPOTLIGHT: Fawning

Fawning, or people-pleasing, is a survival mechanism in which a client ingratiates themselves with their abuser in the hope of mitigating or avoiding further abuse (Walker, 2013). For clients who grew up in narcissistic families, this may translate to being a social chameleon—someone who can subtly morph into whatever version of themselves suits the moment. Chameleons are very good at blending in to avoid drawing negative attention. They are not very good at understanding the difference between being mentally flexible and having no opinions of their own.

While fawning can serve the client in the short term, it causes long-term problems when the client is unable to voice their opinion or tolerate disagreements. They may also be even more susceptible to gaslighting due to their desire to avoid conflict. They may camouflage their true feelings in order to keep the peace, potentially leading to built-up resentment that they have no voice of their own. Eventually, they may hit their personal limit and begin to push back against the expectation that they always yield to the other person. This change may be abrupt and explosive. They may suddenly reject any and all viewpoints besides their own, swinging to the other extreme and refusing to concede lest they fall back into their old ways.

A former people-pleaser may generalize this new mindset across other life domains, causing them to become abrasive, argumentative, or stubborn even in relationships that have not been abusive. Since adult children of narcissists often think in extremes, they will need help finding a healthy middle ground between being a doormat and a wrecking ball. They have had little family experience of assertive communication, healthy disagreement, or respectful conflict resolution. They are used to surviving in the extremes.

When a client presents with rigid boundaries or porous boundaries, the goal is to help them develop healthy boundaries, in which they can assert their wants and needs, set limits without feeling guilty, and share personal information as appropriate. In doing so, it is important to explore the client's value system, as survivors of narcissistic abuse have had little opportunity to develop their own unique sense of self. Support the client in exploring what is important to them outside of the family norms and values they adhered to up to this point. Encourage them to identify the values they were raised with and to be curious about how those values align with their life choices at this time (see the *Values Exploration Exercise* in the appendix). This may be a process that takes several sessions or longer to explore thoroughly.

Most clients will vacillate between rigid and porous boundaries as they work out their values, make their first attempts at setting boundaries, and figure out how to live their life separate from the narcissistic system. Many will believe that the best course of action is to do the opposite of everything they disliked in their narcissistic parent. You can help them explore what *different* could look like without needing to go all the way to *opposite*.

Some clients feel incapable of doing boundary work. They want you to tell them what boundaries to hold because they have been conditioned to take their cues from the most powerful person in the room. In the therapy office, that is *you*. Even though the client may trust you to give them good advice, if they begin setting boundaries only because you have told them to, it becomes a shallow exercise in obedience rather than personal empowerment. Clinicians should be very mindful of the long-term effects of appeasing the client's immediate anxiety by providing advice that shortcuts the work of values identification. The client might feel relief in the moment, but the effects will be short-lived and can damage the therapeutic relationship in the long run. In chapter 9, we further examine how to help clients set effective boundaries.

Overachieving and Perfectionism

If you ask an adult child of a narcissist what it means to be an overachiever, you might get a blank stare. The concept doesn't always land because, to them, there is no such thing as overachieving. What others would consider overachieving is simply normal behavior to a client who is always trying to live up to a narcissist's impossible expectations (McBride, 2008). Anything less means they are slacking off, which is seen as proof of their laziness and moral deficiency.

Of course, most clients won't verbalize it in that exact way. Instead, they will mention how they don't feel like they're living up to their potential or working hard enough. These are the clients who run themselves ragged and become physically ill because they're overextending themselves at work. The clients who have a meltdown when they get a B instead of an A in a single class. The clients who shrug it off when others describe them as gifted or driven because they feel like they're just doing what they are supposed to do.

These are also the clients who "keep score" with their partner or spouse because they feel like they're contributing more to the relationship. And in many ways, they are. So many overachieving clients try to be "super parents" who keep the entire family running with little or no support from the other parent. They may also agonize over less-than-ideal parenting moments, such as when they lose their temper or say something in the heat of the moment, because they fear becoming just like their own parents. When these clients say or do something unkind in a relationship, they will ask if this is evidence of their own narcissistic tendencies and if they are becoming emotionally abusive themselves.

Mentally and emotionally, overachievers may punish themselves for every mistake or imperfection, using negative self-talk to try to push themselves to "do better." Physically, they may engage in overt or subtle forms of self-harm, including skipping meals to punish themselves for their weight or body shape, picking or scratching at their skin, or even cutting themselves to express their rage against the only person it feels safe to hate. Their internalized shame can drive any number of hurtful behaviors and mental patterns, and it is important to remain curious about the source of these behaviors rather than trying to simply reduce or eradicate them.

Bringing the Relationship into the Room

As you learn how narcissistic abuse can manifest in a client's life outside of the family setting, be aware of how these behaviors show up in the therapy room. Adult children of narcissists may be eager to prove themselves as "good clients" and may have difficulty speaking up if an intervention or reflection doesn't resonate with them. They may also feel ashamed if they struggle with or resist a homework assignment. Because these clients try very hard to be the client they *think* you want them to be, they can become resentful of your allowing this.

As the clinician, you have a powerful, influential role in these clients' lives. If ever there was a group of clients for whom it is especially important to bring the relationship "into the room," it is this one. In the context of the therapeutic relationship, you have an opportunity to model healthy conflict resolution, address problematic relationship dynamics in a respectful way, and demonstrate nonaggressive confrontation. A strong therapeutic relationship is crucial in their healing. Don't be afraid to compassionately name what is happening as it happens and to invite the client to join you in processing any frustrations or issues as they arise.

Chapter Takeaways

 Key Points

- Narcissistic abuse has long-ranging effects that can touch on every life domain.

- Clients may not understand what healthy attachment looks like. They may be anxious, avoidant, or a combination of both.

- Clients' perfectionistic and overachieving tendencies can show up in the workplace, at school, in friendships, and in romantic relationships.

- Clients may be excellent chameleons, even in the therapy room.

Therapist Aid

- *Gaslighting Decision Tree* (appendix, p. 144)

- *Values Exploration Exercise* (appendix, p. 145)

Reflection Questions

- Think of a client from your caseload whom you believe to have attachment wounds from their family of origin. How do you see those attachment wounds affecting their current relationships?

- Adult children of narcissists are conditioned to rationalize and overlook harmful behavior. How might you gently explore clients' beliefs about what constitutes healthy and loving behavior?

- *Codependency* is an often misunderstood and misused word by clients and clinicians alike. What might you look for in a client's relationships to determine whether they are at risk of codependency?

PART 3

· · · · · · · · · · · · · · · · ·

Healing Complex
Developmental Trauma

CLIENT STORY: Elijah

Elijah began therapy for the first time at age 40 after cutting off all contact with both of his parents, John and Esther, the year before. During Elijah's childhood, John frequently worked 60-plus hours a week, and Esther resented him for expecting her to run the home and raise Elijah and his two sisters on her own. When Elijah was 10, Esther reached her limit and filed for divorce. She left the children with John, moved to the other side of the country, and got remarried within a year. Her letters and phone calls were regular at first but gradually came less often as she moved on with her life.

A few days after Esther's departure, Elijah's father took him aside and said, "You're going to have to step up now that your mom has abandoned us." Given that Elijah was the oldest of the children, he became responsible for his younger siblings, including getting them ready for school and making dinner, as John was rarely home before 8 p.m. When John did come home, he often closed himself up in his bedroom with a six-pack of beer and didn't come out until the younger children were in bed. He would then sit on the couch watching television and complaining to Elijah about his "deadbeat, lowlife excuse for a mother."

Elijah soon became the default caregiver in his family. His younger sisters looked to him for their physical and emotional needs, and John seemed to forget that Elijah was still a child. Elijah's grades began to slip, but he continued doing his best to take care of everyone at home. After graduating from high school, he went on to trade school to become an electrician. Elijah regularly donated his time and skills to his father and sisters, rewiring their homes or helping them with electrical problems even when it interfered with his paid work.

Elijah's breaking point came after spending a great deal of time and energy on one project for his father. John tried to add another task to the list at the last minute, and when Elijah explained he could not accommodate that, John cursed him out as a "selfish jackass." Standing in his father's house, tools in hand, Elijah had a moment of realization. No matter how much he gave, it was never enough. *He* was never enough. His father would never appreciate him and would never acknowledge the sacrifices that Elijah had made since childhood. Elijah packed up his tools and left the house with the project incomplete.

As Elijah got into his truck to drive away, John ran after him and threw a rock at the truck, shattering a taillight. Later that night, Elijah emailed his father and told him he would not come back until his father apologized and showed some appreciation for Elijah's work. John sent back an insult-laden diatribe and refused to apologize for his actions. Realizing his father might never apologize, Elijah found himself at a crossroads: Should he sweep it under the rug and move on? Or stick with the boundary he had set and see what happened?

Elijah decided to give it a month. If his father cooled down and at least admitted that he'd behaved poorly, Elijah would consider that good enough to resume their relationship. If not, he would have to figure out a plan B. One month went by with no apology. Then another month. Then another. At this point, Elijah realized his father would probably never take responsibility for his actions that day because John had *never* taken responsibility for anything.

For the first time that he could remember, Elijah felt angry. Deeply, thoroughly angry. He had spent 30 of his 40 years alive putting everyone in his family first, at his own expense. And with that anger came the freedom to finally say "enough." The next morning, Elijah called a therapist. "I think I need to cut my dad out of my life," he said, a bit shakily. "I can't do this anymore. Can you help me?"

Even after coming to the realization that his father was too emotionally immature to initiate a reconciliation, Elijah felt extremely guilty at the prospect of cutting off his father. He still felt obligated to look after his dad in the name of family and wondered if he was taking things too far by not just giving John what he wanted, as he had in the past. Despite his stoic exterior, Elijah would often cycle through a mix of complicated, interwoven emotions: anger at his father's selfishness, sadness that things had reached this point, guilt for abandoning his aging father, resentment of the expectation to care for his father, and shame at feeling resentful. And, beneath it all, a deep pain that his father could not seem to love Elijah enough to reach out to him.

CHAPTER 7

Processing Acceptance, Grief, and Attachment Wounds

Elijah's story is one you will hear in many forms when you work with adult children of narcissists. Somewhere along their journey, there is a moment that changes everything: a moment when they stop making excuses for their loved one and begin to see that person's behaviors as hurtful and exploitative. That moment of profound realization is the beginning of one of the hardest and most important pieces of the healing journey. That moment is when clients begin to *grieve*. This grief is multilayered, complex, and confusing. And it saturates every step of the healing process. At its heart, healing from narcissistic abuse is grief work. In this chapter, we will explore what that looks like for clients.

A Critical Step in Healing: Acceptance

Some elements of the healing process for survivors of narcissistic abuse are easy to make sense of. This includes helping clients let go of old, hurtful beliefs about themselves and embrace a more compassionate perspective. While releasing the pain of the past is a crucial step in the healing process, it is not the only one. Clients must also learn to accept the reality of the abuse for real healing to take place. Narcissistic relationships flourish when the victim remains unaware of, or is willing to excuse, the narcissist's abusive behavior. When the victim recognizes the abuse for what it is, their perception of the relationship and of the narcissist changes—forever. The client can't return to ignorance once they understand the reality of the relationship.

Even once the veil of narcissistic abuse has been lifted, though, many clients struggle with acceptance. After all, how can they accept something as uncomfortable—as deeply, profoundly painful—as parental narcissism and the loss of a loving parent-child relationship? For many clients, the mind rebels, throwing up fierce defenses to avoid confronting a reality that is too painful to bear. As humans, we all engage in these types of defenses. We may scroll endlessly through our social media feeds to detach from the news. We may change the subject when someone brings up a topic we're tired of talking about. From the individual to the global, humans have developed many defenses to protect themselves from hurtful realities.

Unfortunately, these defenses have limited utility. Just as denying that we are in the midst of an earthquake doesn't make the ground stop shaking, refusing to accept a loved one's narcissistic traits doesn't change their harmful behavior. Therefore, clients need to reach a baseline level of acceptance in order to heal, and as a clinician, you need to help them sort through their feelings about that acceptance (Thomas, 2016).

To further complicate the matter, there is a widespread misunderstanding of what acceptance means in the context of relationships. Many clients mistakenly believe that in practicing acceptance, they are condoning abusive behavior and giving unspoken permission for the behavior to continue without consequence. However, acceptance does not equal approval. Rather, acceptance is the process of acknowledging reality for what it is, even if the client wishes that reality were different. Acceptance is bittersweet; when the client embraces what *is*, they have to let go of what they hoped *could be*. This is part of the grief process and is often a deeply sorrowful moment of clarity.

Although acceptance involves an element of grieving, it also presents an opportunity for the client to set new expectations for what they can expect from their narcissistic loved one. Acceptance means they can begin to look forward with clearer vision, rather than being constantly caught by surprise when their expectations don't line up with reality. And acceptance creates an opportunity for the client to develop a more honest and authentic relationship with not only the narcissist, but also themselves.

Still, some clients may continue to resist accepting their parent's narcissistic traits even after clarifying the difference between acceptance and approval. After all, acceptance can be a catalyst for many deep and difficult emotions, which is why it evokes some of the fiercest defenses we see in the therapy room. These defenses exist for a reason and are not an indication that the client is being stubborn or unwilling to do the work. Clinicians must understand that acceptance is heavily loaded because of the choices it forces on the client.

Consider the following example: If a client accepts their parent as narcissistic, they must confront their parent's inability to show them unconditional love. If a parent can't love their own child, the client may wonder if there is something fundamentally wrong and unlovable about them, leading them to feel profound shame and despair. In light of these emotions, defenses like resistance and avoidance make perfect sense. Clinicians must be sensitive to how deep this distress can run and hold space for all the emotions the client might feel. Validating a client's emotions honors their reality. It *is* unfair that the client must do so much work to correct the warped perspective they were given. It *is* frustrating that the narcissist seems so unaffected by the client's distress.

While it is always important to validate a client's distress, it is also important to invite curiosity about some of the conclusions they may be drawing from their parent's inability to show them unconditional love. Here are a few examples of the kinds of conclusions that clients may draw, along with suggestions for reframing them.

Inviting Curiosity

Client Fear	Alternate Offering
"If my own mother couldn't love me, does that mean I am unlovable?"	If your mother couldn't love you, could that mean she didn't know how to love?
"If my father doesn't care about me enough to stop treating me this way, does that mean I'm not worth the trouble?"	If your father isn't willing to treat you more kindly, what could that mean about his ability to show empathy?
"If I couldn't be a good enough child for my family to love, doesn't that prove that I'll never be good enough to deserve the love I want?"	If you couldn't "prove" yourself deserving of love to your family, maybe that was never an appropriate goal to give you.

Compassionate curiosity smooths the path to exploring these fears in session. Remember that resistance is a defense mechanism that clients use to protect themselves from further pain. Help your clients cultivate a curious and respectful framework around the risks that acceptance brings. What feels safe about avoiding those risks? What feels scary or vulnerable about the choices that acceptance presents? What is it like to be here, on the precipice of making this choice to see the world through a different lens? Your presence and rapport with your client are crucial in creating a space that feels safe enough for vulnerability. Any change in a narcissistic relationship will bring consequences of some kind, and clients need reliable support to weather the storms.

Grief Is Three-Dimensional

It is easy to imagine that clients will only feel immense relief when they reduce or cut off contact with a narcissistic loved one. After all, they are removing themselves from a source of pain and creating room to build a happier life. But grief is part of the healing process because the clients' relationships were and are important to them (Agglias, 2018). Clients grieve because the love, care, and compassion they felt—and may always feel—for their parent was real. That the relationship has changed or ended does not lessen the pain. In some cases, the pain may feel even more profound because the client could have avoided this loss if they hadn't decided to set new expectations with their loved one. Helping your clients accept this reality and process the grief it brings is some of the hardest and most important work you will ever do.

The complexity of grief in narcissistic relationships lies in the fact that it spans the past, present, and future. Not only is there grief for painful experiences that occurred in the past, but there is also grief for what did not, cannot, and will not happen within these relationships now and in the future. The client is grieving the person they believed they knew, as well as the person they now realize their loved one to be. They are grieving the loss of what they expected to have but now know they cannot. This kaleidoscope of loss makes grief work a recurrent theme whenever certain milestones, experiences, conversations, or family events bring the client's awareness back to this loss time and time again.

In our client story at the beginning of this section, we talked about the many emotions that Elijah felt when he finally had the chance to grieve his parents' separation. He could feel the shock, fear, and sense of betrayal that his mother could walk away and leave him with a father who was incapable of emotional support. He could feel his anxiety and anger at the expectation that he become the new co-parent despite still being a child himself. He could feel the deep well of sadness as he watched his childhood effectively end, and the dread of looking ahead to a life where he was always taking care of someone else. As he looked back over his life through this lens of awareness, he began to identify the losses, real and potential, that he had experienced. Among them were the losses of:

- A childhood as he was abruptly thrust into a caretaking role

- The teenage and adult years he'd expected to have with his parents there to support him and celebrate his milestones

- A stable, loving home where he could rest and be taken care of

- Academic and recreational opportunities due to exhaustion from caretaking others

- A parent who, while alive, removed herself from his life

- Emotional connection, intimacy, and support from his remaining parent figure

- Gratitude, appreciation, and love from his father in adulthood

- His perception of his father as a parent who cared, despite his absence during Elijah's childhood

- Hope for a loving, proud, respectful relationship between an adult child and their parent

- A future he'd hoped for, in which he and his father could repair the relationship and improve it moving forward

Like Elijah, many clients from narcissistic families come into treatment carrying the weight of these losses on their shoulders. While they can likely readily identify some losses, there may also be *shadow losses* that go unnoticed and unprocessed. The losses of what could have been—the what-ifs—are all shadow losses, and they are equally important to process as the more readily identified losses. Elijah suffered many shadow losses, such as the education and career choices he had to give up and the ideal father-son relationship he'd hoped to build. Your clients' healing work will be deepened and enriched by working through all levels of grief and loss (see the *Acceptance and Grief in Narcissistic Relationships* worksheet in the appendix).

Helping Clients *Go There*

Grief and acceptance are tricky, loaded concepts that many clients have a hard time with. Even some clinicians feel reluctant to bring up or address these experiences when they do arise in a session. They may worry that they will reopen a wound the client isn't prepared for, move too quickly, or offend a client by telling them they need to accept their narcissistic parent. These are all reasonable concerns and worth thinking about as you move through the delicate layers of grief work. As always, we recommend following the client's lead in terms of readiness to explore the topic at hand. With that said, questions and discussion prompts, when used appropriately, can open up or deepen the conversation around grief and acceptance. Here are a few suggestions:

- **What does acceptance mean to you in the context of a narcissistic relationship? That is, what does it mean to accept your narcissistic loved one?** Help your client differentiate between accepting that a loved one has narcissistic or emotionally immature *traits* and accepting their manipulative or abusive *behaviors* as normal or deserved.

- **Is acceptance the same thing as approval? Why or why not?** Remember that acceptance does not indicate approval. Acceptance is simply facing the reality before us, rather than resisting reality because we don't like it. Accepting a loved one as narcissistic does not mean the client is expressing their approval of the other person's behaviors, attitudes, or expectations.

- **If you accept that your loved one is narcissistic, what does that mean for you? What does that mean for your life?** Acceptance brings the client to a crossroads that can't be avoided. If they accept that their loved one is narcissistic, they are confronted with a choice: remain in a cycle that hurts them or change the dynamics and face the consequences.

- **What is the hardest part of acceptance for you? What can you accept more easily?** Some clients can easily accept that a narcissistic parent has toxic behaviors and personality traits, but they stumble when confronted with the other parent's failure to protect them. Some clients may have difficulty accepting the potential fallout that can occur with this secondary relationship and struggle to grieve the loss of their idealized version of this relationship.

- **Many people find that acceptance opens the door to grief. Has that been true for you?** Clients often unconsciously avoid accepting their loved one as narcissistic because doing so means they must come to terms with a painful reality. They must lose the illusion of the relationship they thought they were in and come to terms with the relationship they are actually in. Acceptance requires letting go of the illusion. This loss is real, even if the relationship was not.

- **Are there things you have already grieved in accepting that your loved one is narcissistic? Are there things you have not yet grieved or don't want to grieve?** Clients who have already begun to mourn the loss of the relationship with their narcissistic loved one may still have difficulty facing present or future losses. Many hold out hope for a miraculous change of heart. Although this is highly unlikely to happen, it is understandably hard to give up all hope of such a change.

- **What aspects of the grieving process do you wish you could avoid? What makes them especially hard?** Some clients will reject any feelings of sadness that come up in their grief work. They may resent themselves for crying or feeling lonely, disappointed, and hurt. These clients may feel like they have already paid their emotional dues and believe that sadness is a reflection that the narcissist has "won."

- **How does grief show up for you? What kinds of emotions, thoughts, and body sensations express your grief?** Grief is not only felt as sadness but can include a multitude of emotions, like loneliness, anger, guilt, betrayal, shame, rage, hate, self-loathing, longing, worthlessness, and regret. Grief can also show up in the form of self-blaming thoughts or ambivalence about what the client thinks they do or do not feel. Finally, grief can present in somatic symptoms, such as headaches, fatigue, joint and muscle pain, flushing, stiffness, or upset stomach.

- **Is there anything beneficial or healing about expressing grief? Does accepting and grieving the reality of your relationship bring any relief?** As clients cycle through their grief, they may come to a place of appreciation for any wisdom they have unearthed through this difficult process. Perhaps they discover a newfound respect for their own resilience or find gratitude for a sibling who helped them out. Maybe they find relief in expressing their anger in the safety of the therapeutic environment. It can be helpful to connect the experience of processing grief with the growth that can come from it.

Attachment Wounds

Narcissistic parents treat relationships as transactional and teach their children to perceive relationships as an act of service. The unpredictable anger, manipulation, and rejection that are common in narcissistic families also make relationships a source of danger and a threat to a child's sense of self (Gibson, 2015; Green & Charles, 2019). Over time, children develop attachment wounds in relation to the most important people in their lives: their caregivers. Because a child's attachment with their caregiver provides the blueprint for all relationships going forward, adult children of narcissists come to view relationships as fundamentally unstable and unreliable. In turn, they begin generalizing the protective behaviors they used to survive their family of origin to *all* relationships, even if these new relationships don't pose a threat.

This is the very nature of posttraumatic stress: the struggle to differentiate between past experiences of threat and what is occurring in the present moment. When the threats involve the most important relationship in a person's life, this can translate to difficulty forming loving, trusting, and stable relationships (Grossman et al., 2017). As noted by Bessel van der Kolk (2014), clients affected by relational trauma are conditioned to assess threats to their safety with an exacting eye. They may fixate on small details in a relationship that justify them "ruling out" a partner or ending a friendship because they equate minor conflict with the significant threats inherent in their parent-child relationships. Their threat perception system is overactive, making it harder to filter out past experiences from what is happening in the present.

On the other hand, some clients may have a hard time discerning who should be "ruled in" to relationships. They may tolerate dysfunctional relationships because they fixate on sporadic examples of when the other person made them feel good instead of looking at the bigger picture of how that person treats them. They may seek out high-intensity relationships to reenact the intensity of the narcissistic roller coaster and struggle to sustain relationships that do not mimic that roller coaster, as they are unused to the stability of a secure relationship.

It goes without saying that attachment wounds can have deep and lasting effects. These clients have internalized the belief that they shouldn't be bothered by their family's hurtful behaviors or that they should let things go instead of working through them. They may feel reluctance, guilt, and shame as they approach their grief work. And for many, the most painful part of the work is accepting they never found unconditional love from their family of origin.

Healing these attachment wounds involves educating clients about attachment and providing them an opportunity to witness secure attachment in the context of the therapeutic relationship. It may also include inner child work, where the client can engage in reparenting their inner child and forming a loving, compassionate relationship with their younger self. Reparenting also allows the client to practice setting compassionate boundaries within themselves and can help them create the experience they want to have in their relationships without perpetuating the shame and abuse from their formative years.

Secure Attachment in the Therapeutic Relationship

In the context of the therapeutic relationship, you have an opportunity to model what healthy attachment looks like, which can feel strange and scary to some clients, especially those who have been indoctrinated to keep family secrets and "put on a happy face." They may need more reassurance and validation than other clients, including reassurance that you are not disappointed with them for the pace of their progress. By treading slowly, building rapport, and providing unconditional positive regard, you can help build trust over time.

Even so, attachment challenges may become present in the therapeutic relationship, as they do in all other relationships. If and when a rupture occurs, the client may not identify it, or they may be too anxious to address the rupture directly. Remember that these clients grew up in an environment where conflict was dismissed, invalidated, and swept under the rug. Therefore, be mindful of any changes in the client's affect or behavior that point to a rupture, such as sudden withdrawal, blank affect, or changes in body language. If you notice any such changes, you want to acknowledge it and "bring it into the room." This gives you an opportunity to work through any relationship fractures in the safety of the therapy room. You may be the first person with whom these clients have an opportunity to experience what healthy rupture and repair looks like.

As a client works to heal the wounds from their family of origin, they will be able to develop a more secure attachment with you and, eventually, with other people in their life. It is good to help the client remember this when they fear that their childhood experiences have damaged them so profoundly that healthy relationships are impossible.

Modeling and Embracing the Loving Inner Parent

The therapeutic relationship has a prismatic quality that is unique from any other relationship. In the therapy room, you can be many things, including a sounding board, a source of validation, a reality tester, and a holder of hard space. You can also be the closest thing to a loving parent that some of your clients have ever experienced. You can model the ideal, loving parent that they have not known and, in doing so, give them a chance to begin identifying these features in their internal relationship to themselves.

Helping your clients develop self-compassion is foundational for this inner child work, as healing cannot come from a place of criticism. The client must be able to see the younger version of themselves who did the best they could with the tools they had, and to feel at least a little bit caring toward that younger part. Reconnecting with this childlike part can be an opportunity for the client to begin redefining their relationship to themselves as they move from self-criticism to self-compassion (Schwartz, 1995). Some clients find it helpful to look at a picture of themselves from childhood that makes them smile or feel fondly toward their childhood self. Others may prefer to use a picture of their own child or of another loved one during childhood, particularly if they struggle with self-criticism and anger toward themselves. Regardless, your role as a secure attachment base is foundational. Experiencing your compassionate, validating support can be the first broad strokes of developing their own self-compassionate inner monologue.

Inner child work and reparenting extends beyond helping clients develop a loving acceptance of their younger selves, although this can be powerfully healing. Clients will also need to challenge unrealistic expectations of perfection and fears of being an imperfect parent. They must gently and lovingly challenge the beliefs that they can and must be perfect and develop a greater degree of self-acceptance that encompasses their humanity. In chapter 9, we will go into more detail on how to help clients work through parenting-related fears.

Final Considerations

Because grief is such a holistic experience that can manifest in many ways, it is important to help clients connect to their emotional, cognitive, physical, and spiritual experience. Clinical approaches that are more cognitive or behavioral in nature may not be as effective in this area. We encourage you to deepen your understanding of more depth-oriented models that embrace the wholeness of being a person. Some models we have found particularly effective are the Hakomi method, somatic experiencing, mindfulness practices, neurofeedback, internal family systems (IFS) therapy, gestalt therapy, eye movement desensitization and reprocessing (EMDR), and brainspotting. This is far from an exhaustive list, of course, and there are many wonderful approaches to deep trauma healing.

In the next chapter, we will discuss mind and body approaches in more detail, but we recognize and respect that there are too many wonderful and effective paths to healing to capture all of them in any single book. We encourage you to be mindful of attending to all levels of the client's felt experience with whatever theoretical model or approach you use.

Chapter Takeaways

 **Key Points**

- Healing from narcissistic abuse *must* include acceptance and grieving.

- Grief is a nonlinear process that may be revisited throughout the client's journey.

- Grief is multidirectional and includes mourning what did and did not happen (past), what is and is not happening (present), and what will and will not happen (future).

- Acceptance is not the same as approval, and clients may struggle with the concept. Psychoeducation is very important to avoid giving clients the belief that they need to tolerate or allow continued abuse in the name of acceptance.

- Acceptance and grief work involve healing and reparenting the wounded inner child. This is tender, deep work that can be very taxing for the client—but also richly rewarding and transformative.

 **Therapist Aid**

- *Acceptance and Grief in Narcissistic Relationships* (appendix, p. 149)

Reflection Questions

- Many clients resist acceptance because they believe it means they are giving the narcissist a free pass to get away with their abusive, manipulative behavior. How might you address a client's anger, hurt, and betrayal if they believe they are being asked to just "let it go"?

- How do you as a clinician feel about inner child work and restorative reparenting experiences within the therapeutic relationship? Knowing that this is an important element of healing from narcissistic abuse, are there areas where you could grow to better serve these clients?

- How can you help your clients understand the serious, long-term effects of childhood emotional abuse on their adult attachments while maintaining a sense of hope for healthy relationships as an adult?

CHAPTER 8

Regulating, Validating, and Reprocessing Traumatic Memories

Trauma can have a profound and multidimensional impact on the client's relationship with themselves. In light of the relational trauma that adult children of narcissists have experienced, it comes as no surprise that they often come to therapy with a strained, detached, or complicated relationship with themselves. They may present with body dysmorphia, an overidentification with their mental or emotional struggles, low self-worth, and a poor sense of self-efficacy. Many of these clients learned to dissociate during distressing or overwhelming situations in childhood, escaping into a distant corner of their mind while their body remained stuck in the present. As a result, the wounds of their past are felt on all levels of their personhood—on their body, mind, and spirit (van der Kolk, 2014).

To effectively work with clients in processing their traumatic experiences, you must support them in healing on all levels. You must help them regain a sense of connection between their physical, emotional, and cognitive selves. In this chapter, we will examine how clients' traumatic childhoods can cause them to feel disconnected and discuss how you can help them regain a sense of wholeness.

Physical and Emotional Disconnection

Reconnecting with the Physical

Adult children of narcissists grew up in an environment in which their appearance, body size and shape, clothing, and personal style were subject to constant derision, critique, and negative commentary. After years of these judgments, it is no wonder that these clients enter therapy perceiving their bodies as excessively flawed, as constantly in need of improvement, or even as the enemy. For these clients, the body can be a minefield, making them more prone to disordered eating and body dysmorphia. Body judgment may be further exacerbated for clients whose gender does not match the sex they were assigned at birth, as well as for clients with physical disabilities, who did not meet their parent's standards for physical appearance or performance.

Clients of color may also struggle with internalized racist beliefs about the depth or tone of their skin, their facial features, and their hair texture. White and White-passing clinicians must be especially mindful of these social messages and their impact on clients of color. Individuals exist within communities, and the numerous layers of critical messages about their appearance are compounded when a client holds one or more traditionally marginalized identities.

Clients who struggle with anxiety and shame toward their bodies may benefit from a somatic intervention known as *biofeedback*, which uses specific devices to provide feedback on what is happening in the client's body as they experience different emotions. Types of biofeedback include electroencephalography (EEG), electromyograph (EMG), heart rate variability, and galvanic skin response (Khazan, 2019; Lehrer & Gevirtz, 2014). Biofeedback provides a source of external validation for what the client believes they are experiencing, and it helps them develop more awareness of their body. As their awareness and trust in their body grows, they may become less dependent on external validation. Biofeedback requires specific training for clinicians, but it may be worthwhile as an additional way to support your clients in learning to trust their bodies and emotions.

Reconnecting with the Emotional

In addition to struggling with their body image, adult children of narcissists often struggle to identify, validate, or express their emotions without becoming overwhelmed. They are quick to undercut their own emotions through internalized gaslighting and self-criticism. For example, a client might say, "I am really depressed, but I should be happy given all that I have." Even though this client recognizes their depression, they immediately deny its validity because they believe they *should* feel differently. This, of course, perpetuates the depression.

When working with clients who have trouble honoring their emotions, we encourage you to validate both the emotion *and* the client's desire to feel something else. Clients do not have to choose which emotion is "correct" if they are allowed to experience all of their emotions as real and valid. The *Emotional Awareness Interventions* handout in the appendix provides several strategies to help clients reconnect with their emotional worlds.

It is also common for adult children of narcissists to have conflicting, polarized emotions, which they often take as evidence that they don't know what they're feeling. In reality, though, these confusing experiences simply indicate that there are multiple parts of the client being activated by a certain issue or concern. Therefore, you may need to provide psychoeducation about emotions—which includes helping your clients find the language to express their feelings and normalizing the experience of having multiple emotions at one time—in order to process through their trauma. Here is where we have found the language of *parts work* to be particularly effective.

With parts work, you identify a client's conflicting emotions, desires, and goals as originating from different parts of themselves, as opposed to it representing their whole being (Anderson et al., 2017). For example, instead of commenting that a client seems resistant in session, you may say that a part of them feels resistant. Parts language accepts all aspects of the client as equally real, valid, and important. Instead of having to choose a feeling or desire to validate, clinicians can support the whole of the person by honoring all parts.

There are many ways to integrate parts work into therapy and several therapeutic models that utilize parts language. Here are a few ways you might begin to use this kind of language. Whatever specific wording you choose, recognize that humans aren't made to feel only one thing at all times. This will go a long way in helping your clients embrace their complex, nuanced, and wonderful selves.

- "I'm hearing that a part of you wants your dad to say he's proud of you, and a part of you wants to tell him to go jump off a cliff. Both of those parts feel equally strongly, and it makes sense that you would have both of them. What is it like to notice both of these parts of you right now?"

- "You want to feel strong and independent, and you also want to be taken care of because being strong is exhausting sometimes. How is it for you to feel both of those things?"

- "As soon as you talk to your mom, all those old feelings come rushing back from when you were a little boy—anxiety, dread, and the fear that you're going to get yelled at. The part of you that still feels like that little boy has a hard time hearing your mom's voice. I wonder how it would be to get to know that young part of yourself a little better and see if we can't help him to feel safer."

As you work with survivors of narcissistic abuse to help them cultivate greater internal awareness of their emotions, remember that clients experience the world in unique and varied ways. This also applies to how clients process and work through traumatic experiences. Healing from narcissistic abuse is a slow process, and you must tailor your clinical approach to what fits within each client. Here are some additional tools you can use to help clients develop greater internal awareness as they work toward healing.

SPOTLIGHT: Tuning into the Body and Mind

Cognitive Clients

Clients who primarily experience the world through a cognitive lens may have difficulty connecting with their emotions and body sensations. They may be able to rattle off hair-raising tales of abuse and manipulation without so much as a twitch, but only as long as they're allowed to tell the story without pausing to feel anything. You may support these clients in developing greater internal awareness by inviting them to identify one experience in which they knew something "wrong" had occurred within the narcissistic relationship. Ask them to describe how they knew that it was wrong and to name what about the experience was wrong.

As they describe the incident, observe their body language and facial expressions. When they are done, pause to describe how *you* experienced their story. Perhaps you felt sad or angry for the client, or perhaps you noticed tension in your shoulders upon hearing them describe this incident. You may then invite the client to check in with their body and see if they can identify any feelings or sensations within themselves.

Be mindful of the client's response to moving inward and watch for signs of dysregulation. If they start to become overwhelmed, you can return to verbally identifying facts about the experience, allowing them to regulate. As you help the client pendulate back and forth between their cognitive and physiological experience of the memory, it can help them increase their tolerance for a more embodied processing experience.

Physiological Clients

Some clients are more physiologically oriented, meaning they can connect to their bodies more easily but have difficulty identifying their thoughts or feelings. For these clients, you might begin by asking them to notice their physical reactions as they recall an upsetting or hurtful event. Invite them to identify how their body responds to the memory. Is their tongue tightly pressed against the roof of their mouth? Are their legs crossed? Are their hands clenched? Are they biting their lips? As they notice their physical reactions, you might also encourage them to speak for those sensations. If their clenched hands had a voice, what might they say? If their tight shoulders could talk, what would their story be?

As with more cognitively oriented clients, pendulating between the felt experience of the event and the client's verbal description of what happened can deepen and expand their understanding of how the experience affected them. This kind of pendulation can be especially helpful for clients who were gaslit to believe their emotional experience is incorrect or flawed.

The act of pendulating between the cognitive and physical "knowings" of an experience can also help clients resist further gaslighting by providing them multiple data points that corroborate their experience of an event or incident. They can begin to trust their perceptions more readily, which increases their self-confidence and reduces the isolation, internal gaslighting, and shame that many clients struggle with.

We encourage you to think deeply about the experience of having emotions and to treat them as a holistic experience encompassing mind, body, and spirit. Just as we clinicians can help clients reconnect to their bodies, we can help clients learn to recognize the physical sensations that accompany their emotions. Developing the ability to identify the felt sensations associated with their emotions can help clients more clearly distinguish the past from the present, which allows them to safely process past traumas.

Psychoeducation and Insight Building

Being in a narcissistic relationship feels like partnering in a dance that has no set rhythm, style, or pace. Clients may start out in a ballet pas de deux, only to find themselves suddenly stumbling through a quickstep and then staggering into a salsa. As a result, adult children of narcissists have spent much of their lives trying to make sense of their parent's inconsistent and seemingly random rhythm. Even those who only have a new understanding of their family's dynamics will find that they've been unconsciously trying to understand the unspoken for quite some time. Whether clients come to you with a wealth of insight or are just beginning to recognize the problematic dance in which they have partnered, these clients are often thirsty for knowledge that will help them understand and predict the narcissist's behavior. Psychoeducation is a key piece of this process (Fisher, 2021).

Psychoeducation about narcissistic families is incomplete without a solid understanding of the narcissistic parent (Agglias, 2018; Donaldson-Pressman & Pressman, 1994; Hall, 2019). Clients often come into the therapy room feeling hurt and betrayed by a parent who has used deeply personal experiences to devastating effect. And it makes sense—narcissists punish those who defy them in very personal ways by bringing up old pains, using favoritism to maneuver family members, and embarking on smear campaigns. It feels deeply, and intentionally, personal. Yet these attacks are impersonal at the same time. Narcissists lash out when they feel hurt, ignored, or wronged. It is a primal response, much like the reaction of a cornered animal, that is not necessarily as calculated as it may feel. Helping clients recognize this dichotomy is one way to reduce the impact of narcissistic punishments.

It is also important to provide clients with psychoeducation about the goals of therapy, as many clients enter therapy with an understandable but unattainable goal: to change their parent's behavior. Nearly all adult children of narcissists, at some point in their development, will harbor the hope that they can change their parent's hurtful behavior if they can just say or do the right thing. If they can just make their parent understand how hurtful gaslighting is, the parent will stop. If they can just learn how to set boundaries, the parent will come to respect the client and treat them more lovingly. If they can just find the right words to explain the harmful effects of favoritism, the parent will change for the better.

For most clients, though, the reality is that these hopes will not be fulfilled. While we will never say that change is impossible, the odds of a narcissist making significant, lasting changes to their behaviors are slim. For the most part, narcissists are only motivated to change their behaviors if they perceive some benefit to themselves (Lay, 2019). Therefore, it's important to gently and compassionately help your clients reframe their expectations and goals for therapy. The client cannot change their parent, and setting boundaries does not guarantee improvements in the relationship. The client can only control their own work, and they will need to release any expectations that this work will lead to the changes they want to see in their parent. The work of therapy is for the client to heal from their wounds and create a life that works for them, not to reform their parent.

Therapeutic Elements of Healing

Validation

Most, if not all, adult children of narcissists will enter the therapy room with a gnawing fear of disclosing their pain and being invalidated. This fear is valid, of course, because they have been the victim of chronic gaslighting for years. As their clinician, your response to their vulnerability carries a great deal of weight. You may be the only person they trust to witness their pain and help guide their healing. Therefore, it is crucial that your work with these clients begins and ends with validating their lived experiences. Your validation reinforces a new message that runs counter to what these clients were taught: that they have the right to speak for their experience and feel what they feel. None of that can happen without a strong foundation of rapport, support, and validation.

We do want to note that validating a client's experience doesn't mean agreeing with them on every thought, judgment, or observation. We can and do challenge our clients because they are humans just like the rest of us. But challenging problematic beliefs and behaviors is delicate work that deserves careful attention. Clients who have experienced narcissistic abuse can be sensitive if they believe their story is being questioned. If you doubt their experience, it touches on very raw wounds left by chronic gaslighting, invalidation, and dismissal. Although some of the stories your clients share may seem so outlandish as to be impossible, every human experiences life through their own lens, and it is normal to find variation in how people remember events.

Therefore, we encourage you to be mindful of what you challenge and how you challenge it. Instead of questioning a story the client shared, you might observe that some elements of the incident may have seemed surreal to the client as they were happening. Here are a few options.

Validating While Challenging

Instead of Saying	You Might Say
"That is unbelievable. Did your dad really say that?"	"It must have been hard to wrap your head around your father saying that to you. What was that like for you when it happened? What is it like to think about it now?"
"Everyone thinks their mom is a narcissist because it's all over social media."	"Narcissism has become much more widely known in recent years. When you first heard about the concept, what jumped out at you? Was there anything you heard described as narcissistic that didn't fit with what you know of your mom?"
"Don't let them live rent-free in your head."	"It's frustrating when you want to stop remembering those hurtful words and move on, but the memories seem superglued in place. We can work together to relieve that feeling so you don't have to feel so stuck."
"You're making assumptions about your parents' intent, but you can't know that for sure."	"Narcissism is such a strange thing; it can be personal and impersonal at the same time. You know your parents were upset with your decision, which makes it personal on one level. I wonder if there were any other factors, like them feeling embarrassed that they didn't get the response they were expecting. What do you think?"

Above all, be mindful of how much your words matter and remember to give your clients' stories the respect they deserve. Their stories are important, and it is an honor to join them in naming and validating their truth.

Encouragement

Encouragement, while often underrepresented in discussions about healing from relational trauma, is another important nuance of healing (Wong, 2015). While adult children of narcissists are strong, resilient, and capable, they may doubt their ability to do the challenging healing work that lies ahead. No matter where clients are when they start therapy, they will encounter points of fatigue, discouragement, and second-guessing. They may feel defeated when their attempts to set boundaries are ineffective, or depressed as they come to the realization that reducing contact with their narcissist is not going to work for them. Clients will need encouragement to face the pain and work through it without blaming and shaming themselves.

Encouragement from a therapist can provide a welcome boost of energy throughout their journey. With encouragement, you express from your heart that the individual before you is capable, good enough, and worthy of living their life to the fullest. At the same time, you should be cautious about overcompensating with empty platitudes and falling into the trap of toxic positivity or cheerleading. In the context of the therapeutic relationship, encouragement might involve:

- Reminding the client of what they have accomplished or survived so far

- Sharing your confidence that they have what they need to heal

- Reminding them that healing is not linear and it's normal to struggle at certain points

- Sharing your unconditional positive regard for them

- Acknowledging and supporting their drive to become more wholly and authentically themselves

- Letting them know that you see, value, and are enthusiastically in support of them as they are

You may be the first person who has responded to their pain with compassion and patience. Your encouragement may be a rarity for them. Your ability to hold space for them when they feel selfish for needing space may be the confirmation they need that they are *worth* holding space for. You hold the *knowing* that they can do this, even when they aren't sure of it themselves—an invaluable gift from one soul to another.

Done well, a clinician's encouragement can be key in helping the client develop a sense of self-efficacy (Wong, 2015). It can be the positive reinforcement that they need to begin internalizing the belief that they are capable of enacting a desired change. Encouragement builds rapport and trust in the therapeutic relationship, which helps the client believe they can do the hard work they came to you to do. By celebrating their successes and reminding them of their growth, you can help nurture the belief that they are strong, resilient, and capable. By supporting them as they work to change the various relational patterns they are replicating, you can help them shape a life that is distinct from their past.

The Therapeutic Relationship: Important Points to Remember

We all carry internalized biases, beliefs, and expectations about how families should work and how conflict resolution should occur. And because so many of us enter this field as wounded healers, it is common to be triggered by stories and dynamics that remind us of our own unhealthy relationships. In this section, we will discuss some of the key areas for clinicians to be mindful of within themselves when doing trauma processing with survivors of narcissistic abuse.

Know Who Your Client Is

Be very clear from the outset on who your client is. Is it an individual, a couple, or a family unit? Be honest with yourself about your scope of practice and areas of competency. If a client is seeking family therapy to set boundaries and salvage a damaged parent-child relationship, but you don't do much family therapy, this is *not* a client you should see. Family therapy with narcissistic individuals requires a highly specialized subset of skills. Attempting to navigate these complicated dynamics without that skill set puts your clients at risk of further abuse, and your license at risk for practicing outside your scope of competence. We discuss family therapy options in further detail in chapter 10.

In addition, if you are already working with a family and discover during the course of therapy that there is a narcissist in the mix, be wary of triangulation and being asked to take sides. Narcissistic parents will use therapy as a tool to manipulate and coerce family members into continuing to serve as a source of supply, and therapists can become part of the coercion if they aren't careful. Be sure to check in with all members of the family regarding their goals and preferred outcomes. Don't take the word of just one member as a family spokesperson, or you may find yourself colluding with a narcissistic parent to gain more control of their family.

Check Your Biases and Cultural Beliefs

We all have personal beliefs about what makes therapy successful when it comes to family relationships, estrangement, and reconciliation. These personal values are influenced to varying degrees by our own family of origin, our training, our cultural values, and the messages we hear in society at large. Be mindful of how your biases and beliefs inform your work, and be especially mindful when you work with clients from different cultures. If you are a White, middle-class, cisgender, heterosexual clinician, you can't assume you will fully understand the family values of a queer, Latinx, first-generation American from an immigrant family.

It is important to remember that family reconciliation is not always an appropriate goal, nor is estrangement from a family member. Everyone benefits from some level of differentiation from their family of origin, but the degree to which this is desired and valued will vary depending on a multitude of factors. While some clients will find greater relief in going low or no contact with narcissistic family members, clients who deeply value family connection may consider reduced contact a betrayal of their personal and cultural values. Beware of transposing your beliefs about family roles and family structure onto your clients.

Finally, remember that the client's family values and beliefs will drive their willingness or reluctance to explore certain options and interventions. Be very curious and affirming of your client's culture and morals, and support them in exploring how they can protect themselves without betraying important beliefs and values. Setting boundaries for a multigenerational family community may look very different than it would in a single nuclear family unit, and you can help each client figure out what boundaries best suit them. In short, one size does not fit all.

Settle In and Don't Rush

Treating complex developmental trauma is long-term, depth-oriented healing work (Hall, 2019; Hopper et al., 2019). Healing from narcissistic abuse requires working through years, often decades, of complex developmental and relational trauma. This is deep work, which can involve working with a client for several years as they process different aspects of their trauma history. Be prepared to have these clients on your caseload for quite some time. As a clinician, it is imperative that you feel comfortable moving at this slower pace, since some clients will be unprepared for the depth and breadth of what they thought was a different presenting problem. Other clients may want to dive in too quickly and risk emotional backlash unless you can help them pace themselves in processing.

Either way, you should be very mindful of clients' capacity for tolerating difficult emotions before you begin trauma processing, as there is a risk of abrupt termination if they feel flooded or overwhelmed. Since many adult children of narcissists have difficulty identifying and labeling their emotions, they may struggle to tolerate even mild emotional distress. There may be times when these clients are simply too overstimulated with the problems of today to have enough bandwidth for the pain of the past. This is particularly the case for clients who are experiencing a high level of present-day stressors, working in demanding job environments, or still residing with their narcissistic parent. Watch out for the temptation to circumvent that safety-building work, or you risk significantly more backlash within your client's emotional system, causing them to subsequently ghost you or terminate therapy too early.

The effects of narcissistic abuse are deep and far-reaching, touching virtually every corner of a client's life. Healing from narcissistic abuse requires that clients get to know themselves very deeply, feel emotions they have been taught to suppress, and allow themselves to grieve the relationships that have profoundly hurt them. No matter how much they have been hurt and how angry they are, there are always elements of sadness, loss, regret, and longing interwoven with anger and eagerness for change. Be gentle, patient, and compassionate with your clients as they mourn the loss of a relationship they never had and probably never will.

Chapter Takeaways

 **Key Points**

- Healing from narcissistic abuse is depth-oriented work that often requires a long-term commitment to therapy.

- Clients may need extensive psychoeducation to recognize their emotions and body sensations before they are ready to process trauma.

- Clients will need continued validation and encouragement throughout the healing process. They enter therapy with a deep deficit in these areas and may need more than other clients who have not suffered narcissistic abuse.

- Clinicians need to be very clear on who the client is, what the client's goals are, and whether the goals are realistic and feasible.

- Clinicians need to be aware of their personal biases and ensure these are not misaligned with the client's values.

 **Therapist Aid**

- *Emotional Awareness Interventions* (appendix, p. 152)

Reflection Questions

- As clinicians, we all bring our own set of beliefs and values into the therapy room. What beliefs do you hold about the role of family, estrangement, reconciliation, and individuation? How might these beliefs show up in your work?

- Complex trauma work is not quick or painless. How can you help clients understand the scope of the work they are likely to do and address potential discouragement if it seems like too much?

- In order to heal, clients need to have enough emotional bandwidth to withstand the thoughts, feelings, and memories that arise during processing. How can you help your clients become more aware of emotions they normally suppress or avoid?

CHAPTER 9

Action Steps and Interventions

Now that we've set the stage for trauma reprocessing, let's take a look at some action steps and interventions that you can use to help your clients grow and move forward. Clients are the experts on their lived experiences, and they will teach you more about what it's like to live through narcissistic abuse than you can ever imagine. But they are coming to you because, even with all their wonderful curiosity, determination, and resilience, they are stuck. In this chapter, we will walk you through some of the areas where you can support your clients so they can develop a sense of self, work through negative self-talk, learn how to set boundaries, and break generational cycles of narcissistic abuse in their own parenting.

Developing a Sense of Self

Growing up, children of narcissists could not develop an identity separate from their narcissistic loved one (Gibson, 2015; McBride, 2008). To cultivate a relationship with themselves now—which is something they often both fear and desire—they will need to separate themselves from the role they filled in their family of origin. However, clinicians will need to explore each client's values regarding individualism versus collectivism to help them individuate in ways that are right for them. The *Individual Choices and Consequences* worksheet in the appendix can assist with this process. Becoming a fully independent adult who lives separately from their family of origin is not a universal goal, and clinicians should beware of imposing this belief on clients.

As you gain an understanding of your client's values, you can begin to assess where they are in the individuation process. If they desire a greater degree of separation and autonomy, have they taken any steps to create it? This could include setting boundaries with their narcissistic parent, decreasing contact, or being more sparing with the information they share. Remind clients that their efforts do not need to be perfect. For example, if they have identified a goal of setting more consistent boundaries around telephone conversations, and they have held their boundaries in three out of five phone calls, they are making great progress! You can help them take a closer look at what is making those other two phone calls more challenging, while supporting and validating their work.

If the client wants to be more individuated but is struggling to disentangle from their narcissistic loved one, help them identify the barriers keeping them stuck. Are there specific strategies their loved one employs that regularly pull the client back into the cycle? What are the hooks? Guilt? Shame? Claims of abandonment? Fear of repercussions? Gaslighting? Help the client identify where they are still vulnerable and teach them how to recognize the words, tone of voice, and body language that make these tactics so effective.

Remember that underlying all decisions about individuation are the family values and beliefs the client was taught to hold. Even clients who desire individuation may still feel obligated to make a narcissistic parent happy, to cater to them because of their age, or to comply out of fear of incurring their rage. It may be helpful to review some of the implicit and explicit beliefs present in many narcissistic families, and to explore the client's relationship with these beliefs, so you can ultimately understand how these beliefs were developed, how they function today, and how the client wants to change them. These beliefs often include:

- Love and worth are conditional.

- Rebellion against the family can and should be punished through withdrawal of love.

- Envy is an expression of love.

- The client should control and restrict their emotions, as their feelings do not matter as much as the narcissistic parent's do.

- Anyone outside of the family cannot be trusted and will try to undermine family unity given the chance.

- Boundaries are harsh, cruel, or cold. Saying no hurts and rejects others.

- Relationships are only as good as their potential to benefit the narcissistic parent.

It is also important to understand how the client has internalized messages from society at large, as these messages may compound or be at odds with those from the family, creating a potentially turbulent mess of conflict to wade through. As the client learns to separate their personal values from what they were taught, they can review their family of origin's relational blueprint with a more critical eye. This allows them to identify the distortions and messages that no longer fit them and begin rewriting their relationship narrative. Of course, helping the client recognize the scripts they've been following is only one piece of the puzzle—the next is to decide which to keep and which to release.

Changing the Script

Adult children of narcissists are masters of negative self-talk (Dentale et al., 2015; Gibson, 2015). Their inner monologue can be relentlessly critical, echoing and reinforcing parental messages of shame and blame. They can find a pathway to make most problems their own fault, even if they logically know they are not to blame. This negative self-talk constantly runs in the background, like self-defeating subliminal messaging. Some of the most common forms of negative self-talk include:

- "I'm always wrong." (Self-doubt)

- "I can't do anything right!" (Shame, self-blame)

- "I'll never succeed." (Self-doubt, hopelessness)

- "They don't really love me; they're just being nice/humoring me/dealing with me." (Worthlessness)

- "Even if I tried, I wouldn't be able to get what I want. What's the point?" (Hopelessness, defeat)

- "I'm a fraud. They just haven't figured it out yet." (Impostor syndrome)

Most of these negative beliefs stem from the client's internalized beliefs that they are not, and never will be, good enough to warrant genuine love, approval, and acceptance. Let's look at Derrick's story for an example of these problematic beliefs.

CLIENT STORY: Derrick

Derrick was 58 years old when he finally sought therapy to address deeply ingrained family messages about his worthlessness and lack of potential. After many years of pain and distress, he came to identify his mother as narcissistic and his father as an enabler. Derrick was angry with both of them but struggled to move beyond repeating stories of his mother's mockery and verbal abuse. Her words seemed like a self-fulfilling prophecy of his failures in life.

"My mom told me for years that I wasn't smart enough, talented enough, or driven enough to succeed at anything. And she's right, apparently, because what have I done with my life? Any time I've even *thought* about trying something, I just heard her voice in my head, telling me I'm an idiot to even think of trying it. Well, congratulations, Mom, you got what you wanted. Maybe if I'd had a supportive mother at any point in my life, I could have made more of myself. Instead, I just proved her right and did nothing with my life."

Derrick wrestled with very polarized feelings about his mother's words. On the one hand, he felt anger and resentment toward her for saying such disparaging things when she should have been supporting him. On the other hand, he felt shame and anger toward himself for having apparently fulfilled his mother's low expectations. Although he'd had various jobs over the years, Derrick had never developed a fulfilling or lucrative career. He often daydreamed about how his life could have been different if he'd pursued his original career aspiration of becoming a pediatric surgeon.

Derrick was trapped by his mother's perception of him as incapable and unmotivated. With her voice ringing in his ears, he turned away multiple opportunities to pursue career paths he might have found exciting—all because he couldn't shake the belief that she was right about him. Derrick had to live in his mother's reality because there was no one to help him challenge it.

To heal, clients need to unlearn the way they've been taught to think about themselves. They need to disentangle themselves from their narcissistic parents' negative perceptions. In therapy, you can help clients do so by first drawing their attention to the beliefs that underlie so much of their self-perception. For many clients, these negative beliefs are background noise; they are so used to thinking poorly of themselves that it feels normal. Bringing those thoughts forward by reflecting them back to the client helps break the cycle of automatic negative thinking. Once the client is able to recognize their negative self-talk, you can begin exploring their beliefs and how the client came to hold them—and from there, you can work with them to develop self-compassion (Westphal et al., 2016).

In Derrick's case, his therapist, Andi, helped him recognize his negative self-talk by interrupting and asking him to pause and repeat his self-defeating statements. Derrick was startled by the interruption, jarring him out of his automatic pattern of self-deprecation. When he repeated the statements ("I'm an idiot, I'm not driven enough, I'm not talented enough, Mom was right"), he seemed to actually *hear* himself more clearly. Andi then asked Derrick to pause and notice the emotions that came with those negative messages. Along with identifying the thoughts and emotions, she also asked him to complete a body scan, observing his physical reaction to his self-talk.

Once Andi helped Derrick tune into how his self-talk sounded and felt, she asked him to rate the truthfulness of each statement on a scale from 0 ("not true at all") to 10 ("completely true"). As Derrick considered each belief, he came to realize that his beliefs were not supported by evidence in his life. At the same time, he noticed a reluctance to accept that these beliefs were wrong. With Andi's help, he became curious about this internal conflict, noticing his ambivalence. Andi then helped him explore his fears about what could happen if he were to release a false belief. Derrick's fears included statements like:

- "If I stop thinking I'm an idiot, I might think too highly of myself and become a narcissist."

- "If I let myself believe I'm doing my best and I don't need to try harder, I might become complacent."

- "If I stop believing I'm not talented, I might find I've missed great opportunities because I was too scared to go for them."

- "If I'm not talking harshly to myself, I might not hold myself accountable for anything and turn out just like my mom."

Like many clients, Derrick's healing journey included recognizing his black-and-white thinking as a legacy of his family of origin. Andi helped him explore the middle ground between shame and self-aggrandizement through role-play and thought experiments. For example, Derrick learned that he could accept a colleague's praise for having come up with a clever solution to a problem at work by simply saying, "Thank you." When he noticed negative self-talk try to get in the way, such as "You're being a glory hound by accepting that praise," he practiced responding with an alternative thought: "It feels nice to be appreciated by my coworker."

For many clients, this is slow and painstaking work. They often don't have a "lightbulb moment" that suddenly frees them from their negative self-talk. They inch toward freedom little by little. Practicing alternative thoughts and talking through likely scenarios that clients may encounter can help build up their confidence to check and challenge these thought distortions and negative beliefs.

Increasing Safety by Establishing Boundaries

Whether or not a client intends to remain in contact with a narcissistic loved one, it is important to help them develop and maintain boundaries that protect them from further narcissistic abuse. In doing this work, clients need to understand that setting a boundary involves more than simply telling the other person to stop a hurtful behavior. While this is certainly part of setting boundaries, it isn't enough to enact the kinds of changes that clients are hoping for.

At the most basic level, a boundary is a line that separates and defines two distinct entities. Boundaries serve as a clear marker of what is and is not acceptable to a person. Although many clients believe that drawing this line in the sand will cause the distressing or hurtful behavior to end, this expectation sets clients up for disappointment and frustration. Instead, it is more likely that the narcissist will respond with backlash, which is why drawing this line is only the first step. In order for boundaries to be effective, they must address four primary elements: (1) the client's personal values, (2) the problematic behavior that needs to change, (3) how the client will respond if the behavior continues, and (4) how they will respond to backlash. The *Boundary Basics* worksheet in the appendix can assist clients with this process.

Step 1: Identify the Value

Boundaries are based on what is important to the client and what they wish to protect. Therefore, the client must ask themselves what values are being violated, or what values they feel are important to protect through boundary setting. When the client can understand how their personal values drive their decisions about what they will and will not tolerate, it will clarify what boundaries they need to set. For example, if a client—let's call her Alma—personally values privacy and autonomy, she may set a boundary by telling family members to wait for an invitation before entering her apartment.

Step 2: Identify the Problematic Behavior and the Need for Change

The next step is for the client to identify the behavior, dynamic, or pattern that violates their personal values. In the previous example, Alma set a boundary based on how she valued her privacy. The problematic behavior in this case was that Alma's family habitually showed up at her door and let themselves in without her consent, which violated her autonomy and privacy. By entering without permission, her family members were invading her personal space and prioritizing their desire to drop in over Alma's wants and needs.

Step 3: Identify the Consequence if the Behavior Does Not Change

After identifying the problematic behavior and the need for change, the client must determine what consequences they are willing to impose if someone refuses to abide by the boundary. For example, Alma decided that if her family continued to drop by unannounced, she would not answer the door. If they entered her home without consent, she would escort them out and lock the door behind them. And if they continued these intrusive behaviors, she would consider it trespassing and contact her apartment's security officer to escort them off the property. It is critical that clients put their words into action when enforcing consequences. If a client sets a boundary but then fails to address any boundary violations, this will actively undermine the client's credibility.

Step 4: Identify How to Respond to Backlash and Boundary Violations

One of the biggest challenges that clients face in setting boundaries is dealing with the fallout from their narcissistic loved ones, who are not used to being put in their place. Narcissistic parents will resort to their usual tactics—guilt trips, gaslighting, and dismissing, to name a few—to pressure the client to back down on the boundary. For example, Alma's family laughed when she told them she would no longer open the door if they showed up unannounced, and they almost immediately violated her boundary by showing up three days later without warning. Alma was forced to put her consequences into action right away, locking her door and leaving her parents on the doorstep for over 30 minutes before they eventually left. As they waited, their response shifted from irritation to rage at being so "disrespected," and they eventually shouted insults at her while banging on the door.

Experiencing her family's wrath was distressing for Alma, as it is for many clients. If Alma had not been prepared for her parents' anger, she might have buckled under the pressure and let them in. Although she would have undermined herself in doing so, this is a very common struggle for clients who are not used to standing up for themselves. Therefore, it is important to help clients prepare ahead of time by developing a solid plan to deal with potential fallout. Process their feelings about how their family responds to their boundaries, and normalize any backlash and uncomfortable confrontations that may occur (see the *Individual Choices and Consequences* handout in the appendix).

Boundaries: Levels of Contact

There is no one-size-fits-all approach to setting boundaries, and clients may need to hold different levels of boundaries with different loved ones depending on their circumstances. Let's look at the three basic levels of contact and what boundaries might look like at each level.

Level 1: Ongoing Contact

At this level, clients remain in regular contact with their narcissistic loved one. They may reduce the frequency of contact somewhat but continue to see or talk to that person regularly. Clients who choose to remain in ongoing contact with a narcissist will need to develop a strategic safety plan to protect themselves from any ongoing abuse and exit the situation when it becomes too much. This can involve attuning to their physical and emotional warning signs of distress, creating parameters for interactions (e.g., setting ground rules that name-calling is not allowed), developing a plan to decrease physical risk factors (e.g., parking at the end of the row so as to not get blocked in if they need to leave a family party quickly), and learning to disengage with attempts at manipulation.

For example, Tanesha is fully aware that her mother is a narcissist, but she does not want to withdraw from her family altogether. "I know who she is and see her for who she is," she says, "But I'm not the kind of person to walk away from family. I need to figure out how to handle her when I see her so I don't lose my integrity and get drawn into the same pointless arguments." Therefore, Tanesha and her therapist developed several safety strategies, including limiting phone conversations to once or twice per week and ending the call after 20 minutes, attending family functions with a friend or partner whom she trusts, strengthening her relationship with her younger siblings by engaging with them separately from their mother, and ignoring or changing the subject when her mother tries to provoke an emotional reaction. Although it is still exhausting to be around her mother, Tanesha feels more confident approaching these visits with some concrete coping strategies.

Level 2: Low Contact

At this level, clients significantly reduce contact with their narcissistic loved one due to ongoing or escalating emotional abuse. Many clients are reluctant to cut ties with any family member, regardless of their behavior, but don't want to risk being triggered by frequent conversations or physical proximity. Low contact may be a good option in this case. Clients may contact their loved one occasionally (for example, visiting on holidays or having very brief conversations from time to time), invite them to meet at a public place for a specified length of time, and only offer very limited information about their personal life in conversation.

For example, as a child, Dev thought of his single mother as nothing short of heroic for raising three children without any financial or moral support from his negligent father. But as he grew older, he began to notice his mother's narcissistic traits. She would lash out at him for disagreeing with her, use personal disclosures he had given in confidence against him, and talk negatively about him to other family members.

After one too many incidents of verbal cruelty, Dev decided to go low contact with his mother. He stopped attending family gatherings apart from one or two holiday events per year and stopped sharing personal information with his mother. When he did speak to her on the phone, he kept the conversations to no more than 10 minutes, or shorter if she was being rude or demeaning. Dev and his therapist also worked on preparing him for flying monkeys who might try to pressure him into reengaging with his mother more frequently. He needed to confront his guilt at feeling like he was abandoning her, while valuing his own well-being enough to protect himself from someone who caused him pain.

Level 3: No Contact

At this level, the client completely stops engaging with their narcissistic loved one. No contact means they do not respond to outreach from the narcissist, do not initiate contact, and generally do not attend family functions or events where the narcissist is likely to be. No contact may be permanent or for a set period of time, although resuming contact is often risky for the client. If a narcissist's behavior is problematic enough for the client to completely sever contact for any period of time, that is often an indication that it is unlikely to change in the long run, regardless of potential consequences.

Many clients enter therapy expressing a desire or plan to go no contact, but not all actually do so. Cutting off contact with a family member can be a daunting task that is easier said than done. There is great potential for collateral damage, as other family members who don't fully understand or support the client's decision may rally around the narcissist and go no contact with the client themselves. Many clients, in turn, waver in going no contact because they are afraid to lose everyone they love as the penalty for cutting off contact with an abusive relative.

For example, Miri went no contact with her father after nearly 50 years of narcissistic abuse. She had tried numerous times to set boundaries, reduce her engagement with him, and limit his opportunities to behave hurtfully. She had resisted cutting off contact because she was afraid of his scorched-earth response and of the possibility of losing her mother and siblings as well. Going no contact was a last resort, and one for which she bitterly resented him.

"He pushed me to this point because he was so unwilling to contain his cruelty the tiniest bit. He didn't even have to be nice to me—I would have accepted him ignoring me. But that little bit of consideration was too much to ask, so here we are." Miri grieved the loss of the potential repair in her father-daughter relationship, knowing that going no contact would almost certainly trigger his narcissistic wounds of rejection. And she was correct. Miri's father erupted with rage upon receiving her letter stating that she would no longer communicate with him. He immediately disinherited her and left a furious voice message telling her she was dead to him.

Miri's mother contacted her separately, aghast that Miri would even consider cutting off contact with one of her parents. She confirmed Miri's fear that her parents would stand as a united front, causing Miri to become cast out from the entire family. It was an inevitable piece of collateral damage due to her parents' enmeshment, but it still hurt her deeply.

For most clients who choose to go no contact, this truly is a choice of last resort. Once the narcissist's wounds around rejection, abandonment, and shame have been triggered, they are unlikely to forgive the client for walking away. Their attention may eventually shift to someone else in the family, but they will not forgive. Clients who are considering going no contact must be prepared for intense, prolonged backlash and rejection by not only the narcissist but other family members as well.

There are also some cases when going no contact is simply not an option, such as when a client is co-parenting with a narcissist, partnered with an adult child of a narcissist who is not yet aware of the dynamic, or financially dependent on a narcissistic parent. In these situations, clients must work to practice acceptance, use coping strategies to protect themselves from further abuse, and develop autonomy within the constraints of the relationship or environment. Much of this is also applicable when working with minor clients, particularly teens, being raised by narcissistic parents.

When No Contact Is Not an Option

- **Acceptance:** When a client wishes to go no contact, but it is not possible right now, it is important to help them process the anger, resentment, grief, anxiety, and depression that may accompany this reality. They must grieve the future they had hoped for—where they could be free of the narcissist—and instead determine how much actual contact they will need to have: ongoing and frequent, or low contact and situational.

- **Coping strategies:** Clients who remain in contact with a narcissist need to learn coping skills to manage their reactivity to the other person. The gray rock method is one useful technique in which clients make themselves as uninteresting and unremarkable as possible to deflect the narcissist's interest and attention away. For example, the client may keep dialogue to a minimum (only responding with brief, one-word answers), show no emotion when engaging with the narcissist, and present themselves with a detached and noncommittal attitude. When using this method, clients must be mindful not to take the bait when the narcissist tries to stir up conflict. Not every snarky comment or insult requires a response; remember that less is more. Clients can also benefit from desensitization protocols like EMDR, brainspotting, biofeedback, exposure and response prevention (ERP), and other trauma treatment models to reduce reactivity to distressing behaviors.

- **Autonomy:** To whatever degree possible, the client must work to decrease dependence on the narcissist and develop their own sense of agency. For example, if the narcissist is providing them with monetary support, they should take steps to work toward financial independence. They must also work to develop a sense of identity distinct from the narcissist by focusing their energy into their own hobbies, interests, and skills. If a client's connection to the narcissist is time limited (e.g., in the case of minor who is waiting until they are old enough to live independently, or a co-parent who is waiting for their child to outgrow the custody agreement), the client will also need to develop the independent living skills they will need in the future.

When to Relax Boundaries and Levels of Contact

Clients often want to know if they will need to maintain these boundaries or levels of contact forever, or if their narcissistic loved one will eventually learn to respect the client's wishes. The answer to this question is very dependent on the degree of narcissism present and the specific subtype of narcissism.

For example, if a client's loved one is a vulnerable narcissist with a lower degree of narcissistic traits—perhaps they are a bit more self-absorbed and lacking in insight than the average person but not excessively power hungry—there is a chance that a low-contact boundary could eventually be relaxed with evidence of sustained behavior changes. The narcissist may still complain that they are being treated badly, but they will adjust their behavior if they value ongoing contact more than winning every battle. However, someone with more narcissistic traits, or who has a more grandiose presentation, may be less willing to bend to the client's wishes. Either way, if someone has enough narcissistic traits to require lower contact to manage them, the client should be aware that this will be an ongoing or recurring issue and plan accordingly.

Ending the Cycle: Adult Children of Narcissists as Parents

Parenthood can be a tumultuous experience for adult children of narcissists. Some choose not to have children not because they don't want to be parents, but because they are deeply afraid of hurting their children the same way they were hurt. Others choose not to have children because they understand that becoming a parent could mean having to revisit their childhood wounds, and they don't want to have to do "even more work" on themselves. Everyone has a limit, and for some adult children of narcissists, having children would push them beyond theirs.

Those who do decide to have children often wrestle with fear or anxiety that they will replicate the unhealthy relationship dynamics they themselves experienced. For example, they may fear that they won't be a good parent, that they will hurt their child, that they will be unable to bond with their child, or that their strained relationship with their own parents will prevent their kids from having a grandparent. The following are some talking points you can use to help clients explore and work through these parenting fears.

Parenting Fears

Concern: "I won't be a good parent. I wouldn't know what to do for a child."

Areas to explore:

- What do you expect from yourself as a parent?

- What does it mean to be a "good parent," and is there a difference between a good parent and a perfect one?

- What would it mean to be a "good enough parent"?

- What kind of skills do you think a good or good enough parent needs? Do you have any of those already? How could you develop any that aren't as strong?

Concern: "I'll hurt my child like my parents hurt me."

Areas to explore:

- All parents will hurt their children sometimes because all parents are imperfect human beings. We all make mistakes and do things wrong. What would it be like for you to allow yourself to be imperfect?

- What patterns or behaviors are you most worried about replicating?

- What would you most want to give your child that you did not receive in your childhood?

- What are the differences between how you approach relationships and how your parents approach them?

Concern: "What if I can't bond with my child? I don't know how to do healthy attachments."

Areas to explore:

- Many parents worry about bonding with their children; it makes sense for you to wonder about that as well. What worries you most about whether or not you can bond with your child?

- Sometimes there are parts of us that want something very much, and other parts that are very scared of getting it. Could that be the case for you? That some parts want to feel a parent-child bond and others are afraid of it?

- Sometimes we worry that getting something good in the present will only make us more aware of not having had that good thing in the past. Could there be parts of you that are afraid you'll have renewed grief over your attachment wounds if you are able to form a healthy attachment with your child?

Concern: "I'm no contact with my parents, so my child won't have grandparents."

Areas to explore:

- What are your beliefs about the role or importance of grandparents in a child's life? Is it important to you to have a multigenerational home, or for your child to spend a lot of time with their grandparents?

- If a child's grandparents are critical, overbearing, or manipulative, what is the potential for them to harm your child as they harmed you?

- If narcissistic grandparents undermine you by criticizing your parenting, ignoring your boundaries, or gaslighting you about your parenting choices, how might that affect your child? Your relationship with your child? Your relationship with yourself?

While you want to help your clients process through their fears, it is also important to understand that these concerns have some validity to them. Remember that adult children of narcissists are all but guaranteed to have their own "fleas" show up in parenting, even if they are the most intentional and insightful of clients (McBride, 2008). These clients have been the victims of relational trauma, and when trauma transcends generations, it unfortunately becomes the burden of the next generation and all those that follow.

For many clients, this trauma can show up as childlike parts that have become stuck in the moment of wounding, causing the client to react to present-day triggers much the same way they did when the original wound occurred. Until the client is able to recognize the dysfunction and make a conscious effort to change it, they may have fleas that can show up in a number of developmental stages and behaviors, such as:

- Stages of differentiation (e.g., infants gaining mobility, preschool years, adolescence, and early adulthood)

- Temper tantrums, especially if the client's parents were very harsh or strict with them about their own emotional expression

- The natural and age-appropriate egocentrism of children and adolescents

- Feeling rejected or unappreciated by their children

- Receiving critical or unsolicited feedback about their parenting choices from in-laws, neighbors, friends, family, society, and so on

These fleas may escape the client's awareness until the stressors of parenthood cause them to flare up. This can be extremely distressing for the client who is determined to parent very differently than they were parented, and addressing the fleas that escape the client's awareness can be a tricky balance for the clinician. The following client story illustrates how this might play out in a therapy session.

CLIENT STORY: Diego

Diego, an adult child of a narcissistic father, has been trying to teach his 7-year-old son, Luca, to tie his shoes. The trouble is, Diego's attempts to teach Luca always seem to end in frustration for both of them, followed by Luca becoming extra clingy for a few days. After Diego's therapist, Joaquin, probes for more details about these interactions, it becomes clear that when Diego becomes frustrated with Luca, his response is to withdraw affection. Diego doesn't want to lose his temper and hurl insults at Luca, as his father did to him, but his withdrawing into silence makes Luca feel insecure. He then follows Diego around, trying to reassure himself that his father still loves him.

Joaquin points out this observation to Diego, noting that when he withdraws in frustration, Luca may interpret this as "Papí is mad at me and doesn't love me anymore." Diego initially becomes defensive with Joaquin, arguing that he withdraws to protect Luca from his anger rather than screaming at him the way he was screamed at in his own childhood. Diego doesn't want to be anything like his father and takes offense that his therapist would suggest he might be replicating a harmful cycle in any way. Joaquin nods, recognizing the shame beneath the anger.

"It's so important to you to be a better father than your dad was to you," Joaquin acknowledges. "It's hard to hear me point out something you're doing that might be hurting your son when that's the opposite of what you want to do. I know this really matters to you, and I think we can explore some other ways that you could handle teaching Luca to tie his shoes without ending up in this frustrating situation. Let's talk about how it might look to practice coregulation skills so Luca will know that you two are in this together and that you care about how he feels."

Diego wanted to be more supportive, but he had to recognize how his own fleas were impacting his interactions with Luca before he could change the pattern. He had to dig a little deeper to find the childhood wound beneath the present-day trigger of an irritating aspect of parenting. Once he did, he could begin to address it.

As Diego's story illustrates, a client's own relational trauma can be sharply accentuated when a child comes into the world. So often, adult children of narcissists try to be the opposite of their narcissistic parent, which leads to other extremes in parenting. Of course, every parent is human, and every parent will make mistakes. No matter how insightful we are or how good our intentions are, it is impossible to exist in relationships without hurting others sometimes. Adult children of narcissists can be highly sensitive to the potential for hurting their children and may feel deeply ashamed over even very minor relationship ruptures. It is important to remind clients that while individual incidents can be hurtful and deserve to be addressed, it is the repetitive cycle of idealization, devaluation, discard, and hoovering that breaks down relationships.

Chapter Takeaways

 Key Points

- Healthy relationships in the aftermath of narcissistic parenting require a combination of internal healing work and external boundary work.

- Clients may need psychoeducation and support in identifying the beliefs and values they inherited from their family of origin. These beliefs often prevent them from developing a sense of self and keep them embroiled in negative self-talk.

- Boundaries are not one-size-fits-all and will need to be developed for and by each client.

- For adult children of narcissistic parents, parenting can be deeply challenging, frightening, and triggering, but it also carries great potential for the client's continued healing.

Therapist Aid

- *Individual Choices and Consequences* (appendix, p. 140)

- *Boundary Basics* (appendix, p. 154)

Reflection Questions

- Many clinicians prefer to work with insightful, self-aware clients who have a keen sense of their inner world. Many adult children of narcissists *are* insightful, but their inner view is distorted by the critical, devaluing, and abusive messages they have internalized. How might you help these clients broaden their self-awareness to include an acknowledgment of their positive traits and skills?

- Clients and clinicians alike often misunderstand how to set and maintain boundaries. What kinds of common mistakes or misunderstandings have your clients struggled with?

- Family trauma can be inherited and passed down through multiple generations of a family line. What do your clients know about their family trauma history? How have domestic and global events—such as economic recessions, wars, civil rights movements, and political factions—contributed to or affected their family history?

- How have the factors listed in the previous question impacted *your* family trauma history? How does your own inherited trauma inform your approach as a clinician?

. . . .

PART 4

Transference, Countertransference, and the Person of the Therapist

CLIENT STORY: Cee

Yvonne was a seasoned trauma therapist with a wealth of experience helping survivors of intimate partner violence and emotional abuse heal and move forward in life. When Cee—a physically disabled, nonbinary adult child of narcissistic parents—contacted her to begin therapy, Yvonne felt she would be a good fit for Cee's needs. She quickly found herself drawn to Cee, who presented with stoic affect and guarded body language.

Cee consistently participated in therapy, talking openly and easily about the problematic dynamics that characterized their family of origin. However, Cee described these experiences without showing any signs of distress or even varying their tone of voice. They were polite and courteous, answering questions without resistance, but seemed to exist behind an invisible shield that deflected any attempts to tease out their emotional state. Concerned that Cee might not have felt safe showing emotions in their family of origin, Yvonne was determined to make sure they knew the therapy room was a safe place to "feel all their feels," but Cee continued to remain an enigma.

After they'd met weekly for several months, Yvonne became frustrated with Cee's polite deflections, feeling like they'd made little to no progress in their time together. Beneath the frustration, Yvonne felt a fear she hadn't experienced in decades: What if, despite her training and years of clinical experience, she was not really a strong clinician? What if Cee remained emotionally detached because Yvonne was failing as a therapist? Yvonne knew her reaction had to do with more than just Cee, but she couldn't figure out why she was feeling such strong countertransference. Her frustration and self-doubt built until she began to consider terminating sessions with Cee and referring them to someone else.

Fortunately, Yvonne decided to seek peer consultation before making a decision. She met with a trusted colleague who was also part of the queer community, Jesse, and poured out her confusion, frustration, and anxiety over working with Cee. As Yvonne talked, she noticed a familiar twisting sensation in her gut that she hadn't been aware of until just now. Before she'd even reached the conclusion of whether or not to terminate with Cee, Yvonne let out a relieved laugh. She'd identified at least part of the problem: Cee, in many ways, reminded Yvonne of her emotionally stilted relationship with her mother and Yvonne's many unsuccessful attempts to foster a closer connection with her.

Jesse listened thoughtfully, validating Yvonne's desire to be a good therapist and her fear that she was not helping Cee enough. Then he pointed out something Yvonne had not been expecting: "Yvonne, you're a middle-aged, able-bodied, cis woman working with a 20-something disabled queer person. You're a wonderful, caring therapist, but you can't expect to do trauma work with someone from multiple marginalized populations if you aren't going to address the elephant in the room first."

Yvonne's face burned as she realized she'd neglected these significant factors when she focused on increasing Cee's emotional expressiveness. Jesse's observations, particularly as a member of the queer community himself, made her feel even more ashamed for having missed them. She had been so focused on her belief that Cee needed to be able to emote more openly that she'd assumed Cee shared that value without checking with them first.

"And the perfectionism that's driving you crazy, that's a legacy from your family of origin, too," Jesse pointed out. Yvonne pushed down her irritation as he spoke, wanting to defend herself and explain why she'd overlooked the differences in identity, background, and privilege between herself and Cee. But his words made her pause and reflect. She wasn't normally so defensive, but both Cee and Jesse had evoked this internal response. Was there more work for her to do around accepting herself as imperfect? Was there even some unexplored bias or prejudice about how she was received by someone from a different community, such as an LGBTQ+ individual or someone with disabilities? Taking a deep breath, she let her muscles relax for the first time in the conversation.

"Jesse, I appreciate this feedback so much. I was feeling so defensive with my client, and again with you when you pointed out what I missed or didn't handle well. I hadn't realized how much of my own stuff I had brought into the room with me. No wonder Cee didn't want to express very much. I didn't even stop to think about whether it would be safe for them to be vulnerable with someone like me. And I wasn't aware of how much my values were playing into my interpretation of Cee. Thank you for helping me find that clarity."

Yvonne's first action after talking with Jesse was to schedule an appointment with her own therapist. Her next was to seek training opportunities to deepen her awareness of how her own privilege and biases influenced her work as a therapist. And her third action was to bring the relationship into the room in her next session with Cee.

"Cee, I owe you an apology. I got caught up in what I thought you needed to do in therapy without really acknowledging how my privilege and biases shape that belief. I apologize for placing my beliefs ahead of your safety; that was not okay for me to do. If it feels okay for you, I would like to learn more about how you would like our sessions to feel." Yvonne hoped they would be able to repair the therapeutic relationship, but she felt prepared to accept Cee's decision if they did not wish to.

"Thanks for acknowledging that," Cee responded. "I get why you'd want me to open up more and talk about my feelings, but I don't know if I'm there. I don't know if I *want* to be there. I don't want to cut off my family, so I don't see the point of digging into painful memories that will just bring up bad feelings. Can you still help me if we don't go into all the old stuff?" Yvonne nodded, accepting Cee's boundary around processing past trauma and expressing their emotions openly.

"Yes," she said. "We can absolutely do good work without going into the past, and I hear that you really don't want to look backward right now. We can focus more on helping you develop concrete coping skills, like learning how to disengage from no-win conversations and handle other family members. It is likely that any memories that still hurt you will continue to do so until you feel ready to work through them. That said, I support your decision to focus on something else in our work. This is your healing journey, and although we work together, you get to decide what we're building."

Cee accepted Yvonne's apology and stated they would consider what Yvonne had said about eventually processing old trauma wounds. Cee then shared how difficult it was for them to show emotions openly in front of others, as it subjected them to backlash from their parents. Yvonne began to understand Cee's nonreactive affect as a protective coping strategy. Yvonne had been inadvertently trying to change something about Cee without realizing how necessary that trait had been in their life. Gradually, as Yvonne showed that she was committed to supporting Cee and tailoring therapy to their life experience, Cee began to open up a little more about the pain caused by their family of origin.

Cee might never be the kind of client to cry their way through a whole box of tissues in one session, but when Yvonne stopped trying to push Cee to be more emotionally expressive, Cee became more emotionally *open*. Yvonne felt her defensiveness and second-guessing decrease as her relationship with Cee became more authentic. She felt more appreciation for Cee's resilience and less frustration with their emotional reticence now that she could see it as a valuable safeguard against further abuse. Yvonne made it a point to resume regular peer consultation after this experience.

CHAPTER 10

Clinical Considerations for the Client and Therapist

Yvonne was not a bad therapist. She genuinely wanted to help and support Cee in healing. Her problems lay in two primary directions. First, she failed to acknowledge the differences in life experience, privilege, and personal values between herself and her client. And second, she was unaware how her own family of origin issues affected her engagement in the therapeutic alliance. Both are concerns that many therapists will find relatable and that they must acknowledge and explore in the therapy room. In this final chapter, we will examine these issues in more depth.

Power and Authority in the Therapeutic Relationship

Advice Giving

One of the first lessons many of us learned in graduate school was that the therapeutic relationship is not a peer-to-peer relationship. There is a power differential, with the therapist being in a position of authority over the client. In this inherently unbalanced relationship, the therapist is perceived and treated as the expert. Clients often enter therapy believing that, as the therapist, you will be able to tell them what to do with their narcissistic loved one by the end of the first session. They believe you will be able to listen to a few stories, conclude what level of contact would be best for them, and instruct them on how to respond to provocation or manipulation. Some clients will be very disappointed, and even angry, if you do not provide direct advice and directions.

Whether you are a social worker, a psychologist, a marriage and family therapist, a licensed professional counselor, or any other mental health professional, a cornerstone of our shared ethical guidelines is that we *do no harm*. Adult children of narcissists have been trained to accept the word of an authority figure and to assume that any misgivings are a result of their own errant thinking. Because of the trust they place in us, we are in a position that carries the potential for harm or healing.

Therefore, when clients ask you to give them advice, we encourage you to be transparent about your role as a clinician, including your boundaries around telling clients how to handle a problem. Here are a few statements we have found helpful when this issue arises. Working with adult children of narcissists may mean repeating these statements regularly, so don't be afraid to develop a response and practice it often!

- "I can completely understand why you'd ask me whether I think it's worth staying in contact with your narcissistic parent. It's a hard decision to make. I can't tell you what to do because, at the end of the day, I don't have to live with your decision; *you* do. What I can do is help you explore all your options, process all your feelings attached to this decision, and support you in making the choice that's right for you. How does that sound?"

- "I can't tell you whether or not your narcissistic ex will ever become a more agreeable co-parent, unfortunately. People are too complicated to make an absolute statement like that. But we can take a closer look at your ex's past behavior and patterns so you can make an informed decision about how to manage those when they show up. We can always revise our strategies if things change."

- "I know it's frustrating when you want a simple answer or set of directions and I'm not giving you one. We therapists can be annoying like that. But there's a reason we do this, and it's not just to be annoying. I don't want to just tell you what to do because then I'm participating in the same cycle you're here to break, where someone else makes decisions for your life and you feel disempowered and stuck. I'm here to help you come to the decision that is right for you without taking away your power to choose."

Clients may still feel frustrated or disappointed when you don't give them the answer they're hoping for. That's normal, and you can process that with them in the moment. We encourage you to bring the relationship into the room and address their feelings in the moment. Acknowledging disappointment and validating the client's right to feel this way can be a great step toward the autonomy and agency you want to help them develop.

Problem-Solving at the Expense of Deeper Work

Television shows tend to fall into one of two formats over the course of a season: (1) episodic shows that follow the problem of the week or (2) serial shows that follow a continuous arc. In the problem-of-the-week format, characters face a different issue in each episode, requiring various solutions specific to that issue. There may or may not be any connecting threads tying these issues together, and the skills the characters use may or may not be applicable to future issues. In continuous arc shows, characters may still face unique challenges each week, but the characters' progression is tied to an overarching issue that reaches some kind of final resolution in the season finale.

When it comes to therapy, many clients will gravitate toward a problem-of-the-week format in that they will focus on specific incidents of narcissistic abuse and will want to talk through each one as a stand-alone event. While allowing clients to share their story is a necessary aspect of validating their experience, you will eventually need to help them progress past storytelling and transition into a continuous arc model at some point. This involves helping them recognize the overarching patterns that each incident fits into, including the stages of idealization, devaluation, and discard. As a clinician, you are trained to see the connecting threads, and part of your work with clients is to teach them to do the same.

Being a "Good Client"

Adult children of narcissists usually try very hard to be good people—and therefore good clients. Some also harbor the fear that they are not a good person, or that they are actually a narcissist in denial, so they engage in people-pleasing behavior to counter their perceived badness. People-pleasing clients don't turn off their desire to make others happy when they enter the therapy room, especially when they view you as an authority figure who holds all the answers to their problems.

In their work with you, they be overly appreciative of and compliant with your suggestions or interventions. They may worry that they aren't progressing fast enough, that you secretly disapprove of them, or that you will abandon them. To further complicate matters, many of these clients have a hard time receiving positive feedback because they have been victim to so many bait-and-switch tactics throughout their lives.

While it may seem the obvious choice to simply reassure these clients—to let them know that you enjoy working with them and that you don't view them as "bad"—we encourage you to instead explore their people-pleasing behavior as it manifests in the therapy room. For example:

- If the client were to displease you, what are they afraid would happen?

- If you decided to terminate the therapeutic relationship and refer the client to someone else, what meaning would the client take from that? What would the client believe about themselves in such an event?

- How do people-pleasing behaviors show up in the client's other relationships?

- What does it feel like for the client to talk about this concern with you in the present moment?

The fear of being perceived as "bad" is a rich subject to explore with clients. Developing insight into the function of their people-pleasing behavior serves them to a much greater degree than simply providing them with verbal validation as the therapy "expert." When they understand how their shame and internalized negative beliefs contribute to their fear of being (or being perceived as) bad, they can process through the experiences that led them to adopt those beliefs. They can heal from the inside out.

If you attempt to override this internalized belief by simply reassuring the client that they are not bad, they may agree with you for the sake of pleasing you—all while secretly harboring doubt or worrying that they've now fooled even their therapist into thinking they are a good person. As much as clients wish you could change their people-pleasing patterns through external validation, you cannot. In order for it to stick, clients must learn to believe they are intrinsically good, worthy, and lovable before they can care less about others' (including your own) perceptions of them.

Supporting the Client's Autonomy

Many clients will enter therapy looking for tools to stop a narcissist's behavior, to feel less upset by the narcissist, and to respond to gaslighting and manipulation. They will ask for concrete, tangible interventions in the hope that this will be enough to change the relationship in the long run. However, we know that this is not going to be as effective as these clients are hoping. We know that they will continue to be triggered by painful memories. We know that coping tools are not magic wands that fix a broken relationship. But clients often don't know this, and they are coming to us looking for a simpler solution than the one they really need.

You always want to respect your clients' autonomy, even when you're concerned about them getting stuck in their healing because of their focus on coping skills (Hopper et al., 2019). For example, in the vignette at the start of this section, Yvonne recognized Cee's right to make their own decisions and honored Cee's autonomy in choosing their treatment goals. Yvonne also acknowledged that focusing on coping skills would limit some of the results Cee could expect from therapy, as they would not be addressing the pain of the past that continued to be triggered in the present. Clients have a right to make this decision, and clinicians have a responsibility to make sure the decision is an informed one by explaining the various options and their likely outcomes.

Transference

Every therapeutic relationship has the potential for transference to develop, and clients who present with a history of relationship trauma and insecure attachment are almost guaranteed to transfer some emotions and expectations onto their therapist. While you may feel wary of this dynamic, transference can be a gift to clinicians, as it allows you a glimpse into the client's relational framework in real time. And for clients, transference with a therapist can be a rare opportunity to experience rupture and repair in a secure, healthy relationship. Therefore, instead of perceiving transference as evidence of poor boundaries, we encourage you to view it as a useful vehicle for exploring the patterns that clients play out in their lives outside the therapy room.

When it comes to working with adult children of narcissists, many of the transference themes we have seen center on power and authority in the relationship. Clients may be quick to abdicate their power in the therapy room, deferring to the perceived authority of the therapist rather than asserting their own desires and preferences. They may try to outsource any decision-making onto the therapist for fear of making the wrong decision and anxiously ask the therapist to give them an estimation of how long they will be in treatment, when they will start to feel better, and where they are in the healing process. If they don't feel like they are progressing fast enough, they may blame themselves or worry that the therapist will be disappointed (especially the people-pleasing clients we discussed earlier). Some clients may feel frustrated with the therapist for not making them feel better quickly enough, although they may not feel they can voice this directly for fear of angering the therapist.

Clinicians can bring the relationship into the room and increase client insight by pointing out transference as it happens. Be prepared, though, that clients may have mixed feelings about exploring their transference. They may be ashamed of their feelings, worried that they have crossed a boundary, or feel a desire to take care of the therapist (who is one of their only secure attachment figures). Clients who grew up in a household where sexual experiences and emotional intimacy were a source of enmeshment may even sexualize the therapist as they become more emotionally vulnerable in sessions.

It is normal and realistic for transference to be a primary focus of therapy at times, so don't be afraid to thoroughly explore these themes if and when they arise. By identifying suspected transference, you are letting the client know that you are paying attention and that you care about their experience of therapy. Addressing transference also supports the client in becoming more mindfully aware of their experience in the here and now.

Countertransference

Let's be real: Most clinicians are motivated to get into the field, at least in part, by their own experiences with mental illness or the experiences of someone close to them. Many clinicians took on a quasi-clinical role long before they entered graduate school, functioning as emotional caretakers, parentified children, scapegoats, or golden children. For clinicians coming from narcissistic families of origin, working with clients from the same population can be rich and rewarding work. It feels good to provide the support and validation we may have needed but did not receive so that someone else won't have to struggle as much as we did. And at the same time, this work can be intensely triggering.

Adult children of narcissists often present with narcissistic or borderline personality traits, which can be triggering for clinicians as they navigate the client's manipulative behaviors, lack of insight, and splitting. Clinicians can become confused and disoriented when trying to track confusing emotional reactions, conflicting emotional energies, and subtly moving goalposts during the session. And clinicians who have fleas of their own may feel agitated or defensive when confronted by these same behaviors in their clients. They may also become frustrated with clients who fail to follow treatment recommendations, appear ambivalent about making change, and repeatedly return to the same concerns without apparent progress. Clinicians should practice mindful awareness of how their thoughts and feelings toward their clients may be evidence of growing countertransference.

As with transference, there is the potential for clients to benefit if countertransference is addressed in session, but only if there is a strong therapeutic alliance in place. To do so, the therapist can reflect on how the client's words or actions affected them, taking responsibility for their own feelings while acknowledging the client's influence. If a clinician's countertransference is particularly strong, or if they are no longer able to maintain the unconditional positive regard needed to remember that the client's problematic behavior is an attempt to meet a need, they should seek consultation or supervision before bringing countertransference to the client's attention.

CLIENT STORY: Mei

Tiana is a therapist who has been working with a 25-year-old client, Mei, to process overwhelming emotions, fear of abandonment, and self-harming behaviors. She has been diagnosed with borderline personality disorder and has a complex trauma history, including childhood emotional abuse and neglect. Mei was raised by a narcissistic mother and a depressed, emotionally distant father. She sought therapy to learn how to have healthier relationships and has spent a great deal of time talking about her strained relationships with her parents.

Recently, Mei seems to be unconsciously avoiding the grief and pain she feels over her narcissistic mother's behavior. Instead of acknowledging her feelings, Mei takes her frustration out on Tiana and complains that Tiana isn't helping her enough. Although Tiana doesn't show it, she is bothered by her client's assertions. She worries that she isn't doing a good job as a therapist because she isn't fixing the problem quickly enough. Sometimes she worries that if Mei is working this hard to avoid the pain, it might be too big for either of them to handle. Tiana also feels resentment that Mei blames her instead of taking responsibility for her own healing.

Tiana hates hearing those old "not good enough" messages start up again as she struggles through every session with Mei. Tiana has worked hard to heal from her own experiences with critical and rejecting parents. She wants to be a good therapist and to relieve her client's pain, but her inability to help Mei is making her question her skills as a clinician. And although she tries very hard to keep her feelings to herself, she suspects Mei is beginning to notice.

Here we see both transference and countertransference in action. Mei is projecting her avoidance onto Tiana and blaming her for feeling stuck. Mei is afraid of her own pain and wants Tiana to get her past it. Tiana, in turn, feels pressured to fix Mei's pain, which triggers her own fears of not being good enough. She resents Mei for not confronting her grief and for expecting that Tiana do everything for her. Mei has abdicated her power to Tiana, and Tiana has accepted it but not willingly.

As a clinician, you must always remain mindfully aware of your own expectations in the therapy room, which can help you clue into more subtle forms of transference and countertransference. For example, you may find yourself wanting to problem solve or help a client at the expense of supporting the client's empowerment and autonomy. You might also respond to a client's timidity by becoming overly protective and taking on too much of the client's work for them. While your nurturing therapist parts may want to respond to a client's desire to be taken care of, this is not always what is best for the client.

Intersectionality and Marginalized Groups

Environmental and communal trauma are the bedrock on which all individual traumas rest for marginalized clients. This includes clients who have been subject to discrimination and persecution on the basis of their race, ethnicity, religion, gender identity, sexual orientation, ability level, education, socioeconomic status, and more. Therefore, you cannot address individual or family trauma without also acknowledging the role and impact of institutional and cultural trauma, as these macro experiences form the framework in which these clients experience their individual and familial relationships.

In addition, you cannot dismiss the multiple experiences of discrimination and unequitable treatment that clients often endure on many levels at the same time. For example, a Black woman from another country who speaks English as a second language may be exposed to discrimination based on at least three layers of her identity: being perceived as female, being a person of color, and being an immigrant. Clinicians can acknowledge these multilayered experiences of trauma and discrimination by using an intersectional framework in their approach with clients.

Marginalized clients often experience forms of trauma that go unrecognized or undiscussed by others (even by some clinicians), such as religious trauma, political trauma, and medical trauma. For example, a transgender client who was raised by narcissistic parents may have suffered the medical trauma of being forced into conversion therapy. Similarly, a gay woman raised in a politically conservative religious community will require multiple layers of work in developing self-compassion, self-acceptance, and healing from gaslighting and rejection.

A client may shift back and forth between the pain points they associate most strongly with their narcissistic loved one and those they associate most with their other identities, or they may feel these traumas are too entwined to distinguish. Depending on the client's emotional and mental bandwidth, they may shy away from the most painful experiences or pick at them inconsistently. We encourage you to be curious about any frustration this may cause and to have mental flexibility in learning how your client's various identities intersect and inform their healing work.

In addition, if you are a therapist who holds multiple privileged identities (e.g., White, cisgender, male, or physically abled), it is crucial to explore how your privilege impacts the therapeutic alliance. Be humble and curious, particularly when working with clients whose cultural values may differ from yours. Be mindful not to assume shared beliefs and values. Continually do your own learning without relying on your clients or colleagues to provide free emotional labor to educate you.

For therapists of color, or for those who exist in other marginalized communities, it is important to establish a strong and dynamic system of self-care to protect against the vicarious trauma inherent in this work. While vicarious trauma is a constant concern for therapists of all backgrounds, it is particularly risky for those whose individual trauma experiences may be triggered through their clients. This trauma can get triggered not only when working with clients from marginalized identities, but also when working with clients whose values around independence, family estrangement, or privilege diverge from your lived experiences.

Group and Family Therapy Options

The secretive, face-saving nature of narcissistic relationships can leave clients feeling isolated and othered. It is for this reason that we highly recommend group therapy or other support groups for adult children of narcissists, whether used as an adjunct to individual therapy or on its own. The group format is a wonderful way to help clients work on relationship dynamics while receiving support and encouragement from others (Gibson, 2015; McBride, 2008). However, thoroughly screening group candidates is vital to ensure that the group space is safe and supportive for all members. Clinicians must also be prepared to model compassionate but firm boundaries as needed for any discord within the group. Let's look at a few group options in more detail.

Short-Term Therapy and Workshops

Adult children of narcissists almost universally share a passion for learning about narcissistic abuse and how to recover from it, making them voracious consumers of information. Psychoeducational groups and workshops can be a great resource to help clients begin to understand what they've been through without having to dive into the feelings that they may not be ready to process yet. These groups can also expose clients to others who have had similar experiences, providing a sense of belonging and community in their recovery.

Some clients will also benefit from short-term skills-based groups, which are focused on building healthy coping skills in response to toxic behavior. These groups have both a psychoeducational component (e.g., learning to recognize gaslighting or identifying manipulative phrases and behaviors) and a behavioral component (e.g., learning basic boundary-setting skills), which can be extremely beneficial at any stage in healing. For clients who are not ready to do the deeper work, these skills will help them feel empowered and boost their confidence. For those who have already begun their healing, developing these skills will support and enhance the deeper work they are doing internally.

These short-term groups are, by necessity, limited in scope and time investment. Clients may benefit from attending multiple sessions with different areas of focus, or even from repeating the same topic multiple times for deeper understanding and processing. Clinicians should be very mindful of their goals and limitations in conducting short-term groups. These will not be deep processing groups, and clinicians should be transparent about what these groups will and will not address in their informed consents. Safety and privacy are needed to process deeper traumatic experiences, and doing that in the context of a brief workshop or a short-term group is generally not advisable without specific safety protocols and training.

Long-Term Process Groups

Another avenue to fill in some of the gaps from individual therapy is a longer-term process group that focuses more deeply on understanding and healing from narcissistic abuse. These process groups offer clients an opportunity to work through the realities of narcissistic abuse alongside a cohort of peers who can relate. Unlike short-term skills-focused groups, process groups focus on deepening clients' understanding and insight into their wounds. Both types of groups can be helpful and productive, and both naturally address different facets of recovery.

In a process group, the clinician may hold a more nurturing, "good parent" role, which can be very meaningful and supportive for the group members. The clinician encourages and moderates conversations around challenging topics, creates and maintains safety within the group, sets the tone for group members to process emotions, and models healthy boundaries in the leader-to-participant relationships. This leadership role can also provoke transference within group members, who regard the clinician as a leader or parental figure. These topics can be richly rewarding for group processing, and clinicians should maintain openness to bringing transference "into the room" for compassionate discussion.

Clinicians should also keep an eye out for countertransference in process groups, particularly toward clients who react positively or negatively to the therapist as the "parent" of the group, or group members who react to one another. Depending on your client population and communication style, it may be helpful to co-lead groups with a second therapist to address transference and countertransference through multiple lenses. Again, we encourage clinicians to be open in sharing their responses to clients—while also being sensitive to clients' fears of rejection—and to process relationship dynamics in the moment. These can be wonderful learning opportunities for clients and provide a place to practice new relational skills and expectations.

Clinicians have many wonderful clinical models to utilize in a process group. Gestalt therapy, psychodrama, and parts work can all be used effectively in groups to help members identify and work through relationship trauma. We strongly recommend that process groups be considered long-term commitments and that cohorts remain together for the length of their group cycles. To promote and maintain safety, we advise running process groups for a minimum of six to eight weeks, though longer cycles of three to six months may be preferable depending on your client population. If a client is interested in groups but unable to make this commitment, they may be a better fit for short-term groups and workshops. Firm boundaries around commitment to the group are an important part of the screening process, as well as in ensuring that the group provides the safety needed for the group members to be vulnerable together.

Family Therapy with Narcissistic Parents

In general, family therapy with a narcissist is contraindicated due to the risk it presents to the non-narcissistic client (Donaldson-Pressman & Pressman, 1994; McBride, 2008). Clinicians must understand that narcissistic abuse is real abuse and that doing therapy with an actively abusive family member presents serious risk to the client's welfare. The narcissist may hijack the session to discredit the client's assertions of abuse, either by presenting the client as the problem or by painting themselves in a favorable light. An unwary therapist who is tricked by the narcissist's charm can become complicit in further gaslighting their client, often causing irreparable damage to the therapeutic alliance.

There are some clinicians who do exceptional work with highly narcissistic individuals, but they are truly a rare breed. Clinicians who work with narcissists must have extremely firm boundaries, rock-solid confidence, and a willingness to confront individuals who have zero tolerance for confrontation. These extra-specialized clinicians also understand that progress with narcissists will be very small and very slow due to their lack of insight and empathy, and that the risk of terminating will be higher than average. If you are not this clinician, that is okay. In the vast majority of cases, your clients will be best served if you educate them about the risks of family therapy with a narcissistic loved one and help them set more realistic expectations.

Family Therapy with Emotionally Immature Parents

In *some* cases, a family member who is emotionally immature but who is lower on the spectrum of narcissistic traits may be a good candidate for couples or family therapy. These family members don't necessarily meet the criteria for narcissistic personality disorder but still use problematic behaviors like poor boundaries, gaslighting, and the silent treatment to get their way. As clients, these individuals will require a great deal of patience, validation, and gentle challenges to confront their dysfunction. They may never be able to admit that they've done anything wrong, but if the relationship is important enough to them and they have enough self-awareness, they may be willing to change make surface-level adjustments to their behavior. Adult children of emotionally immature parents should still be mindful that their parent may not be able to generalize a specific behavior to a more global relationship shift and that these behavioral changes may be impermanent.

Family Therapy with the Nuclear Family

Adult children of narcissists can benefit tremendously from couples or family therapy with their nuclear family. As clients learn to reframe their expectations for themselves and others, they may appreciate the support of a therapist who can help them establish healthier parameters and expectations with their children and partners. Family therapy can also be an opportunity to model and practice building attunement, trust, and honesty in a safe and supportive environment. For clients who want to end a legacy of intergenerational trauma, this can be transformative.

The Person of the Therapist

Working with adult children of narcissists can be incredibly rich and rewarding work. It can also be painful, triggering, and exhausting. We know you care deeply about the individuals, couples, and families that sit across from you, pouring out their pain in hopes of finding relief. You carry their stories home with you. You fume to your peers about how unfair your clients' lives have been. And you may find yourself revisiting memories you would rather not as you recount the people, relationships, and experiences that led you into this helping profession in the first place.

Therefore, as we near the end of this guide, we want to acknowledge the individual on the other side of the office: the clinician. Just as the client brings their history into the room, so do you as the clinician. Understanding who you are and how you arrived here is just as important as understanding the client's story (see *The Person of the Therapist* in the appendix). You must have a deep, compassionate understanding of yourself that goes beyond your favorite theoretical orientation because this work can and will stir up your stuff. This is true whether you are new to the world of narcissistic abuse or an old pro by virtue of firsthand experience. Your inner child will be triggered during this work. Your inner parent will be triggered during this work. Your deep grief will be triggered during this work.

Pay attention to what wounds you carry and how your clients provoke them. Be mindful of how you spend your time and energy outside of the therapy room. Be generous with yourself in making time for rest and recovery. It is an act of care for your clients, as well as for yourself, to practice what you preach and turn your mindful awareness inward. You and your clients alike will benefit from your being a model of self-love and self-compassion.

Chapter Takeaways

 **Key Points**

- Adult children of narcissists can benefit from many approaches to therapy, including group therapy and workshops, as long as the model or approach supports their autonomy and validates their lived experience.

- Clients are multidimensional individuals who may have experienced many forms of discrimination and trauma outside of the family of origin as well as inside. Remember that clients are part of a society that may mitigate or reinforce harmful messages from the family.

- Clinicians can do wonderfully deep, rewarding work with adult children of narcissists—and they deserve the same kind and loving approach they show their clients. Don't forget to care for yourself, especially when clients stir up your own memories and experiences.

 **Therapist Aid**

- *The Person of the Therapist* (appendix, p. 156)

Reflection Questions

- Group therapy can be a wonderful experience for clients who feel isolated and alone in their experiences. What opportunities or barriers do you see in providing group sessions for your clients?

- Many therapists are trained to believe that family therapy can be effective to reintegrate estranged adult children and heal family rifts. Are there any messages or teachings about family therapy that you may need to revisit, question, or unlearn to best serve your adult clients?

- It is often easier to focus your compassion and kindness on your clients than to turn it inward, but working with adult children of narcissists can be triggering for clinicians who come from similar backgrounds. How might your inner child need your care as you work with these clients?

....

Therapist Aids:
Handouts, Worksheets, and Assessment Tools

Glossary of Toxic Relationship Terms

Here is a nonexhaustive list of frequently used terminology to describe traits, behaviors, patterns, and roles in narcissistic relationships.

Codependency: A relationship dynamic in which two people become deeply enmeshed and depend on each other's dysfunctional behaviors to feel secure, leading to the loss of an individual's sense of self in service to the role they fulfill in the relationship.

DARVO: An acronym for a pattern of manipulation often seen in gaslighting, standing for deny, attack (or accuse), and reverse victim and offender.

Double bind: A no-win situation where someone is manipulated into having to choose between two bad options.

Enmeshment: A relationship dynamic in which two individuals have very weak or nonexistent personal boundaries and are excessively involved and invested in one another.

Fauxpology: A false "apology" that deflects guilt or responsibility from the guilty party onto the person who was wronged.

Flying monkeys: Friends, family members, or acquaintances who are recruited to do someone else's dirty work and who pull the victim back into a negative cycle if they begin to pull away. A reference to the classic novel and film *The Wizard of Oz*.

FOG: An acronym standing for fear, obligation, and guilt.

Gaslighting: An emotional and mental manipulation strategy to make the victim question their experiences, perceptions, and beliefs. The term comes from a stage play and film titled *Gaslight*.

Golden child: In families with multiple children, the golden child is singled out for the narcissist's love and approval, and others are often compared to them unfavorably.

Grandiose narcissist: A subtype of narcissism marked by elevated self-esteem, exploitative and antagonistic behavior, social extraversion, and a focus on external measures of wealth, status, and popularity.

Gray rock: A technique in which the intended victim minimizes their appeal to a narcissist by presenting with a bland, uninteresting appearance and manner.

Hoovering: A technique to pull someone back into the patterns and cycles of a toxic relationship. This is often accomplished by a temporary improvement in the narcissist's behaviors—a promise of "turning over a new leaf"—to convince their victim that they have changed. When the victim returns, the abusive behavior resumes.

Invisible or lost child: In families with multiple children, one child (or more) may be pushed to the background where they are rarely noticed (positively or negatively).

Love bombing: A technique in which the narcissist lavishes gifts, praise, and positive attention on a victim to pull them into the fantasy of the perfect relationship.

Low contact: Partial estrangement or very limited interaction with a narcissistic relative.

Malignant narcissism: A subtype of narcissistic personality traits in which manipulative behavior is more intentional and the narcissist shows traits of sociopathy, such as receiving pleasure or amusement from the pain they cause others.

Narcissism or narcissistic personality traits: A set of traits including an inflated sense of self-importance and superiority; excessive need for praise, admiration, or reassurance; lack of personal boundaries in close relationships; manipulative and emotionally abusive behavior designed to control others; lack of insight into how one's behaviors affect others; difficulty accepting criticism; lack of empathy; and envy of others' success.

Narcissistic abuse: A persistent pattern of manipulative, abusive, and controlling behaviors that occur within a relationship, with the primary goal being the promotion of the narcissist's well-being at the expense, and to the detriment, of others.

Narcissistic rage: A term used to describe the punitive anger narcissists may express when crossed, disregarded, or challenged. Sometimes referred to as "scorched earth."

Narcissistic supply: The process of drawing time, energy, and attention from others in order to meet the narcissist's need for admiration, validation, and status.

No contact: Full estrangement from a narcissistic family member.

Parental alienation: When a narcissistic parent drives a wedge between their child and the other parent by gossiping, discrediting or devaluing them, or pressuring the child to demonstrate loyalty to the narcissist.

Parentification: When a child is thrust into adult responsibilities at an early age due to their parents' inability to maintain healthy boundaries. Parentified children may be expected to take care of their parents rather than the other way around.

Projection: When a narcissistic or emotionally immature person cannot acknowledge their own feelings and tries to paint them onto someone else.

Rug sweeping: A pattern of ignoring unresolved conflict by pretending nothing happened and failing to acknowledge any pain or harm caused during the conflict.

Scapegoat: A family member designated as the black sheep or loser of the family. Scapegoats often bear the emotional brunt of family stressors.

Smear campaign: A way of punishing those who deviate from the narcissist's wishes by spreading malicious rumors (real, exaggerated, or fabricated) about the other person in order to turn others against them.

Stonewalling: Refusal to engage in conversations to resolve a conflict; a form of giving the silent treatment that narcissists employ to shut down conversation with someone they have harmed.

Triangulation: When two members of a relationship draw a third party into their conflicts, placing unfair expectations and burdens on the third party to resolve their problems. In narcissistic or emotionally immature families, the third party is often a child.

Vulnerable narcissist: A subtype of narcissism in which the narcissist is motivated by secretive self-loathing or shame and manipulates others into a nurturing, protective, and caretaking position.

Karpman Drama Triangle

The Karpman drama triangle (Karpman, 1968) is a useful tool to demonstrate how clients may become trapped in dead-end dynamics with a narcissist. Each point of the triangle represents one of three roles that a participant may hold: victim, persecutor, and rescuer. Despite a fervent desire to change the pattern, it is very common for clients to feel stuck and remain unaware of how they are perpetuating the cycle (Fjelstad, 2013; L'Abate, 2009). As you review each of the three roles in the triangle, help your client explore how and when they may have played each role. Please note that some of these terms can be difficult for clients to accept. For example, they may become defensive when asked to consider if they've fulfilled the persecutor role or identify strongly with the victim one.

However, it can also be a deep, rich, and rewarding process to help the client explore hard questions around fulfilling a role that holds negative connotations for them. For example, if the client has ever been a persecutor, what bothers them most about having played this role? What might it mean to them, or about them, if they have been a persecutor? As this kind of healing work is by necessity depth work, these kinds of questions can be a great way to dig a little deeper into the client's self-identity, internal messaging, and self-concept.

The Triangle

These roles are not static, and participants may shift between different roles throughout the cycle of conflict. For example, a victim may be pushed into a persecutor role in angry defense, or a rescuer may become a victim when they feel burned out and unappreciated.

Rescuer

Core belief: "Let me help you."

In the rescuer role, participants feel responsible for improving the victim's life. They feel compelled to step in to try to fix the problem, despite the usually short-term nature of the fix. While well-intended, rescuers may perpetuate the victim's sense of helplessness and contribute to their own burnout.

Persecutor

Core belief: "It's all your fault."

In the persecutor role, participants blame victims for their problems and criticize rescuers for trying to solve them. Persecutors are quick to find flaws and place blame, but they do not take responsibility for their own aggressive or bullying behavior. Their rigidity may be an attempt to maintain boundaries by refusing to take on the rescuer role.

Victim

Core belief: "Poor me."

In the victim role, participants feel helpless, powerless, and trapped. They believe they are at the mercy of everyone and everything around them. They take no responsibility for their current circumstances, nor do they feel capable of changing their circumstances.

Additionally, the role that a participant fills is dependent on the perspective from which you are seeing the conflict. While one person may perceive themselves to be the victim, their partner may feel *they* are the victim. Identifying the role that a client fills both from their own perspective and from that of the narcissist can be enlightening, as it provides some insight into how the narcissist perceives their conflicts. The following client story illustrates how the triangle might play out between a narcissistic father and his daughter.

CLIENT STORY: Melody and Dwayne

Melody grew up with a narcissistic father, Dwayne, and an emotionally absent mother, Lucretia. While Lucretia rarely got involved in any relationship conflict, Melody and Dwayne frequently found themselves rotating through the roles of the drama triangle.

Melody generally identified herself as the victim in her conflicts with Dwayne. Cold and critical, he routinely pressed her to "step up" her chore completion, shamed her for her C average in math, and complained about her being ungrateful for everything he did for her. Melody perceived her father as the persecutor based on her experience of his criticism and complaints.

As Dwayne continued to needle her about her grades and lack of appreciation, Melody would eventually become angry and lash out in her own defense. She would move into the persecutor role and say things to Dwayne that she knew he felt self-conscious about. Later, seeing how hurt Dwayne was, she would feel remorseful and then move into the role of rescuer, taking on extra credit assignments to raise her math grade so he wouldn't be embarrassed by her poor performance.

From Dwayne's perspective, he was the victim in both the initial and second phase of the conflict (whereas Melody was the persecutor). He felt victimized by Melody's low math grades, which made him feel embarrassed and insulted. When she became defensive, he again felt victimized because he felt that she was being irrational and cruel.

However, whenever Melody brought home a higher math grade, Dwayne would move into the rescuer role and express concern that she was staying up too late to complete extra credit assignments. "Melody, honey, you need to keep some perspective. It's just one class; it's not worth ruining your health over!" Melody, stunned by her father's sudden attitude reversal, would feel the anger building again as she thought about the many hours she spent doing extra credit assignments to appease Dwayne. The anger would come to a boil, and the next cycle would begin again as she'd start to yell.

When working with clients to identify the roles they play in their relationship conflicts, it is important to be clear about the difference between playing a persecutor or a victim and being abusive or victimized. Perception is powerful, and narcissists will often accuse their victims of being abusive even though the client was not actually abusive. Narcissists filter all interactions through a self-aggrandizing lens and rarely, if ever, see themselves as doing anything wrong.

Finally, adult children of narcissists may swing between two extremes. At one end, they may be reluctant to accept that they sometimes fill a persecutor role in appearance or reality. At the other end, they may believe that filling the persecutor role at any point means *they* are the narcissist. A lifetime of chronic gaslighting has conditioned these clients to believe that they are the problem in most conflicts. Supporting them in coming to a more nuanced understanding of how they have been harmed *and* how they have participated in a painful dynamic will require your patience and compassion.

Money Mindset Exploration Exercise

Narcissists frequently use material wealth and financial power to pressure, manipulate, and coerce others into following their wishes. Clients raised in these families may develop distorted views about money, power, and their own value. This exercise is designed to assist clients and therapists in exploring and bringing to light any subconscious beliefs about money. It may also help you explore several relevant themes, including but not limited to:

- Personal worth and value

- Wants and needs

- Favoritism among siblings

- The importance of appearance

- Social status

- Prioritizing

- Work-life balance

- Education and career paths

- Present-day investments

- Debt

- Gambling addiction or reckless spending

- Shopping addiction

Use the following worksheet in session or ask the client to complete it between sessions. Discuss their answers to each question and explore the thoughts, feelings, body sensations, and memories they noticed while answering each question. This may serve as a jumping-off point to explore other related experiences, to clarify their emotional connection to money, or to gain insight into family values and expectations around money.

Exploring and processing these questions may take place over multiple sessions. Often, questions about money and material goods touch on some of clients' deepest moral beliefs and convictions. If the client comes from a religious background, there may be additional layers of messaging to explore regarding money, wealth, greed, and materialism.

Money Mindset Exploration Exercise

Narcissistic parents often get what they want by using money, power, or social influence to persuade others to follow along. Some narcissists use money to show favoritism or to maintain an appearance of superiority or importance (Grapsas et al., 2020). When money is used to manipulate, control, or create an elaborate facade, it can taint and distort your perspective on the use and value of money. In this exercise, you will explore how your family's relationship with money may have influenced your beliefs and expectations around money.

Answer the following questions in as much detail as you feel comfortable with. Reflect on any thoughts, feelings, memories, or bodily sensations that arise as you work.

1. What is the earliest you can recall becoming aware of money in your family of origin? Describe the memory and note any emotions, physical sensations, or beliefs connected to it.

_____

_____

_____

_____

2. When you think about money now, what is your immediate response? Note if you feel excited, worried, full of dread, angry, or any other emotional response. Don't worry about whether it seems to make sense. Try to notice the response without judging it.

_____

_____

_____

3. How do you feel about money in general? Do you see gathering material wealth as an opportunity to enhance your life or as a quest doomed to failure? Do you loathe money as evidence of greed or view it as a neutral tool to be used however it most benefits the individual?

_____

_____

_____

_____

4. Can you recall a time in your family of origin when money was used in a way that felt unfair, confusing, or unequal? Describe your memory or memories, and notice what emotions come with it as you think about it now.

_____

_____

_____

_____

5. If you had to condense your family's money habits into a few rules or ideals, what would they be? Think about how your family used, valued, and talked about money. Did they idealize it? Demonize it? Bemoan their lack of it?

_____

_____

_____

_____

6. What is the most upsetting memory you can recall in connection to money? What makes this memory the worst for you? Describe the memory or incident and how it felt at the time. Were there lingering consequences or repercussions? How do you feel as you think about it now?

_____

_____

_____

_____

7. Have you ever been the recipient of a disproportionately large or small monetary gift? For example, have you ever been the sibling to receive a new gaming system while your brothers or sisters received new socks? Or were you the one getting new socks instead? Describe how this felt.

_____

_____

_____

_____

8. How did your family perceive the connection between money and personal value? Some narcissistic families value members primarily based on their material wealth (or the appearance thereof). Were there any messages of this nature within your family?

_____

_____

_____

_____

9. Can you think of any ways that your parents' relationships with money may have harmed you? Are there any ways those relationships may have helped? Perhaps you had to get an after-school job very young because your parents couldn't afford your tuition after buying another luxury car. Or perhaps their need to flaunt their wealth meant you had access to the best private education. Explore all sides!

_____

_____

_____

_____

10. If you could change your mental and emotional relationship with money in any way, how would you change it? What associations would you dissolve? Which might you develop?

_____

_____

_____

_____

Narcissistic Abuse Tactics

Learning to recognize patterns of abusive behavior in narcissistic relationships is necessary for meaningful change to be possible. These behaviors keep victims off-balance and disoriented, making it harder for them to be assertive. Here are some of the most common tactics narcissists use to limit, control, coerce, and manipulate those around them. Which of these have you encountered in your relationships?

Accusations	Invalidating	Silencing
Blame shifting	Love bombing	Silent treatment
Comparison	Lying	Smear campaigns
DARVO	Mockery	Stealing credit
Double bind	Playing the victim	Stonewalling
Dismissing	Projecting	Talking over you
Encouraging competition	Rationalizing abuse	Teasing (mean-spirited)
Fauxpology	Ridiculing	Triangulating
Flying monkeys	Rug sweeping	Undermining
Gaslighting	Scapegoating	Withdrawing affection
Ignoring	Scorched-earth rage	Withholding money

Family of Origin Levels of Awareness Assessment

When working with narcissistic families, there are many ways to encourage exploration and curiosity at whatever stage of awareness the client is in. You can explore the family structure and norms without labeling anyone as narcissistic or calling out problem behaviors. Here we have included some sample questions you might use to get to know a client's family background, along with examples of how adult children of narcissists at different levels of awareness might answer each one.

How would you describe your family overall?

- **In-denial client:** "We were super close until my sister, Josie, decided to cut us off after she had a baby. My parents were so supportive and caring, but she just seems to think the worst of people."

- **Unaware client:** "I thought we were fine before Josie cut us off after she had her baby. She kept saying my parents were overbearing and that they were undermining her. I guess I just thought they were being supportive, but she saw it differently."

- **Not-quite-ready client:** "I mean, I guess we're a pretty normal family for the most part. Josie cutting us off after she had her baby was pretty shocking. She says Mom and Dad are overbearing and intrusive. I guess they can be kind of over the top, but I don't know if I'd go all the way calling them narcissists like she did."

- **Aware client:** "Growing up, I thought we were really close, but now I realize we were actually enmeshed. My mom is very demanding and entitled, and my dad is her flying monkey. My sister, Josie, cut my parents off after she had her baby because Mom wouldn't stop undermining her and criticizing her parenting, except she called it 'being supportive.' My mom is probably a narcissist, and my dad doesn't stand up to her, so I guess he's not much better."

How did your parents or caregivers approach their jobs or careers?

- **In-denial client:** "My dad works so hard to provide for us. He has really sacrificed a lot for our family. He deserves to be proud of his accomplishments!"

- **Unaware client:** "My dad worked a lot when I was a kid. He still really prides himself on his work ethic, even though he's had a hard time with the unstable job market. He's had a lot of bad bosses and coworkers."

- **Not-quite-ready client:** "Well, he was kind of a workaholic, but he had to do what he had to do with a family to support. He's had a lot of different jobs, and I think he's had a hard time finding the right fit. He starts off liking his boss and his coworkers, but it seems like things eventually go sour. He can be a bit abrasive when he's stressed out."

- **Aware client:** "My dad lives for his career. He has always prized his work life over his home life. He liked having this image of being a noble single dad busting his butt to take care of his kids.

He couldn't stand being contradicted, though, so he never lasted long at any job before he'd quit or get fired because he went off on someone for not doing things the way he thought they should be done."

What are some things your parents or caregivers struggled with?

- **In-denial client:** "I think my parents are misunderstood a lot. They aren't bad people, but they can be intense. I guess people just don't know how to handle their intensity, but it's not a flaw. It's just who they are."

- **Unaware client:** "My parents seem to have a hard time in their social life. I don't think they've found the right friends yet. They were abandoned by a lot of people they thought were their friends, so I think they often felt lonely."

- **Not-quite-ready client:** "They try really hard to maintain friendships, but it seems like things never work out. They've lost a lot of people they thought were friends, but who couldn't handle their emotional intensity. I suppose they don't always handle things the best way, but no one's perfect, right?"

- **Aware client:** "My parents have driven away every friend they've ever had because they always have to be right, call people names when they get mad, and can't be wrong no matter what. My dad hit a neighbor's parked car once and went off on the neighbor for parking badly. The neighbor was parked right up to the curb; my dad just cut it too close when he went by."

Depending on how narcissism aware your clients are, you may receive a wide range of responses to these questions. The accompanying worksheet includes these and a number of other questions to help you explore your clients' family backgrounds with them. Listen for clues to the client's stage of awareness in their answers.

Getting to Know Your Family of Origin

Have you ever been in a room where a strong scent or odor was present? Have you noticed how, if you're in the room for long enough, you may stop noticing that scent, even though it was very strong and noticeable when you entered? This concept is colloquially known as becoming "nose blind." The only way to correct nose blindness is either to step outside the room with the strong smell and then return, or to bring conscious attention to your sense of smell.

The same principle at work in nose blindness—that familiarity can lead to decreased awareness—can also be applied to family dynamics. You might call this "relational blindness." In this exercise, you will revive your relational awareness through a series of questions to help you think about your family in a more conscious way.

1. How would you describe your family overall?

_____

_____

_____

_____

2. What are some things your parents or caregivers struggled with?

_____

_____

_____

_____

3. When did you feel most loved, connected to, or close to your parents? You can name a specific time or incident, or talk about larger themes or patterns (e.g., feeling especially loved whenever you got a good report card).

_____

_____

_____

_____

4. When did you feel most disconnected, distant, or unloved by them? You can name a specific time or incident, or talk about larger themes or patterns (e.g., feeling distant whenever you disobeyed a rule).

_____

_____

_____

_____

5. How did your parents or caregivers approach their jobs or careers?

_____

_____

_____

_____

6. How did your parents or caregivers respond when you needed something? This could have been in response to a single event or an ongoing need, such as material necessities or help with homework.

_____

_____

_____

_____

7. If you have siblings, what is their relationship like with your parents or caregivers?

_____

_____

_____

_____

8. If you could change one thing about the way your family works, what would it be?

_____

_____

_____

_____

Individual Choices and Consequences

Many children who grew up in narcissistic families struggle with individuation as a result of parental pressure, enmeshment, and the fear of being punished for making their own choices. Those who struggle with people-pleasing in particular may have very little sense of identity because they always feel the pressure to do whatever will make their narcissistic parent happy. The following exercise can help you explore your sense of individuality and determine how it has (or has not) developed throughout your life.

1. Describe a time when you wanted to make a decision that went against your parent's wishes but did not.

_____

_____

_____

_____

2. What prevented you? What did you feel would happen if you did?

_____

_____

_____

_____

3. Now describe a time when you did actually go through with making a choice that your parent did not agree with.

_____

_____

_____

_____

4. How did you feel making that decision?

_____

_____

_____

_____

5. What happened? How did your parent respond?

_____

_____

_____

_____

6. How did you feel after their response?

_____

_____

_____

_____

7. Did you maintain your decision? Why or why not?

_____

_____

_____

_____

8. What did you learn or take away from this interaction with your parent?

_____

_____

_____

_____

Assessing Family Norms in Conflict Resolution

Exploring how conflicts were resolved in the client's family of origin can help them understand how they show up in conflicts today. Below are some questions that can be useful in helping clients recognize the beliefs they have internalized as a result of how their family of handled, or ignored, conflicts.

1. Tell me about a time that you were in conflict with your narcissistic parent (even if it seemed very small or minor). What happened?

   Invite the client to describe the conflict and the outcome of the disagreement or discussion.

2. How did you know the conflict had ended and the issue was resolved?

   Ask the client to identify any specific words, phrases, actions, or other behaviors that signaled the conversation was finished (e.g., "This conversation is over"), whether or not there was a resolution.

3. Did you feel like the issue had been resolved?

   Ask the client if they felt the issue had been addressed satisfactorily, or if it was swept under the rug with no meaningful changes.

4. Was this conflict followed by any kind of reconciliation? Or was it followed by a rejection?

   Explore whether the client received love and affection from their parent following a disagreement, or whether they received the cold shoulder (e.g., the silent treatment or passive-aggressive comments about a sibling being pleasant and agreeable).

5. Did your parent acknowledge the conflict?

   If the client's parent did not initiate the conflict, did the parent consider it a real issue?

6. If your parent did not acknowledge the conflict, how did they respond to you (e.g., gaslighting, minimizing, or denying)?

   Did the client's parent dismiss their concerns as immaturity or grudge-holding, or otherwise minimize them?

7. If your parent was still angry or upset after the conflict ended, what happened?

   Did the parent punish the client for the parent's anger? Did they take it out on others in the home? Withdraw affection?

8. Did other family members acknowledge the conflict (and any residual anger)? If so, what did they say or do?

   Ask the client whether their concern was equally invisible to other family members. Did anyone address the elephant in the room, or was it treated as a "you problem" by everyone else as well?

9. Did your narcissistic parent ever apologize for mistakes, hurtful words, or their behavior during a conflict?

   If so, did they take responsibility for themselves, or did they deflect responsibility with a fauxpology ("I'm sorry you feel that way") or by redirecting blame?

10. What did you do with the feelings you couldn't share with your parent? How did you manage your feelings?

    Explore whether the client had any space in the family to express their upset feelings, or whether they were expected to handle those on their own by isolating or stuffing them down.

11. As you think back to what you learned about conflict resolution in your family of origin, is there anything you want to do differently now? What might this change look like?

    How does the client resolve conflict at this point? What could they do differently?

Gaslighting Decision Tree

Clients and therapists alike sometimes find it hard to identify gaslighting when it happens, which makes sense, as the point of gaslighting someone is to create confusion and self-doubt. It can be particularly challenging to differentiate between gaslighting and genuinely different experiences of an event, as any two people may perceive the same incident very differently. This decision tree will help you clarify whether a client is experiencing gaslighting or a simple variance between how two or more people perceive something.

Values Exploration Exercise

In this exercise, clients will explore how their personal values align with or differ from those of their family of origin, their culture, and society at large. Once the client has defined their own set of values, they can begin moving on their authentic path. This practice of moving toward self-identified values further distances the client from the internalized trauma of their childhood and provides a self-generated alternative to living that supports the differentiation process. You can treat this as a formal exercise or allow it to unfold more organically as values questions arise in session. Feel free to revisit this exercise at any time to see how the client's perspective may change over time.

Instructions

1. To begin, have the client choose a value they'd like to explore. This may be one that the client identifies with or that they recall being prioritized in their family of origin, their culture, or society. (We have included an extensive list of potential values at the end of this exercise, which you can use as a jumping-off point.)

2. Clients may write their responses in the following worksheet. In the first column, they should note how their family of origin valued, rejected, or expressed the identified value. In the second column, they should note how this value was treated within their larger community or culture (e.g., at their church, by other members of their racial or ethnic group, etc.). In the third column, they should discuss their current, personal relationship to this value as an individual.

3. After the client completes all three columns, explore how their responses in the third column align with or differ from the other two columns. If there are significant differences, would the client be willing to redefine this value using their knowledge of the past and their presence of today? If so, have them write out a new definition. Then ask them how they would like to feel *after* they embody this new definition.

4. Finally, identify specific actions or behaviors that will support the client's growth in this direction. Understand that clients will not be perfect and will make choices that do not lead them to where they want to feel. That is their humanness. When this happens, encourage them to meet themselves with compassion and to view any missteps an opportunity to learn more about themselves and their own internal landscape.

An example is provided for you on the next page, followed by a blank worksheet you can fill out with clients.

Values Exploration Exercise

Value: _Achievement_

Family of Origin	Community or Culture	Self Today
• Achievement was very important in my family. We always had to be striving for something. There was this sense that achievement was the most important thing, besides money. • We were only worthy of love if we achieved something. That's when we celebrated. • I always felt a of pressure and confusion. • Achievement felt like this undefined quality that took up so much space. It came from the outside—someone else had to tell you that you achieved something.	• My community and culture also views achievement as very important. • Everything is competitive: grades, athletics, extracurriculars. Unless you were the star, you weren't celebrated. • I remember how important it was in my culture to go to a "good college." • Similar to my family, achievement wasn't explicitly defined in my community, but you had to attain something from an external source to be something.	• I hate the word "achievement." It makes me feel not good enough—like my power is taken away from me. I get a knot in my stomach when I think about it. • I continue to try to enact this value by overworking, buying expensive things, and posting pictures online to make it look like I have achieved something. • I don't like anything about the current definition of achievement. For being something so important, it doesn't even have a true definition.

New definition for this value: _To me, achievement should be about doing something new, learning something new, taking steps toward goals, and developing my skills._

How do you want to feel after you embody this value? _I want to feel full of delight and gratitude._

What behaviors will lead you closer to your path? What actions in this moment will bring you closer to the feeling you identified in the previous question? _I will make a gratitude list every day of three things I am grateful for. I will practice meditation daily, opening myself to the possibility of delight in everyday life._

Values Exploration Exercise

Value: _____

Family of Origin	Community or Culture	Self Today

New definition for this value:

_____

_____

How do you want to feel after you embody this value?

_____

_____

What behaviors will lead you closer to your path? What actions in this moment will bring you closer to the feeling you identified in the previous question?

_____

_____

List of Values

Acceptance	Contentment	Fortitude	Loyalty	Sensitivity
Accountability	Contribution	Freedom	Mastery	Service
Accuracy	Cooperation	Friendship	Meaning	Sharing
Achievement	Courage	Generosity	Moderation	Silence
Adaptability	Courtesy	Goodness	Motivation	Simplicity
Aggression	Creativity	Grace	Openness	Single-mindedness
Ambition	Credibility	Gratitude	Optimism	Skill
Amusement	Curiosity	Greatness	Organization	Solitude
Appreciation	Decisiveness	Growth	Originality	Spiritedness
Assertiveness	Dedication	Happiness	Passion	Spirituality
Attentiveness	Dependability	Hard work	Patience	Stability
Awareness	Determination	Harmony	Peace	Status
Balance	Development	Health	Performance	Strength
Beauty	Devotion	Honesty	Persistence	Stubbornness
Boldness	Dignity	Honor	Potential	Success
Bravery	Discipline	Hope	Power	Support
Brilliance	Discovery	Hospitality	Pragmatism	Sustainability
Calm	Efficiency	Humility	Presence	Thankfulness
Candor	Ego	Humor	Productivity	Thoroughness
Capability	Empathy	Imagination	Prosperity	Thoughtfulness
Caution	Empowerment	Improvement	Protection	Timeliness
Certainty	Endurance	Independence	Purpose	Tolerance
Challenge	Enthusiasm	Individuality	Quality	Toughness
Charity	Equality	Innovation	Reason	Tranquility
Clarity	Ethics	Integration	Recreation	Transparency
Cleanliness	Excellence	Integrity	Reflection	Trust
Cleverness	Exploration	Intelligence	Resilience	Truth
Comfort	Expression	Intensity	Respectfulness	Understanding
Commitment	Fairness	Intuition	Responsibility	Uniqueness
Communication	Fame	Justice	Risk	Unity
Community	Family	Kindness	Satisfaction	Vision
Compassion	Fearlessness	Knowledge	Security	Vitality
Concentration	Ferocity	Leadership	Self-confidence	Wealth
Confidence	Fidelity	Learning	Selflessness	Winning
Connection	Flexibility	Levelheadedness	Self-reliance	Wisdom
Consciousness	Focus	Liberty		
Consistency	Foresight	Love		

Acceptance and Grief in Narcissistic Relationships

Accepting your parent as narcissistic is a key element in healing from narcissistic abuse. This acceptance can also be tied to grief, as coming to terms with such a painful reality means letting go of the ideal-parent fantasy that many adult children of narcissists hold. Use these questions to explore your own acceptance and grief, either in a therapy session or as part of your own journaling between sessions.

1. What does acceptance mean to you in the context of a narcissistic relationship? That is, what does it mean to accept your narcissistic parent (or partner, co-parent, etc.)?

_____

_____

_____

_____

_____

2. Is acceptance the same thing as approval? Why or why not?

_____

_____

_____

_____

_____

3. If you accept that this person is narcissistic, what does that mean for you? What does that mean for your life?

_____

_____

_____

_____

_____

4. What is the hardest part of acceptance for you? What can you accept more easily?

_____

_____

_____

_____

_____

5. Many people find that acceptance opens the door to grief. What things have you grieved after accepting that this person is narcissistic? What things you have not yet grieved or don't want to grieve? What makes these elements especially hard?

_____

_____

_____

_____

_____

6. Not only can you have grief for what occurred in the past, but you can also have grief for what cannot happen now and in future. What losses do you grieve in the present, and what do you anticipate feeling grief for in the future?

_____

_____

_____

_____

_____

7. People may grieve the loss of actual experiences as well as *shadow losses*, which are the losses of what could have been—the what-ifs. What shadow losses do you grieve? That is, what are the experiences you never got to see through to fruition?

_____

_____

_____

_____

_____

8. How does grief show up for you? What kinds of emotions, thoughts, and body sensations express your grief?

_____

_____

_____

_____

_____

9. Is there anything beneficial or healing about expressing grief? Does accepting and grieving the reality of your relationship bring any relief?

_____

_____

_____

_____

_____

10. Some people find comfort in recognizing their losses, whether tangible or shadow losses, with a ritual, such as burial, release, or other forms of closure. Is there anything you would like to do to recognize the losses you have experienced?

_____

_____

_____

_____

_____

Emotional Awareness Interventions

Many adult children of narcissists try to reduce their vulnerability by shutting off or limiting their emotions. Reconnecting with their emotional world can be a challenging process, particularly when they are concerned about how painful it will feel if they allow themselves to feel again. Here we lay out several interventions to help you support your clients in getting back in touch with their emotional world at whatever pace they can tolerate.

Rating Emotional Fluidity

This mindful awareness exercise is designed to increase clients' awareness of the natural ebbs and flows of their emotional state. It can also help them identify specific triggers that affected their emotional state. This exercise is particularly effective for clients who report feeling stuck or who have little awareness of their emotional shifts over time.

> **Therapist:** I'm going to ask you to rate how you're feeling right now on a scale of 0 to 10, with 0 being "the most terrible ever" and 10 being "the best ever." Where would you say you feel right now?
>
> **Client:** Umm… maybe a 3.
>
> **Therapist:** Okay, so you're at a 3 out of 10 right now. I will ask you again in a few minutes. Whenever I ask you, you cannot say the same number twice in a row. You can say you're at 3.1 or 2.9, but it can't be a 3.0 again. We'll take a moment to really check in on how you're feeling then and see how that is.

After about ten minutes, ask the client to use the 0–10 rating scale to identify how they're feeling. By not allowing them to simply repeat the same number, you encourage them to pay closer attention to their current state and to acknowledge even the tiniest of shifts. Help your client identify what made them most aware of the differences. Did their breathing change? Were they thinking less critically of themselves? Did they feel a little more relaxed? You can also give this exercise as a homework assignment to increase mindful awareness throughout the week and review in the next session.

"Microdosing" Emotions

Microdosing is a playful term that describes how clients can incrementally allow themselves to feel more intense emotions without being flooded by them. Begin by asking the client to rate the intensity of a current emotion on a scale from 0 to 10, with 0 being "the least intense" and 10 being "overwhelmingly intense." Once the client has responded with their rating, ask them to see if they can increase or decrease the intensity by a small increment, such as 0.3, and to notice how that feels.

Invite the client to check in with their physical experience of this increase or decrease, and to observe any physical sensations they may feel. Clients who struggle to tolerate uncomfortable emotions may especially appreciate this intervention, which assists them in developing a present moment orientation and learning to trust their ability to experience their own emotions (Corrigan et al., 2011). The client can then repeat this exercise periodically to track how their tolerance for certain emotions changes over time.

Reframing Unrealistic Emotional Expectations

Oftentimes, adult children of narcissists will have unrealistic emotional goals, such as the expectation that they be happy all the time. They are used to the emotional extremes of their family of origin and may become anxious and self-critical when they don't feel the way they think they should. In addition, they may believe they are only supposed to feel one emotion at a time, as nuance and ambivalence are not normalized in narcissistic families.

To counter these messages and reframe expectations, it is important to help clients understand that they can experience multiple emotions simultaneously. In doing so, clients can expand their spectrum of emotions and validate the often confusing experience of feeling conflicting things in a narcissistic family environment. Here is one example of how you might help a client reframe their expectation that they should feel differently than they do:

Client: I know I'm supposed to be happy with my life, but I feel so depressed. Why can't I just be happy with what I have?

Therapist: I hear that you want to feel happy, and that seems impossible when you are depressed. Sometimes we think we are *supposed* to feel a certain way, and if we don't, then our feelings must be wrong. Let's consider an alternative: How might it feel to say, "I can be happy about some things in my life and also still feel depressed about others"?

This may be a very new experience for clients, especially if they are not very emotionally aware. We encourage clinicians to be mindful of not negating any feeling in favor of another—for example, don't suggest that the previous client say, "I know I'm depressed, but I have so much to be happy about!" These kinds of "yes, but" statements can feel like toxic positivity. Instead, use "yes, and" statements to validate the client's entire emotional experience, even if certain emotions seemingly conflict with each other.

You can also invite clients to dig a little deeper into the expectation that they "should" feel a certain way and explore the downsides of this quest to feel a particular emotion. For example, clients who were conditioned to "put on a happy face" for their narcissistic parent may desire to feel happy but also find the experience of happiness triggering and impossible to attain. Explore what makes the client's goal of happiness feel this way. And, if they are interested, you might explore an alternative emotional goal: If happiness feels unattainable, does contentment feel better? What about calmness? Satisfaction? Help your client explore alternatives that may feel less anxiety-provoking, laden, or unattainable.

Boundary Basics

Setting effective boundaries requires more than just asking someone to stop a harmful behavior. It also involves identifying (1) your personal values, (2) the problematic behavior that needs to change, (3) how you will respond if the behavior continues, and (4) how you will respond to backlash and boundary violations. Let's walk through each of these four steps to increase your chances of success the next time you set a boundary. You can apply this structure to boundaries in all areas of your life.

Boundary you want to set:

_____

_____

Step 1: Identify the value.

What personal value is being negatively affected by the narcissist's behavior? Examples include the right to privacy, autonomy, age-appropriate access to resources, physical space and touch, emotional energy and labor, time, and attention.

_____

_____

_____

_____

Step 2: Identify the problematic behavior and the need for change.

Name the specific behavior, dynamic, or pattern that violates your personal values. Identify a *specific* harmful behavior or action, as boundaries that are too broadly categorized are subject to interpretation.

_____

_____

_____

_____

Step 3: Identify what will happen if the behavior does not change.

Determine the consequences you are willing and able to enact when the narcissist violates this boundary. This must be something you will actually follow through on; otherwise, you are undermining yourself.

_____

_____

_____

_____

_____

Step 4: Identify how you will respond to backlash and boundary violations.

How will you handle boundary stomps and backlash from the narcissist and other family members who do not support you? Be prepared for people to push back when you try to set a boundary, but also remember that resistance to your self-care does _not_ mean you are doing something wrong!

_____

_____

_____

_____

_____

155

The Person of the Therapist

In the field of psychotherapy, clinicians hold the unique privilege of being the instrument of change. From this position, clinicians can facilitate their clients' healing, which is beautiful and rewarding work. However, clinicians can also be of detriment to the healing process if they carry the same wounds as their clients and haven't done their own internal work. The following series of questions will help you care for yourself so you can continue being the instrument of healthy change that your clients both need and deserve.

1. What narcissistic family concerns cause the greatest reactions in you? What most disturbs your spirit?

   _____

   _____

   _____

   _____

   _____

2. What is it about this specific issue that bothers you the most? Is there anything in your family of origin or other close relationships that mirrors or parallels these relationship struggles?

   _____

   _____

   _____

   _____

   _____

3. What unhealthy, abusive, or toxic messages did you receive from your family or loved ones while growing up?

   _____

   _____

   _____

   _____

   _____

4. What losses, whether tangible or shadow losses, have you had to grieve with your family?

_____

_____

_____

_____

_____

5. What have you avoided accepting or grieving? What are you ready to release?

_____

_____

_____

_____

_____

6. Where does your inner child still carry the wounds of your past? Where is your heart still tender or bruised from past unloving relationships?

_____

_____

_____

_____

_____

7. How will you care for these tender places if they become triggered by your clients' journeys?

_____

_____

_____

_____

_____

8. What are you grateful to your family for? What have they given you that you want to keep?

_____

_____

_____

_____

_____

9. What are your clients grateful to you for bringing to the relationship?

_____

_____

_____

_____

_____

References

For your convenience, purchasers can download and print the worksheets from www.pesi.com/acon

Ackerman, R. A., Hands, A. J., Donnellan, M. B., Hopwood, C. J., & Witt, E. A. (2017). Experts' views regarding the conceptualization of narcissism. *Journal of Personality Disorders, 31*(3), 346–361. https://doi.org/10.1521/pedi_2016_30_254

Agglias, K. (2018). Missing family: The adult child's experience of parental estrangement. *Journal of Social Work Practice, 32*(1), 59–72. https://doi.org/10.1080/02650533.2017.1326471

American Psychiatric Association. (2013). *Diagnostic and statistical manual of mental disorders* (5th ed.). https://doi.org/10.1176/appi.books.9780890425596

Anderson, F. G., Sweezy, M., & Schwartz, R. C. (2017). *Internal family systems skills training manual: Trauma-informed treatment for anxiety, depression, PTSD & substance abuse.* PESI Publishing.

Aron, E. (1998). *The highly sensitive person: How to thrive when the world overwhelms you.* Three Rivers Press.

Baker, A. J. L. (2006). Patterns of parental alienation syndrome: A qualitative study of adults who were alienated from a parent as a child. *The American Journal of Family Therapy, 34*(1), 63–78. https://doi.org/10.1080/01926180500301444

Bent-Goodley, T. B., & Fowler, D. N. (2006). Spiritual and religious abuse: Expanding what is known about domestic violence. *Affilia, 21*(3), 282–295. https://doi.org/10.1177/0886109906288901

Cain, N. M., Pincus, A. L., & Ansell, E. B. (2008). Narcissism at the crossroads: Phenotypic description of pathological narcissism across clinical theory, social/personality psychology, and psychiatric diagnosis. *Clinical Psychology Review, 28*(4), 638–656. https://doi.org/10.1016/j.cpr.2007.09.006

Carries, P. J., & Delmonico, D. L. (1996). Childhood abuse and multiple addictions: Research findings in a sample of self-identified sexual addicts. *Sexual Addiction & Compulsivity, 3*(3), 258–268. https://doi.org/10.1080/10720169608400116

Cichocka, A., & Cislak, A. (2020). Nationalism as collective narcissism. *Current Opinion in Behavioral Sciences, 34*, 69–74. https://doi.org/10.1016/j.cobeha.2019.12.013

Corrigan, F. M., Fisher, J. J., & Nutt, D. J. (2011). Autonomic dysregulation and the window of tolerance model of the effects of complex emotional trauma. *Journal of Psychopharmacology, 25*(1), 17–25. https://doi.org/10.1177/0269881109354930

Csillik, A. S. (2013). Understanding motivational interviewing effectiveness: Contributions from Rogers' client-centered approach. *The Humanistic Psychologist, 41*(4), 350–363. https://doi.org/10.1080/08873267.2013.779906

Dentale, F., Verrastro, V., Petruccelli, I., Diotaiuti, P., Petruccelli, F., Cappelli, L., & San Martini, P. (2015). Relationship between parental narcissism and children's mental vulnerability: Mediation role of rearing style. *International Journal of Psychology and Psychological Therapy, 15*(3), 337–347.

de Zavala, A. G., Cichocka, A., Eidelson, R., & Jayawickreme, N. (2009). Collective narcissism and its social consequences. *Journal of Personality and Social Psychology, 97*(6), 1074–1096. https://doi.org/10.1037/a0016904

Donaldson-Pressman, S., & Pressman, R. M. (1994). *The narcissistic family: Diagnosis and treatment.* Jossey-Bass.

Finzi-Dottan, R., & Cohen, O. (2010). Young adult sibling relations: The effects of perceived parental favoritism and narcissism. *The Journal of Psychology, 145*(1), 1–22. https://doi.org/10.1080/00223980.2010.528073

Fisher, J. (2017). *Healing the fragmented selves of trauma survivors: Overcoming internal self-alienation.* Routledge.

Fisher, J. (2021). *Transforming the living legacy of trauma: A workbook for survivors and therapists.* PESI Publishing.

Fjelstad, M. (2013). *Stop caretaking the borderline or narcissist: How to end the drama and get on with life.* Rowman & Littlefield Publishers.

Fossati, A., Beauchaine, T. P., Grazioli, F., Carretta, I., Cortinovis, F., & Maffei, C. (2005). A latent structure analysis of *Diagnostic and Statistical Manual of Mental Disorders, Fourth Edition*, narcissistic personality disorder criteria. *Comprehensive Psychiatry, 46*(5), 361–367. https://doi.org/10.1016/j.comppsych.2004.11.006

Foster, J. D., Campbell, W. K., & Twenge, J. M. (2003). Individual differences in narcissism: Inflated self-views across the lifespan and around the world. *Journal of Research in Personality, 37*(6), 469–486. https://doi.org/10.1016/S0092-6566(03)00026-6

Freyd, J. J. (1997). Violations of power, adaptive blindness, and betrayal trauma theory. *Feminism & Psychology, 7*(1), 22–32. https://doi.org/10.1177/0959353597071004

Garber, B. D. (2011). Parental alienation and the dynamics of the enmeshed parent-child dyad: Adultification, parentification, and infantilization. *Family Court Review, 49*(2), 322–335. https://doi.org/10.1111/j.1744-1617.2011.01374.x

Gibson, L. C. (2015). *Adult children of emotionally immature parents: How to heal from distant, rejecting, or self-involved parents.* New Harbinger Publications.

Grapsas, S., Brummelman, E., Back, M. D., & Denissen, J. A. (2020). The "why" and "how" of narcissism: A process model of narcissistic status pursuit. *Perspectives on Psychological Science, 15*(1) 150–172. https://doi.org/10.1177/1745691619873350

Green, A., & Charles, K. (2019). Voicing the victims of narcissistic partners: A qualitative analysis of responses to narcissistic injury and self-esteem regulation. *SAGE Open, 9*(2), 1–10. https://doi.org/10.1177/2158244019846693

Green, A., MacLean, R., & Charles, K. (2021). Female narcissism: Assessment, aetiology, and behavioural manifestations. *Psychological Reports,* 1–32. https://doi.org/10.1177/00332941211027322

Grijalva, E., Newman, D. A., Tay, L., Donnellan, M. B., Harms, P. D., Robins, R. W., & Yan, T. (2015). Gender differences in narcissism: A meta-analytic review. *Psychological Bulletin, 141*(2), 261–310. https://doi.org/10.1037/a0038231

Grossman, F. K., Spinazzola, J., Zucker, M., & Hopper, E. (2017). Treating adult survivors of childhood emotional abuse and neglect: A new framework. *American Journal of Orthopsychiatry, 87*(1), 86–93. https://doi.org/10.1037/ort0000225

Hall, J. (2019). *The narcissist in your life: Recognizing the patterns and learning to break free.* Hachette Book Group.

Hart, W., Adams, J., Burton, K. A., & Tortoriello, G. K. (2017). Narcissism and self-presentation: Profiling grandiose and vulnerable narcissists' self-presentation tactic use. *Personality and Individual Differences, 104*, 48–57. https://doi.org/10.1016/j.paid.2016.06.062

Hopper, E. K., Grossman, F. K., Spinazzola, J., & Zucker, M. (2019). *Treating adult survivors of childhood emotional abuse and neglect: Component-based psychotherapy.* Guilford Press.

Hughes-Hammer, C., Martsolf, D. S., & Zeller, R. A. (1998). Development and testing of the codependency assessment tool. *Archives of Psychiatric Nursing, 12*(5), 264–272. https://doi.org/10.1016/S0883-9417(98)80036-8

Huh, H. J., Kim, S.-Y., Yu, J. J., & Chae, J.-H. (2014). Childhood trauma and adult interpersonal relationship problems in patients with depression and anxiety disorders. *Annals of General Psychiatry, 13*(1), 1–13. https://doi.org/10.1186/s12991-014-0026-y

Jack, C. (2021, January 12). Sons and daughters of narcissistic mothers: Who fares worse? *Psychology Today.* https://www.psychologytoday.com/us/blog/women-autism-spectrum-disorder/202101/sons-and-daughters-narcissistic-mothers-who-fares-worse

Karpman, S. (1968). Fairy tales and script drama analysis. *Transactional Analysis Bulletin, 7*(26), 39–43.

Khazan, I. (2019). *Biofeedback and mindfulness in everyday life: Practical solutions for improving your health and performance.* W. W. Norton & Company.

Koepernik, T., Jauk, E., & Kanske, P. (2020). Lay theories of grandiose and vulnerable narcissism. *Current Psychology.* Advance online publication. https://doi.org/10.1007/s12144-020-01296-w

Kostyanaya, M. (2019, December 31). Bridging the evidence-based gap: From pathological narcissism to narcissism survivors. *The Science of Psychotherapy.* https://www.thescienceofpsychotherapy.com/bridging-the-evidence-based-gap-from-pathological-narcissism-to-narcissism-survivors/

L'Abate, L. (2009). The drama triangle: An attempt to resurrect a neglected pathogenic model in family therapy theory and practice. *The American Journal of Family Therapy, 37*(1), 1–11. https://doi.org/10.1080/01926180701870163

Langer, E. (2014). *The art of noticing.* The Langer Mindfulness Institution.

Lasine, S. (2002). Divine narcissism and Yahweh's parenting style. *Biblical Interpretation, 10*(1), 36–56. https://doi.org/10.17265/2159-5542/2019.08.001

Lay, G. (2019). Understanding relational dysfunction in borderline, narcissistic, and antisocial personality disorders: Clinical considerations, presentation of three case studies, and implications for therapeutic intervention. *Psychology Research, 19*(8), 303–318. https://doi.org/10.17265/2159-5542/2019.08.002

Lee-Maturana, S., Matthewson, M., Dwan, C., & Norris, K. (2019). Characteristics and experiences of targeted parents of parental alienation from their own perspective: A systematic literature review. *Australian Journal of Psychology, 71*(2), 83–91. https://doi.org/10.1111/ajpy.12226

Lehrer, P. M., & Gevirtz, R. (2014). Heart rate variability biofeedback: How and why does it work? *Frontiers in Psychology,* Article 756. https://doi.org/10.3389/fpsyg.2014.00756

Levy, K. N. (2012). Subtypes, dimensions, levels, and mental states in narcissism and narcissistic personality disorder. *Journal of Clinical Psychology, 68*(8), 886–897. https://doi.org/10.1002/jclp.21893

Masterson, J. F. (1995). *Closet narcissistic disorder: The Masterson approach.* Newbridge.

McBride, K. (2008). *Will I ever be good enough? Healing the daughters of narcissistic mothers.* Atria Paperback.

Meier, J. S. (2020). U.S. child custody outcomes in cases involving parental alienation and abuse allegations: What do the data show? *Journal of Social Welfare and Family Law, 42*(1), 92–105. https://doi.org/10.1080/09649069.2020.1701941

Miller, J. D., Campbell, W. K., & Pikonis, P. A. (2007). Narcissistic personality disorder: Relations with distress and functional impairment. *Comprehensive Psychiatry, 48*(2), 170–177. https://doi.org/10.1016/j.comppsych.2006.10.003

Olson, D. H. (2000). Circumplex model of marital and family systems. *Journal of Family Therapy, 22*(2), 144–167. https://doi.org/10.1111/1467-6427.00144

Piff, P. K. (2014). Wealth and the inflated self: Class, entitlement, and narcissism. *Personality and Social Psychology Bulletin, 40*(1), 34–43. https://doi.org/10.1177/0146167213501699

Rogoza, R., Cieciuch, J., & Strus, W. (2021). A three-step procedure for analysis of circumplex models: An example of narcissism located within the circumplex of personality metatraits. *Personality and Individual Differences, 169*, Article 109775. https://doi.org/10.1016/j.paid.2019.109775

Ross, N. D., Kaminski, P. L., & Herrington, R. (2019). From childhood emotional maltreatment to depressive symptoms in adulthood: The roles of self-compassion and shame. *Child Abuse & Neglect, 92*, 32–42. https://doi.org/10.1016/j.chiabu.2019.03.016

Sarkis, S. M. (2018). *Gaslighting: Recognize manipulative and emotionally abusive people—and break free*. Hachette Books.

Schwartz, R. C. (1995). *Internal family systems therapy*. Guilford Press.

Shafti, S. S. (2019). Malignant narcissism: Concealed side of psychopathy. *Biomedical Journal of Scientific & Technical Research, 22*(1), 16310–16315. https://doi.org/10.26717/BJSTR.2019.22.003686

Shin, H., & Youn, N. (2020). How insecure narcissists become cultural omnivores: Consuming highbrow culture for status seeking and lowbrow culture for integrity signaling. *Psychology of Aesthetics, Creativity, and the Arts.* Advance online publication. https://doi.org/10.1037/aca0000303

Simonič, B., & Osewska, E. (2020). Traumatic bonding in intimate partner violence: A relational family therapy approach. *Family Forum, 9*, 71–90. https://doi.org/10.25167/FF/1092

Stanton, K., & Zimmerman, M. (2018a). Clinician ratings of vulnerable and grandiose narcissistic features: Implications for an expanded narcissistic personality disorder diagnosis. *Personality Disorders, 9*(3), 263–272. https://doi.org/10.1037/per0000272

Stanton, K., & Zimmerman, M. (2018b). Unique and shared features of narcissistic and antisocial personality disorders: Implications for assessing and modeling externalizing traits. *Journal of Clinical Psychology, 75*(3), 1–12. https://doi.org/10.1002/jclp.22708

Stocker, C. M., Lanthier, R. P., & Furman, W. (1997). Sibling relationships in early adulthood. *Journal of Family Psychology, 11*(2), 210–221. https://doi.org/10.1037/0893-3200.11.2.210

Thomas, S. (2016). *Healing from hidden abuse: A journey through the stages of recovery from psychological abuse*. MAST Publishing House.

Vaknin, S. (2018). Narcissistic disorders of the self as addictions. *Journal of Addiction Research, 2*(2), 1–5.

van der Kolk, B. (2014). *The body keeps the score: Brain, mind, and body in the healing of trauma*. Penguin.

Walker, P. (2013). *Complex PTSD: From surviving to thriving*. Azure Coyote.

Westphal, M., Leahy, R. L., Pala, A. N., & Wupperman, P. (2016). Self-compassion and emotional invalidation mediate the effects of parental indifference on psychopathology. *Psychiatry Research, 242*, 186–191. http://dx.doi.org/10.1016/j.psychres.2016.05.040

Wink, P. (1991). Two faces of narcissism. *Journal of Personality and Social Psychology, 61*(4), 590–597. https://doi.org/10.1037/0022-3514.61.4.590

Wong, Y. J. (2015). The psychology of encouragement: Theory, research, and applications. *The Counseling Psychologist, 43*(2), 178–216. https://doi.org/10.1177/0011000014545091

World Health Organization. (2019). *International statistical classification of diseases and related health problems* (11th ed.). https://icd.who.int/

Yakeley, J. (2018). Current understanding of narcissism and narcissistic personality disorder. *BJPsych Advances, 24*(5), 305–315. https://doi.org/10.1192/bja.2018.20